THE AMERICAN NEGRO
HIS HISTORY AND LITERATURE

An Arno Press / New York Times Collection

Black Troops in Cuba in 1899

THE BLACK PRESS
VIEWS AMERICAN IMPERIALISM
(1898-1900)

Compiled and edited by George P. Marks, III

With a preface by William Loren Katz

ARNO PRESS and THE NEW YORK TIMES

NEW YORK 1971

LC 70-94141
ISBN 0-405-01985-8

The American Negro: His History and Literature
General Editor
WILLIAM LOREN KATZ

Associate Editor for this volume
Nancy Lincoln

Manufactured in the United States of America

A complete list of the titles in the American Negro Collection
is located at the back of this volume.

CONTENTS

PREFACE

During the middle 1960's Martin Luther King, Jr., Stokely Carmichael and Eldridge Cleaver led a chorus of black dissent against American involvement in the Vietnam war, linking it to racism at home. Their stinging rebukes of United States foreign policy have been carried to the far corners of the world. So pointed, even dramatic, have been their attacks and so widely disseminated by the news media, that one might suppose they were carrying forth a black tradition, and indeed, they were. From Frederick Douglass's castigation of America's war against Mexico in 1846 to W. E. B. Du Bois's oppostion to U.S. intervention in Korea more than a century later, to the black voices of today, criticism of American wars against weaker nations has been an enduring black tradition.

Yet this tradition has, almost without exception,[1] escaped the notice of historians. Most have assumed the opposite and some have claimed that during each and every war black Americans have shown a loyalty unmatched by any other minority in the country. Content with such generalizations, they have then, most untypically, left the matter unresearched. Even John Hope Franklin's careful and balanced text, *From Slavery to Freedom* (New York, 1967, revised edition), which includes a chapter on American imperialism at the turn of the century, fails to mention the black opposition it aroused. And the most recent survey of anti-imperialist thought, *Anti-Imperialism in the United States: The Great Debate, 1890-1920,* by E. Berkeley Tompkins (Philadelphia, 1970), completely omits black sentiments.

This book, therefore, is a revelation. Twenty years ago George P. Marks III began his investigation of the black press's response to the American invasion of the Philippines that smashed its independence movement. In 1951 he published some of his findings in a little-known, short-lived journal edited by black scholar Lorenzo J. Greene.[2] Mr. Marks has extended his research in the present volume, providing the first thorough examination of the way the black press greeted America's initial venture in imperialism. He has had to labor under formidable burdens; entire black newspapers were no longer available and none left a complete run for the period under consideration. The work, therefore, is unfortunately fragmentary and incomplete, but it does conclusively establish a series of black attitudes that is quite distinguishable from that of whites. Further, as the ten-week "splendid little war" with Spain concluded, and the long and sordid guerrilla war in the Philippines began, black press criticism of American foreign policy mounted in fury. The newspaper comments highlighted here are no small discovery, nor are they of significance solely to scholars, for they detail a painful past that is painfully present. Indeed, this collection of clippings presents an inescapable challenge to historians who have ignored or sidestepped its information. At the same time, it reiterates the desperate need in black history for original research and fresh approaches. It will stimulate new research and provoke sharp debate on a vital but neglected topic.

That so many of the black newspapers found American interest in a "free Cuba" hypocritical is hardly surprising. During the last decade of the nineteenth century, as interest in Cuba and overseas expansion rose, black Americans lived under the yoke of a new slavery. Ninety percent lived in the South—landless and voteless peasants. Beginning in 1890, each state of the old Confederacy wrote into law, often into its constitution, provisions for the disfranchisement of its black citizens and their segregation in public schools, conveyances and facilities. In 1896 the Federal stamp of approval was put on segregation when the United United States (*Plessy vs. Ferguson*), and Congress refused to enforce the States Supreme Court ruled it did not violate the Constitution of the Constitutional Amendments guaranteeing black liberty and equality.

In the South, mob action accompanied discriminatory laws and decisions. From 1889 to 1901, when overseas expansion escalated, almost 2,000 black men, women and children were lynched, often with unspeakable brutality. The Right Reverend Hugh Miller, Bishop of Mississippi, justified lynchings, saying "the laws are slow and the jails are full." In North Carolina, where a coalition of black and white voters elected some black office-holders in 1898, Colonel A. M. Waddell, representing the white opposition, said his forces would carry the next election "if we have to choke the current of Cape Fear with carcasses." Five days later he led his forces, now armed, into Wilmington to massacre black officials and terrorize black voters.

For southern blacks the American shock at "Spanish brutality" and enthusiasm for a "free Cuba" must have seemed a cruel joke. Only one week after an explosion sunk the U.S. battleship *Maine* in Havana Harbor, a white mob in Lake City, South Carolina, shotgunned and fired the home and office of a duly-appointed black Federal postmaster, Fraser Baker, killing him and his infant son and wounding his wife, older son and four daughters.[3] As white Americans pondered the question of war with Spain, George Henry White, the nation's lone black congressman, tried unsuccessfully to pass through Congress a resolution to provide the surviving family of Postmaster Baker with a small indemnity. He was not even permitted to address Congress on the bill.

However, racist rhetoric ran rampant in the 55th and 56th Congresses that served from 1897 to 1901. On the day that Congress declared war on Spain, David A. De Armond of Missouri told his fellow congressmen that black people were "almost too ignorant to eat, scarcely wise enough to breathe, mere existing human machines." Congressman Meyer of Louisiana insisted white supremacy was necessary to save "us from the forces of ignorance, lawlessness, vice and irresponsibility." Senator "Pitchfork" Ben Tillman of South Carolina explained how his state saved itself from "black domination":

> We have done our level best; we have scratched our heads to find out how we could eliminate the last one of them. We stuffed ballot boxes. We shot them. We are not ashamed of it.[4]

In ten weeks, United States armed might crushed Spanish power from Puerto Rico to the Philippines. But it would take three long years to smash the Philippine independence movement led by young Emilio Aguinaldo. In words reminiscent of the southern congressmen, the Republican San Francisco *Argonaut* made this suggestion in "grim earnest":

> . . . In pursuance of our imperialist plans, it would be well to hire some of the insurgent lieutenants to betray Aguinaldo and other chieftans into our clutches. A little bribery, a little treachery and a little ambuscading, and we could trap Aguinaldo and his chieftans. Then, instead of putting them to death in the ordinary way, it might be well to torture them. The Spaniards have left behind them some means to that end in the dungeons of Manila. The rack, the thumbscrew, the trial by fire, the trial by molten lead, boiling insurgents alive, crushing their bones in ingenius mechanisms of torture—these are some of the methods that would impress the Malay mind.[5]

While the white press and congressmen were denouncing Aguinaldo, the black press viewed him as a dark-skinned liberator, fighting for independence by expelling a foreign oppressor. Salt Lake City's *Broad Ax* lashed out at U.S. "robbers, murderers and unscrupulous monopolists, who are ever crying for more blood." This black paper explained the fierce guerrilla resistance by noting that "maybe the Filipinos have caught wind of the way Indians and Negroes have been Christianized and civilized" in the United States.[6] In the month that Representative White left Congress, North Carolina state law prohibiting him from ever returning, Aguinaldo was captured by American treachery. Until 1946 American authorities kept Filipinos from choosing their own government; white rule in the South still prevents the election of black men to Congress.

Painful ironies run through this era of racism at home and abroad. Black anti-expansionists thrashed about looking for a political home. William Jennings Bryan and the Democrats opposed imperialism abroad while enforcing white supremacy at home. Bryan, three times the Democratic Presidential candidate, announced: "Anyone who will look at the subject without prejudice will know that white supremacy promotes the highest welfare of both races." The Republicans, supported by most blacks, had become the party of imperialism. The best President McKinley could offer black southerners was this advice: "Be patient, be progressive, be determined, be honest, be God-fearing, and you will win. For no effort fails that has a stout, earnest heart behind it."[7]

In the U.S. Senate, South Carolina's Ben Tillman denounced the hypocrisy of his Republican colleagues who insisted the Filipinos were unfit for self-government and required American control. "In the name of common sense and honest dealing," he said, "if the Philippines are unfit, why are the negroes fit?" He drew another parallel:

> . . . No Republican leader, not even Governor [Theodore] Roosevelt, will now dare to wave the bloody shirt and preach a crusade against the South's treatment of the negro. The North has a bloody shirt of its own. Many thousands of them have been made into shrouds for murdered Filipinos, done to death because they were fighting for liberty.[8]

But the white community remained deeply split over imperialism. Less than two months after Congress declared war on Spain an Anti-Imperialist League was formed by prominent Americans ranging from Mark Twain to Grover Cleveland. By the election of 1900, the Democrats had elevated expansion to a major campaign issue. The division among whites further emboldened the black press's attacks. They undoubtedly benefited from this extra strength when facing either entrenched beliefs or implacable foes within their own community.

To challenge administration foreign policy, the black editors had to flaunt the public views of Afro-America's leading spokesman, Booker T. Washington. He had urged his people to sacrifice their battle for equal rights and accommodate themselves to the white South—and this during an age of mounting mob violence and disfranchisement. An intimate of leading industrialists, who provided him with funds, and a consultant to Republican Presidents, who sought his advice on southern Federal appointments, Washington would soon launch his successful drive to bend much of the black press to his way of thinking.

To emphasize their strong disagreement with the Republican President and administration, the black press forcefully challenged an established black political tradition—unswerving loyalty to the party of Lincoln. One paper printed the advice of Stanley Ruffin of Boston, "a leading Afro-American," who urged black clergymen and editors to declare: "We shall neither fight for such a country or with such an army." Though others never went that far, few failed to express some hostility or suspicion of the administration. In 1898 the Washington *Bee* claimed: "A majority of the Negroes in this country are opposed to expansion." Its opinion, "expansion is a fraud," may well have been the majority view held by articulate blacks.[9]

By 1900 the spokesmen for expansion had become more outspoken and arrogant. On January 9th Senator Albert J. Beveridge, a leading advocate of imperilism, announced: "God . . . has made us the master organizers of the world to establish system where chaos reigns. . . . He has made us adept in government that we may administer government among savages and senile people." Paradoxically, eleven days later, Congressmen White, in a dramatic move to halt U. S. barbarity at home, introduced the nation's first anti-lynching bill to Congress. To halt this widespread and escalating crime, his bill provided the death penalty for convicted lynchers, but it died in committee.

By this time black opposition to imperialism was mounting. Early in October a black paper quoted Howard University professor and black essayist Kelly Miller, saying: "To be plain about the matter, I don't think there is a single colored man, out of office and out of the insane asylum, who favors the so-called expansion policy."[10] Later that month, in an article, "The Effect of Imperialism Upon the Negro Race," Professor Miller concluded: "Acquiescence on the part of the Negro in the political rape upon the Filipino would give ground of justification to the assaults upon his rights at home."

In 1966, during a scholars' conference on black thought at the turn of the century, this editor mentioned black anti-imperialist sentiments and cited the Kelly Miller article. The only response came from a noted white scholar, prominent in historical associations and widely-known for his early work in black history and thought. He insisted "there was no Negro opposition to our foreign policy then," and said he had "been all through the Booker T. Washington papers at the Library of Congress, including his extensive collection of news clippings, and found nothing of the sort." He concluded: "Why mention the Kelly Miller article when the one following it by Frederick McGhee refuted it?"

While this historian may have been correct about the material in the Booker T. Washington papers, he was incorrect in his generalization. And, although the article he cited by Frederick McGhee did follow the Miller article in *Howard's American Magazine* that October, he had either misread or misrepresented its contents. Far from disputing Miller, McGhee, a leading Catholic layman and a prominent black Minnesota lawyer, carried his argument much further. He insisted "the murder and assassination going on in the Philippine Islands under the guise of war with the insurgents" was the cause for "the spirit of mob rule, the prevalence of lynch law, in all parts of our country." In a passage particularly relevant today, McGhee continued:

> . . . Our soldiers wrote home of what fun it was to shoot the "niggers" and see them keel over and die. Then came the famous order, "Take no prisoners," followed by the shameful account of the fiendish slaughter of forty-six Tagals, because one had killed an American soldier. Of the number of women and children killed in attacks upon villages defended by men armed with bamboo spears, this with the profoundly and oft-repeated assertion, of late so prevalent, that the proud Anglo-Saxon, the Republican party, by divine foreordination, is destined to rule earth's inferior races, and if they object make war upon them, furnishes an all-sufficient cause. Is it to be wondered then that so little value is placed upon the life, liberty, freedom, and rights of the American Negro?"[11]

To misread this clear denunciation of U. S. foreign policy required a formidable bias, one our respected scholar shared with many others, despite their training in objective analysis of historical evidence. This volume, then, cannot help but ruffle a few academic feathers. And well it should. Neither complacency nor bias ever produced accurate history. But more important, those laymen who wonder why some black spokesmen today insist on drawing parallels between the shooting of blacks in Orangeburg, South Carolina; Jackson State College, Mississippi; Newark and Detroit, and the massacre at Songmy, Vietnam, should find this volume enlightening.

WILLIAM LOREN KATZ

NOTES

1. The exception is historian Herbert Aptheker, a Marxist who has often quoted black anti-imperialist views. See his "American Imperialism and White Chauvinism" (1950) and "Robber Wars and the Negro People" (1952) reprinted in *Toward Negro Freedom* (New York, 1956) and his monumental *A Documentary History of the Negro People in the United States* (New York, 1951), particularly pp. 821-26.

2. See George P. Marks III, "Opposition of Negro Newspapers to American Philippine Policy, 1899-1900," *Midwest Journal* IV (Winter, 1951-1952). Another contributor to this journal, August Meier, wrote the definitive *Negro Thought in America, 1880-1915* (Ann Arbor, 1963), which does not mention a single black criticism of U.S. imperialism. However, this staggering omission is more typical and traditional than exceptional for historians.

3. As the clippings in this collection demonstrate, the murder of Postmaster Baker drew heavy fire from the black press. It so impressed novelist Sutton E. Griggs that he used it in his revolutionary, if not seditious, book, *Imperium in Imperio*, which he published in 1899 (reprinted in 1969 by Arno Press and The New York Times). In the novel, the Baker assassination leads to a meeting of a secret black congress that considers the seizure, with the aid of an unnamed foreign power, of Texas and Louisiana during the Spanish-American War. As a reward for their assistance in this coup, the ally is to keep Louisiana and Texas is to become a black republic.

4. See *Congressional Record,* 55th Congress, Second Session, Appendix pp. 362-363, 620; Third Session, p. 342; 56th Congress, First Session, pp. 2242, 2245.

5. See Aptheker, "American Imperialism and White Chauvinism," *Op. Cit.,* p. 93.

6. See Marks, *Op. Cit.,* p. 24.

7. See William Loren Katz, *Eyewitness: The Negro in American History* (New York, 1970 revised edition), pp. 372-73.

8. *Ibid.*

9. See Marks, *Op. Cit.*

10. *Ibid.*

11. Kelly Miller, "The Effect of Imperialism Upon the Negro Race," and Frederick L. McGhee, "Another View," in *Howard's American Magazine* V (October, 1900), pp. 87-96. After both articles, publisher James H. W. Howard added this comment: "People who try to cover the cloven hoof of empire with the petticoats of 'Expansion' are as careless of the dictionary as of the constitution. . . . What is proposed to do with [the Philippines] is no more like expansion than the present administration is like Lincoln's."

FOREWORD

This book is a collection of materials gathered from black newspapers during the period from January, 1898 through December, 1900, dealing with attitudes toward the two major aspects of American foreign policy at that time, the Spanish-American War and the question of annexation or imperialism. From 1898 to 1900 there were about 150 weekly Negro newspapers published in the United States. Most of these, unfortunately, were not preserved. The Schomburg Collection of the New York Public Library has perhaps the largest number, twenty-five, but there are no complete sets for any of them in that library or elsewhere. Among the twenty-five at the Schomburg, a considerable number of issues exists only for the following: Washington, D.C. *Bee*; Salt Lake City *Broad Ax* (this paper moved to Chicago in 1899); Indianapolis *Freeman*; Cleveland *Gazette*; and Richmond *Planet*. For the other twenty there are only scattered issues, in most cases no more than one or two. Appendix II to this volume lists an additional thirty-seven newspapers that are quoted in the extant twenty-five.

*   *   *

The titles of articles that appear in quotation marks in the text were created for this volume; the others, and the subheads within the articles, are from the original sources.

*   *   *

I wish to thank Mr. Ernest Kaiser of the Schomburg Collection of the New York Public Library for his valuable assistance in helping me unearth some of the documents in this book; Prof. Sidney Kessler of Glassboro State College, New Jersey, for kindly doing some of the research; Mr. William Loren Katz of Arno Press for his editorial direction; Miss Nancy Lincoln of Arno Press for reading the manuscript carefully and helping to clarify some obscure points; and President Kenneth I. Iversen and Dr. Albert Meder of the Board of Trustees of Union College, Cranford, N.J. for giving me a grant in the summer of 1969 to prepare the book for publication.

GEORGE P. MARKS III

INTRODUCTION

The position of most black newspapers on the Spanish-American War was a cautious and prudent patriotism. Although generally accepting the government's justification of the war—the liberation of the Cubans from Spanish oppression—the Negro press was adamant on the issue of black officers for black soldiers and advised their readers not to enlist unless their volunteer units were commanded, up to the regimental level, by blacks. This goal was successfully achieved only in a few states.

Once the Treaty of Paris was ratified, in February, 1899, and the Philippine insurgents under Emilio Aguinaldo had begun their fight for freedom and independence, there was a division in the black press on the question of annexation. Most of the black newspapers were anti-annexationist* whatever their political orientation in 1899 and 1900. The two most frequently cited reasons were that the American government could not deal justly with dark-skinned peoples as evidenced by its do-nothing record at home, and that governing a people without their consent was contrary to the Declaration of Independence and the American tradition.

The black press reported numerous lynchings and violations of constitutional rights in 1898, 1899 and 1900. The two cases most often referred to were the mob-murder of Postmaster Fraser Baker and his infant son in Lake City, South Carolina in February, 1898, and the anti-Negro and anti-democratic terrorism in Wilmington, North Carolina (erroneously described by C. Vann Woodward in his *Origins of the New South* as a "race riot") in November, 1898. The black press vigorously protested McKinley's silence on these matters in his annual messages to Congress in 1898 and 1899 and his administration's reply that, since these cases had "no federal aspect," it could do nothing. Not being protected in their constitutional rights by a Republican administration, and systematically being excluded by terror and the revision of state constitutions in the South from political and equal rights, the black press generally concluded that the American nation was not wise, just and

*See George P. Marks, III, "Opposition of Negro Newspapers to American Philippine Policy, 1899-1900," *Midwest Journal*, Winter 1951-1952, Vol. IV, No. 1, pp. 1-25.

democratic enough to govern people of a darker hue in the Philippines or anywhere.

The election of 1900 presented black Republican editors with a dilemma that probably reflected that of the Negro voter in the northern and western states—whether to support the Democratic or Republican party. Blacks could agree with the anti-expansionism of the Democratic party but not with its blatant racism and anti-democratic policy in the South (which it often branded "domestic imperialism" or "governing without the consent of the governed"). W. Calvin Chase, Republican editor of the Washington *Bee,* who was a supporter of McKinley, assailed the President for his policy towards the Philippines, yet in 1900, reluctant though he was, he felt that he had no choice but to back McKinley. There were black anti-imperialistic Democrats in the Midwest who admired William Jennings Bryan despite his party's record in the southern states and who could point out that the Republican party's record was no better in that region. Their position was that the Democratic party in their states was a better one for blacks. Leaders such as Bishop Alexander Walters of the AME Zion Church called for the formation of a third, all-Negro party, since he could not support either of the two major parties, the one for its racism and the other for its imperialism. However, when the chips were down in the fall of 1900, Bishop Walters, like many other blacks, "held his nose," and voted for the Republicans and McKinley.

THE BLACK PRESS
VIEWS AMERICAN IMPERIALISM
(1898-1900)

I

THE ANNEXATION OF HAWAII

In 1893 white Americans staged a coup d'etat to overthrow the Hawaiian government, but expansionists in the Senate failed to gain passage of a treaty of annexation. In July, 1898, during the excitement over the war with Spain, Hawaii was annexed by a joint resolution of the House and Senate.

In early 1898 the black press was divided on the issue of Hawaii's annexation. The division is illustrated in the Indianapolis *Freeman*, which in January opposed going into the "land-snatching business;" in March condemned the 1893 overthrow as a "reprehensible act," and asserted that the " 'Negro press' had no sympathy for the Hawaiian annexation;" in June started to reverse itself by saying that annexation was in all probability "a necessity;" in July, claiming that "the interests of the country" were to be served first, stated that "in the name of self-preservation and high philanthropy . . . Hawaii should be annexed;" and finally, by the end of August, concluded by saying that "Hawaii should congratulate herself" on her good fortune.

"No Annexation of Hawaii"

President Dole [of Hawaii] has walked into the shambles and should be sheared. The United States has not gone into the land-snatching business. Let other nations that were born and reared to such practices perpetuate them if needs be. The policy of isolation has kept this country free from the entanglements that keep the European nations ever on the *qui vive*. To annex Hawaii is to gratify sentiment alone. No one expects advantages from these islands thousands of miles remote from the nearest civilization. In other words, Dole is the Hawaiian Islands as the matter now stands. He has secured his elephant, now let him care for it as he best can. If the natives of the islands prefer their exiled queen or her beautiful relative, they ought to be lords of the situation. This, perhaps, is not might, but it is right. Let the government appoint a

1

protectorate over the islands and re-establish the rightful rulers to the country. Success, or the ends do not always justify the means.

Freeman (Indianapolis, Indiana), January 29, 1898

"SENATOR TILLMAN AND HAWAII"

Washington, D.C.—After deciding against Senator Pettigrew in his effort to deliver with open doors a speech upon his resolution declaring the acquisition of the Hawaiian Islands to be inexpedient, the Senate last week, Wednesday, in executive session, resumed consideration of the Hawaiian treaty. Senator White, of California, took to the floor to continue his argument against ratification. He spoke nearly three hours without concluding his remarks. One of the objections to the acquisition of the islands which Mr. White urged at some length was that the population was undesirable, made up largely of natives, Chinese and Japanese, and that the proportion of whites was small as compared with the whole population.

This gave Senator Tillman, of South Carolina, an opportunity to accuse the republicans of inconsistency, which he proceeded to do with great warmth. By their advocacy of the annexation of Hawaii, the republicans were, he said, endeavoring to set up a white man's government in those islands, where the whites formed only an inconsiderable proportion of the population, the great majority being colored. Yet the republicans had been for years howling against the white man's government in the South, and claiming that the colored brother was deprived of his vote.

Gazette (Cleveland, Ohio), February 12, 1898

"AGAINST HAWAIIAN ANNEXATION"

It has been just about five years ago since the first overt acts, having for their object the overthrow of the former native government of Hawaii, took place. Intelligent readers doubtless remember the history of that outrageous and entirely unjustifiable assault upon a weak people by a lot of unscrupulous adventurers, persons who, in point of disposition, were not a particle less piratical than the infamous man-stealers of antebellum days.

It seems impossible that a citizen of the United States, possessing ordinary sense of honor and patriotism, could fail to experience a feeling of shame and disgust upon viewing the dishonorable role which this government was made to play in the diabolical proceeding. There is not the least ground for doubt, but for aid rendered the adventurous buccaneers by the demonstrations made in their favor by our navy—particularly by our man-of-war Philadelphia—their attempt to overthrow the native government would have resulted in ignominious failure, instead of ending in villainous success. It is quite evident that the original actors in that outrage against a people with whom we were in perfect peace counted from the very first on receiving prompt and material assistance from this government. . . . And now the same gang of robbers are moving heaven and earth to induce this government to shoulder the whole burden of their villainy by becoming the receiver of their stolen property. But the worst phase of the matter lies in the fact that it looks as if there were about equal chances that the foul scheme of annexation may yet succeed.

Afro-American Sentinel (Omaha, Nebraska), February 26, 1898

"Against Hawaiian Annexation"

Congressman Johnson [of Indiana] has torn the mask from the Hawaiian mockery. He believes in the principles that established this government, viz., that those who are to govern should have the consent of the people to be governed. The seizure of the Hawaiian Islands was a reprehensible act measured by the well-known policy of this government. The prompt recognition of the Dole et al. movement was racial recognition, which, to say the least, is very small business for our government to be in with its own racial problems to deal with.

Indianapolis *Freeman,* March 5, 1898

"Against Hawaiian Annexation"

It is very noticeable that the "Negro Press" has no sympathy for the Hawaiian annexation hippodrome.

Indianapolis *Freeman,* March 12, 1898

"Against the Acquisition of Hawaii and Cuba"

It is an open question as to whether the colored people of Cuba will be better provided for under the American administration of affairs than they are under Spanish rule.

The spirit of conquest seems to have taken possession of certain men in high places. It was the same mischievous trend of affairs which, during President Harrison's administration, robbed the dusky queen of the Hawaiian Islands of her possessions. It now has a government with that prince of hypocrites, Dole, as president. It is run upon the American plan, Japanese and Negroes not being consulted, while the natives are not thought of.

Desperate efforts are now being made to secure the annexation of these islands to this country. In other words, they wish to hand to us the stolen property, because it is getting to be worthless in their hands and they are desirous of unloading it upon our government.

The next movement was the acquisition of Cuba upon an alleged ground of humanity. The hollowness of this pretext is shown in the desperate, but successful effort made to strike out the clause recognizing the present Cuban Republic (so-called). The officials of this alleged government are composed to a great extent of persons who would be called in this country Negroes.

It would never do to recognize them, so the government of the United States is to intervene, and finally assist in setting up a government which will either be a "carpet-bag government," or will be headed by a man who will be a tool in the hands of the capitalists of New York.

In no case will he be of African descent. The failure to recognize the Cuban Republic will also invalidate the bonds issued by that alleged body. So far this country has spent fifty millions of dollars in "getting ready." It is a matter of guess work what she will spend after she has "gotten ready."

It is a most disgraceful affair at best. It will cause as much disgust to the Cubans as it does to the Spaniards. The unfortunate inhabitants have simply leaped from the "frying pan into the fire" and the coming years will demonstrate whether or not they have chosen the lesser of two evils.

Planet (Richmond, Virginia), April 23, 1898

"Hawaiian Annexation"

Hawaii, it is evident, will be annexed. It is very probable that the present war has shown a necessity for such action which peaceful times could never have demonstrated. All is well that ends well. Hurrah! for the United States and United Islands of America!

Indianapolis *Freeman,* June 25, 1898

"Hawaiian Annexation Approved"

Wednesday, July 6, a majority of the members of the United States Senate voted in favor of annexing the Hawaiian Islands to the United States, and just as soon as the people of those islands decide to ratify the actions of our Congress they will be permitted to hoist the Stars and Stripes, and long may old glory wave over the Hawaiian Islands.

Broad Ax (Salt Lake City, Utah), July 9, 1898

"Hawaii in Other Hands Could Become a Menace"

If Hawaii can become a menace by falling into other hands, we had better end the matter by taking her in.

*   *   *

"Negroes Not Enthusiastic Over Annexation"

The negroes themselves have not been very enthusiastic over the annexation idea. They have felt all along that it was a racial issue to some extent and the further establishing of the decree that eventually the weaker races must succumb to the stronger ones. This idea is being rapidly demonstrated. The question of blood causing unity no doubt had much to do in the matter. But the intent and purposes of our own government are too well known to entertain scruples as to the welfare of the annexed Hawaiians allowing nothing for the sentiments of localities. The interests of the country are to be subserved first all the time, and if the trend of the present war demonstrates that Hawaii can serve this country and better their own condition at the same time, then in the name of self-preservation and that high philanthropy that permeates all the doings of the government in this war, Hawaii should be annexed.

Indianapolis *Freeman,* July 9, 1898

For Hawaiian Annexation

America's borders are not now confined by the banks of the Atlantic and Pacific, but Hawaii . . . has been annexed to the United States, and with the control of the central part of the Philippine Islands and probably some more islands adjacent to Cuba, we will have acquired quite an addition of territory which is quite productive and very valuable in tropical fruit, sugar, tobacco and manila rope. We can see no serious objection to the annexation of the Hawaiian Islands. Senator Tillman of South Carolina and some of his southern compatriots seem to oppose its annexation, simply because most of its inhabitants are colored people and it would give us more trouble to control them as we have our hands full here. We do not agree with the senator from South Carolina because the colored people of America are more law-abiding, more patriotic, than the senator and some of his white friends of the South because when it was the law in the South to enslave the colored man and to sell him as chattel, he submitted and obeyed that cruel law, but when the constitution law made him a freeman and gave him the right of suffrage, you white men did not obey the law; again, when you men passed your unjust and damnable jim crow laws, you asked him to obey them and he does so, and now, when he simply asks the protection of the government, you men from the South refuse that. Now in all fairness, is that patriotism and loyalty?. . .

Iowa State Bystander (Des Moines, Iowa) July 15, 1898

"HAWAIIAN ANNEXATION APPROVED"

Hawaii was formally admitted to the fold of the Union last week. While we are not in favor of dispossessing foreign potentates of their crowns, no matter how trifling or insignificant, yet Hawaii in this instance will have all to gain and nothing to lose. Hawaii should congratulate herself that such a powerful benefactor has rushed to her rescue.

Indianapolis *Freeman,* August 27, 1898

II

CIVIL RIGHTS AND THE
POSSIBILITY OF WAR

The furor caused by the blowing up of the U. S. battleship *Maine* on February 15, 1898 compelled black newspapers to define their position in the event of war. As in every war crisis between 1865 and 1917, blacks asked themselves: Should the Negro, who was deprived of his civil rghts by federal and state laws and adjudications, and treated with "terrible injustice" in the form of lynchings and terror in the South, fight for a government that recognized him as a citizen in name only?

One of the black newspapers that was actively opposed to the war, the Kansas City *American Citizen,* asserted that the United States should not intervene in the Spanish-Cuban War to protect Cubans until it first protected its own citizens at home. It referred to the recent murder of Postmaster Baker and his infant son as an illustration of the lawlessness in the South and to President McKinley's inaction in bringing to trial members of the mob that killed Baker, stating: "Let this government see that all laws are obeyed by our fire-eating southerners before going to war with Spain or any other country." The Washington *Bee* concurred: "A government that claims to be unable to protect its own citizens against mob law and political violence will certainly not ask the negroes to take up arms against a foreign government." The Indianapolis *Freeman* quoted a dispatch from Hartford, Connecticut that said:

> If the government wants our support and services, let us demand and get a guarantee for our safety and protection at home. . . . When we are guaranteed freedom and equality before the law, as other American citizens, then we will have a right, as such, to take up arms in defense of our country.

Some black newspapers questioned the necessity of the war. The *Weekly Blade* (Parsons, Kansas) asked why the United States did not recognize the Cuban revolutionary government, sell them supplies and munitions, and "let them alone to win their independence," rather than actively participating in the struggle.

But some members of the black press supported a war with Spain, feeling that Spain's sins should be punished and the Cubans freed from her oppression. They also felt that a war would give Negroes a chance to prove their bravery and manhood, and thereby earn the respect of white America. For example, the Cleveland *Gazette* voiced the opinion that:

> Of all citizens the Afro-American has a mighty interest at stake. . . . [since his] fondest and most cherished hopes for liberty and happiness are all centered in the instituitons of our country . . . [therefore] let us be ready and willing to do . . . even more than others in the hour of the nation's peril. Thus shall be reaffirmed our claims to equal liberty and protection.

And the *Iowa State Bystander* maintained that the war was "a blessing in disguise" for the black man, because "his real worth will be more respected; . . . his loyalty will establish a friendlier feeling in the South between the two races."

When war was declared in April, 1898, the Richmond, Virginia *Planet* tersely summed up the situation: "The wisdom of it is questioned. However, all loyal citizens must do their duty."

"McKinley's Cautious Cuban Policy Approved"

Because he [McKinley] has shown excellent, conservative judgment in handling the "Cuban" question, many in their blind enthusiasm for the deserving insurgents are now criticising or abusing him. . . . No rash man, or one who cannot consider the manifold interests of this great country as paramount to any desire born of enthusiasm or admiration for a brave, struggling and deserving, but foreign people, is wanted as the chief executive of these United States. No one sympathizes with the Cubans in their grand and heroic and winning struggle any more than the writer (and we also believe the President) and yet we can see good common sense and wisdom and *Right* in President McKinley's Cuban policy.

Cleveland *Gazette,* January 1, 1898

"Civil Rights First"

Let Uncle Sam keep hands off of other countries till he has learned to govern his own. Human life at home is at a low ebb now and should be protected before reaching out to protect others.

American Citizen (Kansas City, Kansas), January 14, 1898

"The Spaniards Suspected of Treachery"

The destruction of the battleship Maine . . . seems at present to point to murder rather than an accident. Spain should be compelled to produce good proof that she was not the cause of the destruction of our warship, and the mere statement that it was a spontaneous combustion should not be accepted by the administration . . . until they have the full details of a thorough investigation. No mere apology can atone for such a barbarous act.

Iowa State Bystander, February 18, 1898

The Maine

Spain feels very sorry about the matter and took good care of all the wounded and helped all she could, yet some people would believe nothing else but that the Spanish sailors did this wickedness. It is true our ship was in Spanish waters, yet we are at a loss to believe the Spaniards would dare do such a cruel deed to a government with whom she is at peace.

It will be hard to decide just what caused the explosion, therefore we wait with bated breath the decision of the investigating committee.

Kansas City *American Citizen,* February 18, 1898

The Maine

The destruction of the battleship Maine has caused the greatest excitement. . . . And if it should be proven that it was not an accident, then Uncle Sam must buckle on his armor and prepare for war.

* * *

"Against Annexation"

The Women's Democratic Club met. . . . The Cuban and Hawaiian questions were discussed at some length by Mr. Ferguson, the president of the club, who gave some good reasons why Cuba and Hawaii should not be annexed to the United States. . . .

Salt Lake City *Broad Ax,* February 19, 1898

The Battleship Maine

The serious catastrophe which took place near Havana on Tuesday, by which hundreds of valiant seamen and millions of property in the shape of one of the best gunboats in the Navy were destroyed, calls for a most searching scrutiny on the part of the American government. The circumstances under which the explosion took place, while they do not point directly to an overt act of violence on the part of the Spanish authorities, yet considering the hostile feeling in Spain to America, this country ought to be certain that Spain completely exonerates herself. In case Spain is responsible . . . full indemnity for lives lost and property destroyed as well as something more for her smartness [can be demanded], although, in our opinion, Mr. McKinley would be little less than inclined to insist upon thrashing Spain and in addition demanding the necessary indemnity. The President, however, is not to be inveigled into war by the jingoism so freely indulged in by some blustering Americans. He will be sure that he is right and will then act accordingly. There will be a hot time if Spain did it.

Bee (Washington, D.C.), February 19, 1898

THE MAINE

The destruction of the Maine was a crime against this nation not yet fully realized; but gradually the civilized world is being awakened to a sense of the appalling deed. No foreign power can justly sympathize with Spain in its base and cowardly treachery. None of the European nations can regard the act with mitigating allowance without compromising its own national honor. Spain has wickedly sinned against Christian civilization and must atone for its offending. Two hundred and twenty-five white Americans and thirty-three Afro-Americans have been wantonly murdered. The colored men of America have immense interests at stake. As a citizen and patriot, let him make common cause with the people and again prove himself an element of strength and power in vindicating the honor and claims of his country in the hour of the nation's peril. The cause of this government is our cause. If die we must, let us die defending a just cause.

Cleveland *Gazette,* February 19, 1898

"CIVIL RIGHTS FIRST"

Let this government see that all laws are obeyed by our fire-eating southerners before going to war with Spain or any other country.

* * *

"POSTMASTER BAKER'S MURDER AND CUBA"

The southern statesmen who plead for Cuba could learn a valuable lesson by looking around their own bloodcurdling confines of butchery. The constitution of the United States declares that each state shall be guaranteed a republican form of government, etc. There is about as much respect for the constitution of the United States in the southern states as there is for the Bible in Hades. The atrocious killing of Baker and his baby at the breast of its mother took place for no other reason than the fact that the President of the United States appointed him postmaster of an office where over half the inhabitants of the town were colored. The Post Office was set afire and then as Postmaster Baker attempted to come out of the burning building he was shot dead; then his wife and two of his daughters received dangerous wounds from which recovery is doubtful. All this the work of highly civilized white South Carolina American citizens. They defy all law, state, human or divine.

Their own hot-headed and ignorant will is law, and this is anarchy. The only reason these high-handed murders have gone on to such an extent is the leniency of the general government in regard to it. It is the duty of the government to look after the safety of the life of its citizens everywhere. No state, black with treason and anarchy, should be entrusted with human life. That government which is powerless to protect the humblest of its citizens should be wiped from the face of the earth.

What will be done about the murder of Baker and his family? Nothing. Every one of those murderers is well known—but not one will even be arrested. The coroner does not even dare indict one of them. The President of the United States will not dare appoint another Negro to that office, because the lawless mob has defied all existing power. To its sulphurious dictum, all law and reason bend the quivering knee. Mob violence is rampant. All else is sinking sand. May God hasten the day of retribution.

Kansas City *American Citizen,* February 24, 1898

SPANISH TREACHERY

Indications point to treachery of the most malignant type in the case of the destruction of the Maine. In case Spanish duplicity has gone so far as to blow up the Maine there is nothing to do but declare war, whip the rascals and make Spain pay for all of the trouble she has caused. Spanish threats can do nothing to bluff this country and it matters but little what speculators may do or say, there will be a hot time if Spain did it. The thousands of patriotic Americans of Caucasian blood who are willing to go to war will be supplemented by thousands of colored men who will vie with them in patriotism and bravery on the field of battle. If he is given but a fair show, the colored volunteer will put up as bold and solid a front, work up to the approved tactics and capture as many flags, positions and men as a given number of his white compatriots will dare do. Let President McKinley and Congress say the word and recruiting will be a land-office business.

Washington *Bee,* February 26, 1898

"WHAT IF WAR COMES"

The truth of this fearful disaster [the destruction of the Maine] must be fully uncovered, and if the dread suspicion of crime and treachery so appalling culminates in the guilt of some Spanish brigand, then Spain must make reparation. If she refuses, then it remains for Americans to do their duty.

Of all citizens the Afro-American has a mighty interest at stake. His proud record, already so gloriously inscribed upon our national banner through the many long and bloody struggles of our country, will again be challenged. Our fondest and most cherished hopes for liberty and happiness are all centered in the institutions of our country. We have been true and loyal in every trying emergency of the nation and we will not shirk a single duty which we owe to this government. . . .

We have never despaired in our hope for the enjoyment of our civil and political rights and we owe it to ourselves to offer our lives and our sacred honors in vindication of our country and the endeared principles for which we contend.

America is the home of our birth. The blood of our fathers mingles in the soil whence we have derived sustenance and support. As citizens and patriots, let us be ready and willing to do out part, to do our full duty, and to do even more than others in the hour of the nation's peril. Thus shall be reaffirmed our claims to equal liberty and protection and ratified more surely the blessings of free government to ourselves and posterity.

Cleveland *Gazette,* March 5, 1898

"CIVIL RIGHTS FIRST, CUBAN INDEPENDENCE SECOND"

After a speech by Recorder P. H. Cheatham before the Congressional Lyceum on Sunday, Feb. 27 . . . the Cuban resolution was taken up for consideration, whereupon after some parliamentary sparing, in which Messrs. W. Calvin Chase, Davis, Frisby, and Brinkley engaged, the first paragraph of said resolution read as follows:

> That the government of the United States of America should promptly recognize the revolutionists of Cuba, who are now honestly struggling to secure their independence of the Spanish government, as composing an independent nation and possessing the rights thereof according to the laws of nations.

To this Mr. Chase offered the following amendment:

> That the United States do not recognize the independence of Cuba until said states are able to protect all American citizens in their civil and political rights at home.

The applause which followed the introduction of this amendment was prolonged and deafening. The amendment was ably discussed *pro* and *con* by Messrs. Davis, Fossett, Brinkley, Tyler, and Frisby. Mr. Chase closed the discussion and moved the adoption of his amendment. Upon a *viva voce* vote when . . . the amendment had been adopted by a vote of 54 to 5, the large audience fairly went wild with applause. . . .

* * *

"THE NEGRO NEEDS FREEDOM AS MUCH AS THE CUBAN"

The United States may play the coward in the Maine explosion by the Cubans, but whether it does or not the American negro must look to his own interest and protection. A government that claims to be unable to protect its own citizens against mob law and political violence will certainly not ask the negroes to take up arms against a foreign government.

The colored man is beginning to learn some sense and will cease jumping after "glittering generals" and imaginary inducements or adventures from political parties. As a matter of fact, the democrats as a whole will not tolerate the negro and it is becoming so that sooner or later the Republicans will shift the responsibility of carrying him, but will no doubt use him to advance their own interest. The negroes favor the independence of any nation. The negro has no reason to fight for Cuba's independence. He is opposed at home. He is as much in need of independence as Cuba is. He is living under a flag that the blood of his ancestors and forefathers fought for and is powerless to protect him. His own brothers, fathers, mothers and indeed his children are shot down as if they were dogs and cattle. Is he living among the brave or is he in the home of his enemies? There is no inducement for the negro to fight for the independence of Cuba.

Washington *Bee,* March 5, 1898

NEGROES READY TO DIE FOR A NON-PROTECTING COUNTRY

Congress was a unit yesterday in voting $50,000,000 to be used by the President of the United States, as he may best see fit for the defence of this nation. There was not a dissenting vote. The result . . . was one united voice of patriotism for the honor of a common country. This is as it should be. The safety of the people should be the supreme desire of any country.

The undaunted patriotism of the Negro finds thousands ready again to lay down their lives for a country that does not protect them!

Kansas City *American Citizen,* March 10, 1898

NEGROES AND CUBA

The prospect of a war with Spain brings a very important question to the front.

Who will be expected to do the fighting? The Negro-haters have declared this to be a white man's country, and the Negroes themselves have enquired, why should not the white man fight for it?

Another question; the cry has been made that the educated and wealthy must rule and vote, then why should not these same elements muster in and fight?

If we are not presumed to be good enough to exercise the right of franchise, why should we be good to exercise the right to enlist in the service of the United States?

If the state governments will not protect us, why should we be expected to protect the state government?

If the national government will not protect us, why should we be expected to protect the national government? Our allegiance to both is based upon a principle of reciprocity and partakes of the nature of a contract.

The repeated violation of the obligation on the one side releases the party on the other side.

These thoughts came to us as we noted the increase of the war-spirit and the talk of sending colored troops to Cuba.

But our people are the most forgiving nation on the face of the globe. No other race living in the republic under similar circumstances would respond in such an emergency, and yet colored troops would rally by the thousands whether called upon by the President, democratic or republican, or by the governor of a state in which they had been ostracized, hounded, murdered, and even denied the right of franchise. Truly, we are a peculiar race of people.

Richmond *Planet,* March 12, 1898

"WHY ANNEX CUBA?"

In the midst of the great war excitement let it not be forgotten that the South Carolina murderers of Postmaster Baker are yet unpunished and that there should be peace at home as abroad.

Suppose this government does purchase Cuba, will it pay? What is in it that this government should be so anxious about? To take in Cuba is but a beginning to swallow up all the West Indies. Do we actually need them for the safety of our republic?

Kansas City *American Citizen,* March 17, 1898

IF WAR SHOULD COME

The rapidly approaching crisis in the affairs of this country as they relate to Spain has been the means of bringing to surface the opinions of many "Negro journals" of the country as to what part the Negro should play in the impending struggle. The consensus of opinions of these journals is not arrayed on the side of patriotism, and if they in any manner reflect the sentiment of their readers, there are about seven millions of people that are indifferent patriots.

"Breathes there a man with soul so dead," etc. says Scott, but he spoke of Scotland. The query naturally arises, under existing conditions could a Negro be more than an indifferent patriot? At first blush the feeling is decidedly in favor of "tabooing" those who could say aught against rushing to arms and joining the fray in defense of home country and honor.

But on the morrow's sober second thought, when the status of Negroes as citizens of the United States is thoroughly canvassed, then comes the slump in the scale of his patriotism. All nations are endowed with that passion from which eventuates love of country, home, fireside or ingle. No nation could have this in greater degree than the Negroes of America, were they permitted fervently to say, "my home, my country." To some the words are a hollow mockery, as tinkling cymbals and sounding brass. To the many the meaning is relative, variable and ever changing.

But notwithstanding all of this, the Negro with canine fidelity will, in this expected struggle as in the past struggles in which this country has been engaged, forge to the front and with his black breast laid bare to the enemy, wring respect out of contempt.

He, as in the past, will not be promoted on the field, decorated with no emblems—insignia of valor. But he, heedless of these failures in the ethics of battlefields, will be no less a soldier.

* * *

"IF THE GOVERNMENT WANTS OUR SERVICES,
LET US DEMAND PROTECTION AT HOME"

Hartford, Conn., Special.—The U.S. recruiting officer is expected in Hartford this week to receive names of men for the prospective Spanish-American war. Great excitement prevails here among all classes, and some of our colored men seem enthusiastic over the idea of enlisting in defense of the government, while some are more reserved and common-sensed, asserting that no colored man should ever offer his services to protect a government that does not protect him. The government of the United States will allow some of her most loyal and true citizens to be burned and butchered and shot to pieces, like dogs, without protection, and go right on ignoring their rights and claims as if all were peace and happiness in the family; and yet, when a foreign war is threatened, these same ill-treated citizens are wont to be rushed to the front in the name of protecting the nation's honor. Such injustice is not tolerated by any other civilized nation; not even is Spain guilty of such discrimination among her own citizens. As a race what means have we for checking such unjust discrimination? Colored men of Hartford, let us think before acting. If the government wants our support and services, let us demand and get a guarantee for our safety and protection at home. We want to put a stop to lynch law, the butchering of our people like hogs, burning our houses, shooting our wives and children and raping our daughters and mothers. In short, as a race, we want indemnity for the loss of ten thousand Negroes who have been lynched and butchered and slaughtered since the civil war. When we are guaranteed freedom and equality before the law, as other American citizens, then we will have a right, as such, to take up arms in defense of our country.

Indianapolis Freeman, March 19, 1898

"DISFRANCHISED PEOPLE SHOULD BE EXCUSED FROM FIGHTING"

The people who are denied the right to vote for their country should be excused from the right to fight for their country. This is equity, if it is not the law.

Richmond Planet, March 19, 1898

"SENDING THE MAINE TO CUBA WAS A THOUGHTLESS ACT"

The feebleness and bad management of our present executive was clearly shown in the Maine affair. What business we had in sending one great war vessel into a hostile port without any invitation is hard to understand. It was the act of a bully. Think of the various hostile factions there and the character of the population; also there are Cuban revolutionists eager to plunge us into a war with their hated tyrant and none too good to have blown up the ship in order to start the game. They are reckless and despairing. To say the least it was a thoughtless act to send the ship there. Mutual invitations should have been interchanged and all done to promote good will. Now this awful calamity has fallen upon us and no one is to be found responsible. . . .

Salt Lake City Broad Ax, March 19, 1898

FALSE PATRIOTISM

Those who are professing such ardent patriotism and indulging in such blooming newspaper correspondence ought at least manifest that medium of modesty becoming persons of such high pretensions. The fact is that there has been no disposition manifested on the part of those preparing for the war to unite the colored brother to assist them in subjugating Spain. The metropolitan journals have been teeming with articles boasting of the bravery and patriotism of the Americans of Anglo-Saxon descent but not a word of encouragement or compliment to the Americans of African descent. Moreover, if the conduct of leading Americans who run things in the South is to be a marker by which to measure our acceptability as soldiers, citizens, or patriots, we need be in no doubt in the matter. The uniform barbarity practiced upon law-abiding colored citizens in the South ought to be a strong reminder that at least in that section the colored brother has no reason to claim this as his country and consequently cannot or ought not enthuse as American patriots. The murder of Baker and his innocent family expresses sufficient proof of this. The nation, though boasting of love of liberty and fair dealing, of protection to its citizens, seems either powerless or indisposed to make its boasting true where the colored citizen is concerned. And until this country is able or shows a disposition to prove to the world that it is the true and honest champion of human rights and the rights of her own citizens, the colored brother shows but slavish disposition to rush forward to prove his fidelity.

The fidelity of the colored people has been fully tested. They have been true under all circumstances. And at all times. It was shown in their manly defense of the Union when assaulted by traitors. It was shown on the plantation while their masters were in the field battling for continued enslavement. But fidelity is at times an expression of race weakness, especially when it is regarded by the erstwhile beneficaries as a species of groveling sycophancy. And judging from our own general treatment, that is about the size of it. Hence while we may be loyal and patriotic, while our blood may boil for revenge upon those Spanish brutes who have spared neither woman or child even in their diabolical butchery, yet common sense and experience ought to teach that severe silence becomes us. When we shall have been treated as men and accorded the rights for which we voted and fought, when we can consistently claim the right as free American citizens to demand the emancipation of others in bondage, then can we afford to publish our loyalty, then can be made haste to prove that we possess our full share of patriotism. It is inconsistent for practical slaves to fight for the freedom of others when a brave stand is necessary in order to procure liberty for themselves. Wisdom dictates silence in this case. Loud boasting will catch no fish.

Washington Bee, March 19, 1898

"McKinley the Peacemaker"

The platform upon which President McKinley was elected declared emphatically in behalf of the Cuban insurgents. Ever since Mr. McKinley's inauguration he has been earnestly and actively engaged upon the grave and responsible problem of relieving the distresses and ending the war in Cuba. Being an advocate of the principle of peace, he has endeavored to bring about the desired results without the sacrifice of lives and prosperity by a war between the United States and Spain. In this ambition he has been sustained by the sentiment of the American people and the endorsement of the world.

The time has come, however, when further delay must seriously compromise the effect of our intervention, whatever form it may assume, and it cannot be doubted that the President has formed a plan that must soon decide the fate of Cuba. That this may be accomplished by peaceful negotiation is still the hope of the President and the wish of the American people. There would be no national glory in our defeat of Spain in an armed contest. Every factor that might contribute to the peaceful but necessary solution of the problem should be welcomed. The recognition of Cuban belligerency by Great Britain and other powers would help the peace cause. Therefore, even the unofficial report of such intended policy is grateful and to our purpose.

Kansas City *American Citizen,* March 24, 1898

"THOSE WHO VOTE SHOULD FIGHT"

The war-scare has cost this country fifty million of dollars. What will a war cost?

We are in favor of those folks who vote and run the government, fighting and run the Spaniards.

Richmond *Planet,* March 26, 1898

"PROTECTION OF RIGHTS CAN AROUSE PATRIOTISM"

There is no want of either patriotism or bravery in the colored American. When the time comes for exhibition of those qualities they will not be wanting. But before patriotism can be aroused the country must place itself in such a position in relation to the rights of man that there can be no doubt that the sentiment of love of country is well-grounded.

Washington *Bee,* March 26, 1898

LET AFRO-AMERICANS PROVE THEIR LOYALTY

We hold to the conviction that in event of a war with Spain Afro-Americans should find resting upon themselves a responsibility equal with that of every other citizen of this republic. The interests involved in the issues of war are important with the Afro-American as with anyone else because, however circumscribed in the exercise of his personal and political immunities, his rights *per se* are as sacred and dear to himself as to any other citizen. As much as we abominate the terrible injustice done the Afro-American under his own government, yet we have never lost sight of the fact that this country and government are his rightful and inalienable heritage, and despite our murmurings we deemed it our duty that every citizen should respond to the demands of the national defense. . . . Very assuredly every intelligent and loyal black man who feels the least personal concern for his surroundings will not only desire a peaceful settlement of the difficulties, but will, in case of an actual break between Spain and our government, feel himself in duty bound to lend all aid, encourage and support his government. . . . Let us not stand upon the asking, but show ourselves ready to maintain intact the government from which we derive our hopes for life, liberty, and happiness.

Cleveland Gazette, March 26, 1898

"HASTY OFFERS OF WOULD-BE HEROES"

Between Spanish diplomatic finesse and American monopolistic jugglery on the one hand and jingoism, braggadocio and real patriotism on the other, the days of war are having a very short time of it. Added to this the hasty and foolish offers of brawn and valor on the part of some of our colored would-be heroes and the indisposition on the part of the war party to accept on the other hand, the effect is still further to complicate matters. After all, the men who haste to run into war are usually the first to run away from it.

Washington Bee, March 26, 1898

WAR OR PEACE

The court of inquiry about the cause of the Maine explosion has made their report and sent it to the President, and he has transmitted it to Congress with no specific recommendation. He has sent his ultimate message to Spain. He furthermore states that he will see that our food for the starving Cubans will be given them upon humanitarian principles, not as a menace to Spain. If Spain objects, he will use naval intervention, such are the state of affairs now, and it looks very much like war. While we do not favor war, yet we think that the time is fully ripe for the United States to free Cuba and get indemnity for the destroying of our vessel.

Iowa State Bystander, April 1, 1898

"NAVAL COURT OF INQUIRY"

War is the only thing that will now give peace. Arbitrations and the like methods may prevent war, but peace cannot be restored. The war fever is raging anew and Americans are spoiling for a fight.

The Naval Court of Inquiry has reported and the Spanish report has been received, and to read the two one can gain only this: For a certainty there was an explosion which blew up the Maine; the ship sunk and two or three hundred persons were killed thereby. It matters not who performed the dastardly deed, whether officially ordered or otherwise, so long as it was a Spanish subject; it seems strange that the Court of Inquiry could not fasten the responsibility upon the Spanish government. Strange, indeed!

Weekly Blade (Parsons, Kansas), April 2, 1898

"APPEALS TO PATRIOTISM"

[The Fraternal Union of America in Omaha passed the following resolution:]

Resolved that we heartily endorse the action of the administration in the stand it has taken thus far in its diplomatic efforts to bring about a peaceable solution of the Cuban question, and the aid it has extended and now is extending toward alleviating the terrible suffering, and be it further

Resolved that we believe the time has come when some more decisive action should be taken, and we request our senators and representatives to insist that the United States demand the independence of Cuba and that the inhuman policy of starvation and butchery pursued by Spain should cease forthwith, and in the name of humanity and liberty enforce such demand immediately, peaceably if possible, by force if necessary.

Omaha *Afro-American Sentinel,* April 2, 1898

THE CRY IS WAR

War is imminent. The forces are being marshalled land and naval for the purpose of settling forever that question as to whether this government will stand idly by and permit untold misery, slaughter and devastation to be heaped upon a brave but comparatively weak nation struggling to be free. There is but little question as to what the outcome will be. Spain, a nation historically brutal and domineering but astute in diplomatic craft, has at last reached a point where loud boasts and tyranny will not count against the prowess and magnanimity of an indulgent but positive nation. The stars and stripes will soon float over the citadel hitherto bedecked with the ensigns of Castillian pride. The rumor that the colored men are to do the fighting and suffer the loss of life is one born of cowardice and hate.

The black allies may be willing to do their part toward defending the honor of the nation and publishing its heroism and magnanimity to the world but they will and must do so by the side of their fairer brother. The slurs cast against a law-abiding, patriotic class of American citizens and the suggestion to put them to the front for the purpose of killing them off is as base and cowardly as any that have ever emanated from the blackest-hearted rebel the country has ever known. The conduct of the black ally will be as heroic and commendable in this contest as he has in every other contest which involves the liberty, honor and prosperity of the country and it is hoped that the results which will accrue to him in his capacity as an heroic citizen may be greater than those which it has hitherto been his fortune to receive. The villainy of suggesting that the colored soldier be used for slaughter merely has no place in the hearts of good citizens, as the events of the near future will certainly show. We will not be led as lambs to the slaughter but will fight like intelligent men knowing the responsibility resting upon us and believing in the ultimate acknowledgment of our rights to civil and political liberty.

*   *   *

THE WAR CLOUD

The war cloud is growing larger and larger every day. Spain's treachery is proverbial and the Maine disaster is only a sample of the sincerity and friendship of a weak, bankrupt, and effete nation. The butcheries which have been perpetrated upon the Cubans, the ingratitude shown by DeLome toward a nation which was profuse in its favor, all attest to the utter debasement of a nation which has long since lost its usefulness. Spain can "smile and smile and be a villain," can put on the calmest exterior to hide the blackest of crimes and can threat and brag when even at the point of beggary. Spanish diabolism and ribaldry have gone so far that "Uncle Sam" is becoming tired and is in a most splendid mood to thrash the deception and blood-thirstiness out of the gay deceivers. The crime of the Maine disaster must be avenged. America's noble braves have been slain in the house of their professed friends and the traitors guilty of the crime should suffer. The lives of our brave seamen and the insult to our flag cannot be atoned for by indemnity. The nation's murdered must be avenged by a chastisement severe and bloody if you please. War must be declared, Spain's treachery must be rebuked and the world informed by example that it is not well to abuse American confidence and outrage American sentiment.

Moreover, such atrocities as are being enacted in Cuba must be rebuked. The slavery to which the Cubans are subjected would be bad enough, but when the lives of the people are considered no more than those of sheep and oxen, when helpless women and children and innocent babes are butchered simply to satisfy a native bloodthirstiness of the Spaniards, it is time for this country to interfere and assist Cuba to be free. As President Lincoln was appealed to wipe out the stain of human slavery from the fair name of the country, so is President McKinley looked upon as the salvator of the Cuban patriots and the avenged wrongs against American interest and American honor.

Washington *Bee,* April 2, 1898

"Negroes Eager to Fight Spain
Should Also Fight Southern Brutes"

It does seem to us that in order to appear consistent these same negroes who exhibit such commendable readiness to assist in driving out the cowardly and treacherous Spaniards ought to show equal readiness when occasions arise—and such occasions certainly occur often enough —to kill off some of their drunken, cut-throat neighbors who make a pastime of hanging, shooting, and burning men, women, and children. Men who submit to the constant perpetration of such brutal and horrifying atrocities without an effort to properly punish the wretches who inflict them would, we suspect, make rather poor soldiers where earnest fighters were needed.

Let the negroes of South Carolina and other Southern states where crimes too cruel and infamous for Indian savages to commit are daily perpetrated by American-born caucasians, offer their services to their governors to wage war on these vile pests of civilized society.

Omaha *Afro-American Sentinel,* April 2, 1898

"Restrained Patriotism"

Colored troops are moving to the front. They should remember the conditions of mankind are not equal in this republic and there will be no return for too strong patriotic zeal.

Kansas City *American Citizen,* April 7, 1898

"American Soldiers Needed At Home, Not in Cuba"

That Louisiana Senator who tendered his resignation to take effect on a declaration of war, and too, for the purpose of going to the front to defend his nation's flag, has in him the stuff that makes up a true American. . . .

Some journals and some people have criticised President McKinley for not jumping head-long into war with Spain, but although Congress was at the stampeding point, by his master mind and executive will President McKinley held that august body in check longer than anyone dreamed he could do, he believing in the everlasting truth that peace is far better than war.

*   *   *

Some of these hot-headed war "ranters" could do infinitely more good by making some arrangements to put a stop to the cruelties and inhuman treatment accorded the Negro in the South than they can by trying to force President McKinley into declaring war with Spain. Give the Cubans what they ask for, and keep the American soliders at home to maintain the peace which is so badly needed at home.

* * *

"Don't Fight Spain, Give Gen. Gomez Aid"

There are thousands of Americans getting ready for war to free Cuba, but Gen. Gomez begs of us not to go to war with Spain, but asks that the United States do no more than recognize the Cuban government in order that they may purchase from us their supplies and munitions of war, and let them alone to win their own independence. Why not do as they ask? The evidence goes to show that Gen. Gomez knows his business. They have been giving the Spaniards a merry chase for four years with almost empty hands. These are facts. Then why need we put up our soldiers for targets when they are not needed?

Parsons *Weekly Blade,* April 9, 1898

"The Patriotic American Must Remember Injustice to the Negro"

We believe that the true American has a right to take up arms and go after Spain's dishonor, but they have for a long time forbidden the colored race equal justice before the law in many states.

Kansas State Ledger (Topeka, Kansas), April 9, 1898

"Justification For War"

This country and Spain are about to lock horns over the inhumanity of Cuban suffering by Spanish butchery; suffering humanity is the highest cause for which nations are justified in waging war. Looking at it from that standpoint we have a righteous cause; therefore we should be thrice armed for the fight. When the cry of a stricken people finally reaches the courts of heaven a deliverer comes from some source. It always has been and it always remains so.

* * *

"McKinley's Message Evaluated"

The message of President McKinley to Congress on Monday concerning the Cuban situation shows the greatest care, research, and forethought. It is a painstaking document, embodying the greatest labor and patience. It very clearly shows perplexity and great anxiety on the part of the writer to dwell within the bounds of precedent. It shows the profoundest interest in the subject matter under discussion and a conscientious desire to deal out exact justice mixed with as much mercy as possible. It burns with patriotic desires for the high standing of our republic among the nations of the world. It is alive with the essence of philanthropy which stands appalled at Spanish cruelty. . . .

It is a valuable state paper. But as a bold, vigorous, aggressive and progressive document, it was disappointing. It lacks the fervor and zeal of righteous convictions in a cause of momentous consequences. It conveys the lack of a sufficient cause for a possible action. The thread woven all through the subject is its weakest part. While this is true, on the other hand there is a closing which seems estranged from the general tenor of the subject and that is a seeming resignation to undertake in good faith whatever is thought best to be done. There is also shown a lack of definite outline and settled conclusions, which exhibits a timidity that throws the responsibility for action on other shoulders and full conclusion to follow rather than lead out in the matter.

Kansas City American Citizen, April 15, 1898

"AMERICA SHOULD STAND BY CUBAN NEGROES"

Gen. Weyler's plans in blowing up the Maine have been revealed. . . . this government should shoot his hide full of holes. . . .
Johnny get your gun.

*　*　*

War with Spain means a good deal; we understand that a great amount of the people in Cuba are Negroes, then we hope to see this government stand by them and protect them from all hazards.

Kansas State Ledger, April 16, 1898

THE POVERTY AMONG US

It has been proposed in Congress and since recommended by President McKinley to make an appropriation of large sums of money estimated at a half million dollars to feed Spanish subjects in Cuba.

Why not an appropriation of an equal amount to feed United States citizens in this country?

We have just passed through an era of hard times. The mills and factories have been idle, industries of all kinds paralyzed.

Money has been in hiding, and the cry of want has been heard throughout the land. In no section of the country has this been more manifest than in the Southland.

Mothers with hungry little ones are begging for bread. During the bleak days of winter, the scant furniture has been used for firewood. Our jails have been filled with persons charged with stealing coal.

The fences in certain neighborhoods have disappeared. Poverty stares all in the face. To-day, thousands and tens of thousands are without the means of earning a livelihood.

Disease has stalked in the wake of starvation and the graveyard is a place of constant visitation by the relatives of those who have gone on before. What is true of the colored population is equally so of the whites.

To add to our miseries, those in good circumstances are now clamoring for war with all of its attendant evils. Already, we are taxed to the "breaking point," and it is now proposed to levy a war tribute, not upon the wealthy but upon the working man. The rich one is beyond the reach of this species of oppression.

By sharp practices, he evades that to which we have to submit.

Oh, no, Congress and Mr. President! Send the half million of dollars to the citizens of the United States.

Open up the ships and the freight-cars to them. Give them a barrel of flour and a "turn" of meat and let them have an opportunity to regard with favor the beneficence of the United States Government.

When the nation was in distress, we came to its rescue; now we are in distress, let it do likewise.

Despite the sneers of the favored classes, the yell for a change of our peaceful policy, the words that are as true and lasting as the eternal hills shine forth in brilliant characters, telling a story pathetic and pitiful, but firm and unwavering, "Charity begins at home."

Feed the starving thousands of the United States, Mr. President, and let the nations of the world provide for those of their own nationalities.

*   *   *

THE PRESIDENT'S MESSAGE

President McKinley's message as transmitted to the two houses of Congress makes the best of a bad case.

It is unquestionably a powerful plea for peace while breathing threatenings of war.

He shifts the responsibilities of the situation upon Congress, and asks at the same time that it be transferred to his shoulders again.

It is a diplomatic stroke to gain time, knowing well as he does that each day's delay tends to bring peace between the two nations.

It is a pleasant surprise to that large conservative element, who up to this time has been unable to see sufficient justification for the shedding of blood and the expenditure of treasure.

The argument against the declaration of independence for, or the recognition of the belligerency of the alleged Cuban government, is one of the most striking characteristics of this truly remarkable document. It is a bombshell, thrown into the camp of the war-party, and will tend to cause endless debate in the Senate.

One striking feature, in fact, the sum and substance of the whole document, is its demand for peace.

It reminds one of Lincoln's attitude; the Union without slavery or the Union with slavery, but the Union.

So it is with President McKinley. Peace without Spanish authority, or peace with Spanish authority, but peace.

In the four reasons given as the grounds for intervention, viewed from a truly statesmanlike viewpoint, we failed to find one which would justify us in a court of international law. In fact, all of them would set a precedent which in the coming years may react upon us with telling effect.

If upon the grounds of humanity then England or Spain has the right to stop the lynchings in the South or to decide that Louisiana, Mississippi, or Texas have not a civilized form of government and its citizens and foreigners are not secure.

If upon the ground of protection to our own citizens then the principle specified above would again apply. Moreover, Spain is liable both for the lives and property of the persons referred to and has never shirked that responsibility.

If upon the ground of injury to trade or commerce, our four years' rebellion would have terminated with disastrous effects to our own national government, for England occupied at that time the same relative position as we now do to Cuba, and would have been justified according to this reasoning in landing English troops upon American soil.

If upon the ground that we are compelled to observe the laws of neutrality by preventing filibustering expeditions against a friendly power, then agreements amount to nothing when we get to the worst of the bargain.

Our first honorable course would be to announce our nullification of this section of international law to the nations of the world.

A noticeable feature too of the message is the request for the power to perform an act which will result in a declaration of war against us by Spain, while at the same time refraining from a recommendation for a declaration of war against Spain by us.

We have never been able to see where we could do more or go further than to recognize the belligerency of the Cuban insurgents. With the confession by the President of the United States that this is out of the question in view of existing conditions, to our minds our case ends.

The nations of the world might intervene in Cuba in the interest of humanity without being chargeable with the desire for selfish aggrandizement. One nation so doing would be open to grave suspicion, even though it be the United States of America.

From a standpoint of diplomacy, the Spanish statesmen have proven themselves masters.

Every excuse for interference has been removed, every reason for war swept away.

Richmond *Planet,* April 16, 1898

"SPAIN SHOULD GET A WHACK AT SOUTHERN WHITES"

We mind not war with Spain so much if it was possible to let Spain get a good whack at all the rebel fire-eating plugs in the South who would rather go to Hades than see a Negro stand on an equal footing with them. But as it is, the Negro is to stand up in the front row to protect a country that doesn't even respect him as a citizen.

*   *   *

If war is declared on Spain by this country, the ones who have been so loud in a desire for war will be the first to squeal: "I told you so!" and when the war wouldn't down in the first few rounds, you'll hear: "I didn't have a thing to do with that business."

*   *   *

"WHY IS WAR WANTED BY US?"

It seems strange that the United States can't recognize the belligerency of the Cuban insurgents and let them buy from us their munitions of war and let them fight out their own salvation as well as to declare war against the same power that the Cubans are fighting. Why is war wanted by us?

Just as has been predicted, Congress is not now so rampant for war. While President McKinley had the matter in his hands, there was a mad scramble for war, but now that these jingoes had a chance to declare war, they exercised their prerogative by declaring war on President McKinley because he didn't declare war on Spain.

Parsons *Weekly Blade,* April 16, 1898

"AGAINST WAR"

The Charleston *Enquirer* of South Carolina has taken a decided stand against the war party in this country, and what's more it is about right. The United States has its own odds and ends to look after. . . .

*   *   *

"FOR CUBAN INTERVENTION WITH NEGRO SUPPORT"

[From Dr. Frank J. Webb's speech in the First Baptist Church, Washington, D.C. on March 27, 1898:]

For years I have been an ardent advocate of American intervention in the Cuban problem and . . . with Maceo and Gomez in favor of Cuban liberty. [There are] three reasons why we as a nation ought to intervene. . . .: (1) Commercial, (2) Moral, (3) Fraternal sympathy. In Cuba Americans have $50,000,000 capital invested. . . .

Shall the descendants of the heroes of the Delaware and New Orleans stand idly by and forget what LaFayette and Rochambeau did for our struggling ancestors?

The cause of the illustrious Maceo is just: Cuban liberty is right. The opportunity for intervention is now. . . .

. . . What stand shall we black men of America take? Is . . . this the hour for us to secure revenge for the lynching of so many of our forefathers and our brothers. . . . Are we to allow the cries and groans of our cremated brothers and our assassinated sisters to ascend to high heaven unavenged? Shall we not in time of war demand an eye for an eye and a tooth for a tooth?

No. . . . I hurl such traitorous thoughts away in scorn and anger.

I think, fellow citizens, in spite of trials and humiliations we love our country's flag. My feeble tongue voices the sentiment of our race when I say 10,000 times "No" to any such revengeful idea. We are all Americans. . . .

Indianapolis Freeman, April 16, 1898

"NEGROES SHOULD SUPPORT THE WAR"

A committee called on McKinley yesterday, led by ex-governor P.B.S. Pinchback of La., and pledged the support of the colored race and said the loyalty of 9,000,000 of his race would assist.

*   *   *

Probably before another issue war will be declared, as McKinley sent his ultimatum to Cuba and demanded a reply not later than Saturday; already large armies of the National Guard are concentrating their forces in Florida near Key West. It is true that war is destructive, yet we are justifiable, and every true American will sanction the course that our government has taken. Young single men that are anxious to win military fame should tender their service and march toward the Torrid Zone.

*   *   *

CUBANS WILL BE FREE

So decided Congress last Monday night at 2 o'clock. Our country will intervene. McKinley has ordered the Spanish army to leave the island, where she has caused so many people to suffer, starve, and die an ignominious death; she has spilled many a loyal patriot's blood . . . the prayers of an enslaved nation have at last been answered by the patriotic, loyal, Christian nation of America. While the American government has no particular ill will for Spain, yet her treatment of the Cubans was so shocking to the moral conscience of Christian nations . . . that the Americans said it must be stopped and Cuba . . . must be free. We are only sorry that her freedom has not come sooner.

Iowa State Bystander, April 22, 1898

Civil Rights and the Possibility of War

"Is War With Spain Justified?"

In the war for Independence, this country was struggling for life and liberty itself. . . .

In the War of 1812, we were struggling for national honor and dignity—a just and equitable right.

The civil war . . . for national unity and the freedom of the republic—a righteous cause. . . .

In the war with Mexico . . . for the rights of a country we had just purchased. . . .

But what shall we say of this war with Spain?

*   *   *

"Negro's Duty to Support the Government"

However we may differ regarding the justness of the cause for war, when the majority decides for, it then is the duty of every citizen to lay aside all personal feeling and enter heartily into the country's cause and [do] all in our power for the success of our cause. . . .

It is a thrilling sight to see soldiers going forth to die for their country. It kindles the sparks of patriotism that have lain dormant for years.

Kansas City American Citizen, April 22, 1898

"The War a Blessing in Disguise"

Los Angeles, California.—As in other cities the Negro is discussing his attitude toward the government in case of war—shall he go to war and fight for his country's flag? Yes. Yes, for every reason of true patriotism. It is a blessing in disguise for the Negro. He will if for no other reason be possessed of arms, which in the South, in face of threatened mob violence, he is not allowed to have. He will become trained and disciplined. . . He will get honor. He will have an opportunity of proving to the world his real bravery, worth, and manhood. . . .

Indianapolis Freeman, April 23, 1898

"Negroes Await the Call"

The President and Congress have at last come to an understanding and war is practically declared. The system of mobilization is going on rapidly and patriotism is increasing in intensity every day. Spain in her dastardly conduct has diplomatized itself into a dilemma out of which she will hardly emerge without much smoke and rents in her garments. The President in his usual wise manner will conduct a vigorous campaign and Congress will not be behind in responding to every demand. The colored soldiers are at the front and thousands of valiant colored men are only waiting for Uncle Sam to say "come on boys" and a howling response will be forthcoming.

Washington Bee, April 23, 1898

"BLACKS NOT OVERPARTICULAR TO STOP SPANISH BULLETS"

Heretofore all colored men who enlisted in the army of the United States have been hustled off to a colored regiment. Under the present circumstances the government should be made to understand that if the great United States could not recognize the Negro as an American citizen and soldier, qualified to stand shoulder to shoulder with any white man, that the black was not overparticular to stop Spanish bullets. Now is the time to make Uncle Sam toe the mark and show his colors.

Parsons Weekly Blade, April 23, 1898

"THE WAR WILL HELP THE NEGRO"

In many respects we think that the present war will help the colored man in America, that is, his real worth will be more respected; his help is needed; his loyalty will establish a friendlier feeling in the South between the two races, his bravery and patriotism in the hour of need, (notwithstanding his own mistreatment), may serve as a lesson to their southern brothers as to what loyalty, true and equal manhood is, and we hope will hereafter be more willing to grant equal justice and freedom to their neighbors and citizens. Then again, the freedom of the colored people in Cuba will have a healthy influence in bringing better conditions for our race in general.

Iowa State Bystander, April 28, 1898

"LOYALTY OF THE NEGRO IN WAR"

It is all unnecessary for any negro self-constituted committee, or any other committee to go to the Executive Mansion and inform the President that 9,000,000 of negroes in the United States are loyal to this government and are willing to fight for Cuban Independence when the record of past generations and past wars will show that the negro has always been loyal and true to the flag that has given him his liberty and freedom.

President McKinley has always found the negro willing and ready to obey his country's call to arms.

We have a class of colored men in this country who must be taught a lesson and be informed that the Constitution of the United States provides for the punishment of traitors and the moral law for the extermination of cowards.

As an evidence of the negro's loyalty we call the attention of our readers to the spontaneous action of ex-Senator Henry Demas and the colored citizens of Louisiana. . . . [See article below—Ed.]

We also call attention to the enthusiasm of the colored citizens of Washington City, as well as everywhere else in the United States.

* * *

"LET BLACK GENERALS COMMAND BLACK TROOPS"

President McKinley has an excellent opportunity of doing what no other President has ever done. He has an opportunity of distinguishing and endearing himself in the hearts of the American negro. There are several distinguished major-generals and other military officers [to be] appointed. The negro is to do his share of fighting in the coming conflict with Spain. All indications point to the negro's valor and patriotism and his willingness to shoulder his gun for Cuban liberty and to uphold the honor and integrity of our American republic. There are negroes in this country who are capable of commanding an army and would do themselves credit if appointed. Generals need not be graduates from West Point or any other military academy. Let President McKinley appoint such a man as Henry Demas, Col. M. M. Holland, or Major Fleetwood. The last named were voted medals of honor for bravery. The negroes don't intend to be dirt workers and scullions in the fight. Let black generals command black troops and Spain will be thrashed in a week.

* * *

"DEMAS' BLACK BRIGADE"

Mr. [Henry] Demas did not make an ass of himself by coming to this city [Washington] and pledging the loyal black soldiers of his state to the American government or by telling the President or the people that he could raise in Louisiana black soldiers to fight the Spaniards like a few lily-white black republicans from the state have done in our Sunday afternoon literary societies. Mr. Demas went right to work to raise a regiment of black soldiers in his state . . . and in a few days will have a sufficient number to meet any Spanish invasion. Jim Lewis, who has been looking for an office since the fourth day of March, can now return to Louisiana and be high private in Demas' black brigade instead of visiting our Sunday afternoon literary societies telling people what he can do. Jim, you cannot do a thing, not even talk sensibly. Return home, Jimmie, and show to the President that you are really in earnest. Don't let your patriotism all be on paper with a string tied to it. You are needed at home. The boys want you. Demas' black brigade is waiting for you.

Washington *Bee,* April 30, 1898

"NEGRO SERGEANT FALSELY IMPRISONED IN KEY WEST"

The action of the white police officer at Key West, Florida in ordering Sergeant Williams of the 25th United States Infantry to put up his revolver, is without a parallel in the history of any nation.

The attempt to arrest him, which was finally successful and his assignment to a "lock-up" was an outrage, the like of which we hope never to hear of again.

The right to carry firearms is one of the guaranteed provisions of the Constitution of the United States, the only requirement being that they shall not be concealed.

This colored soldier is at Key West for the purpose of defending the lives and property of the citizens of Key West, Florida.

We noted with undisguised admiration and satisfaction the action of the twenty-five colored soldiers who repaired to the City Hall and demanded the surrender of their officer at the point of the bayonet, and gave the sheriff just five minutes in which to comply with this demand.

It would have been far better to have been sent to the guardhouse than to Cuba.

We trust to see colored men assert their rights. If the government cannot protect its troops against insult and false imprisonment, let the troops decline to protect the government against insult and foreign invasion.

It is a poor rule which does not work both ways. If colored men cannot live for their country, let white men die for it.

*   *   *

WAR HAS BEEN DECLARED
BY THE UNITED STATES AGAINST SPAIN

The Senate and House of Representatives took this extreme step on Monday last.

The wisdom of it is questioned. However, all loyal citizens must do their duty.

                                        Richmond *Planet,* April 30, 1898

III

THE DEMAND FOR BLACK OFFICERS:
"No Officers, No Fight!"

Prior to the Spanish-American War, there were four black military units in the regular army, the 9th and 10th Cavalry and the 24th and 25th Infantry, all organized after the Civil War. They spent their time in the West subduing Indians and now they were to fight with great proficiency and courage. In 1898, after President McKinley's first call for 125,000 volunteers, only 2,000 blacks were accepted. Thinking that the liberation from inhuman Spanish rule of fellow black men in Cuba was a just cause for the war, and believing they could improve their position in American society, many blacks formed volunteer companies and battalions, under the command of black officers. These volunteer units were rejected in most states, especially in the South. A campaign to get black officers above the rank of lieutenant in the regular army was launched by the Richmond *Planet*, which coined the slogan used throughout the war: "No Officers, No Fight!"

By June, 1898, a congressional act permitted the organization of up to ten Negro regiments, but the War Department and McKinley ruled that no black officer in those regiments should have the rank of captain or above. Only four regiments were formed, the 7th, 8th, 9th and 10th U.S. Volunteers, but none of these saw action in the war. The only black man in Congress at the time, Representative George H. White of North Carolina, spoke twice to McKinley about appointing black officers above the rank of lieutenant but was told both times that nothing would be done.

Only North Carolina, Virginia, Ohio, Kansas, Illinois and Massachusetts permitted black officers above the rank of lieutenant. There were about 100 black second lieutenants appointed in the volunteer companies, and six noncommissioned officers of the regular army were commissioned on the battlefield. But for the duration of the war, the black press kept up its campaign of discouraging enlistment under the battle cry: "No Officers, No Fight!"

NO OFFICERS, NO FIGHT!

President McKinley has called upon Virginia to furnish her quota of troops which is estimated to be three regiments. An interesting question has been raised, owing to the presence in the state of two colored battalions, the First being commanded by Major J. B. Johnson of this city and the Second by Major W. H. Johnson of Petersburg, Va.

An effort is being made to muster in the men without the field and staff officers.

The idea is to deprive them of the honors to which they are justly entitled. Major J. B. Johnson out-ranks his white fellow officers in point of service.

It is now proposed to place in charge of these troops white officers and to form a regiment with a white colonel.

The cry should be: "No officers, no fight!" It is the duty of the national government and especially of the state military officials to form a regiment in this state and promote Major J. B. Johnson to the position of colonel.

He is thoroughly competent and his military abilities are conceded by all who are in the least qualified to judge.

Colored men must contend for their rights now, or they will lose them hereafter.

*   *   *

"NEGRO OFFICERS NEEDED"

Now that we are in the midst of war and destruction our soldier lads are in great demand. . . . We should like to see our colored soldiers out in full . . . we mean a full company, battalion or regiment with their own officers from Captains, to Colonels and Generals. If this cannot be done, let the Regimental or Field Offices come from the regular army and not white men from some of the states who have no interest in the colored soldier but to force him to the front to see him die, and they draw big pay and get big honors. We gladly welcome the organization of more companies. This should have been done long ago, but prejudice and jealousy have been the great barrier, but the day of necessity is near at hand and will force all such enemies to the rear. Let not the Governor be puzzled or worried but call out the colored companies, issue commissions to colored men to organize other companies for the Regiment with colored regimental officers. . . .

Richmond *Planet,* April 30, 1898

"NEGRO OFFICERS NEEDED"

There should be a black Brigade in the U.S. service officered and manned by colored men.

There should be a Negro major general of Negro volunteers. Would it not be a fine sight?

When the President calls out fifty thousand colored troops, will these noble sons of Ham be officered by whites or colored?

If you or any of your people think the Negro is afraid of battle, just arm and equip him and then stand aside and watch results.

The only Negroes in the army of the United States are two regiments of cavalry and two of infantry—4,000 in all. There are none enlisted in the new call.

Kansas City *American Citizen,* May 6, 1898

"No Officers; No Fight!

The Richmond, Va., *Times* in its issue of the 17th inst., in commenting upon the statement of this journal relative to the part our people should take in this war says:

> Here is something for the colored people to think about. One paper complains that as good American citizens the Negroes are not receiving proper recognition at the hands of the Federal government in the bestowment of offices. Another one declares that the Negro should not fight except he can fight in his own way. Is that good citizenship?

We are not entering into a discussion as to whether it is good or bad citizenship, but we are very much concerned as to whether we are being treated in a good or bad way.

A country that will not accord to a citizen his rights and make good to him its guarantees releases him from any obligation to comply with his part of the contract. This is equity and it is law.

Where he is denied the right to muster in and is turned down in the matter of military appointments simply on account of his color, he has a right to decline to submit to such indignities and require the offending parties to muster him in as a conscript.

He does not ask to fight in his own way, but insists upon fighting in accordance with the laws of the land and the dictates of justice.

As to whether our attitude will do the Negro more harm than good, that is a matter of opinion.

Certain it is that the other policy has been observed for thirty years with the result that insult has been added to injury, and the cry against us has been taken up virtually by the nation itself.

If this be treason, make the most of it.

The *Times* says:

> The real friends of the Negro are men like Booker T. Washington who advise them to keep out of politics and to turn their attention to the improvement of their mental, moral, and material condition. It seems to us that the Negro should have learned by this time that holding office, instead of being a benefit to him, almost invariably gets him into trouble.

We agree with you. Mr. Washington has not as yet organized a regiment or sent a company to the front.

We have not done so either. We, too, advise them to keep out of politics as a race, and to let the white men do the fighting, while they turn their attention to the improvement of their mental, moral, and material condition.

There may be glory in war, and honor in politics; but nothing will materially and permanently elevate us but much learning, more money, increased business and a thorough knowledge of all the trades.

When the white folks want us, they will call for us. We are not under obligation in waging wars of conquest.

We are pledged to stand ready to repel the invasion of a foreign foe. We are not rushing forward now to die. We have done our part of that kind of serious business, for sixty thousand victims of the Ku-Klux Klan, the white-caps, the lynchers, and miscellaneous hordes of red-handed murderers are sleeping beneath the sod, and souls, Mr. Editor, "go marching on."

Our patriotism is unquestioned, our bravery unsurpassed, and we are not on trial in this particular before the nations of the world.

However, we insist upon it that it is right before expediency; officers before a fight and for this reason we have voiced the cry: No officers; no fight!

Richmond *Planet,* May 21, 1898

"SHOULD NEGROES ENLIST?"

The St. Louis, Mo., *American Eagle* disagrees with this journal and the New York *Pilot* in our position on the enlisting question. It says:

> Brothers Mitchell and Jones are both a little off. Gentlemen, we cannot win along that line. We feel the insults that are given us and the abuses that are heaped upon us just as much as you gentlemen do. It hurts! It cuts to the quick; but we cannot right public wrongs by committing another public wrong.

We fail to see where our attitude can be called a public wrong. There is nothing in the Constitution of the United States which requires us to engage in a war of conquest.

If it is, why should we be asked to volunteer? Why not muster us in regardless of our wishes?

The nation's honor is not at stake, neither is the government in peril. Then, under what obligations are we to be hanging around the front door of the war department gazing at the sign "Negroes not wanted! Negro officers not thought about!"

Spain, so far as her crimes are concerned, is no more guilty than the United States of America when gauged by the stern rule of comparison.

The two hundred and fifty years of slavery, leaving in its wake broken-hearted mothers, quivering fathers, sobbing children, and streams of blood drawn by the lash, tell a story almost too horrible for reference.

Peace did not bring a cessation of the evil, and murders of the most outrageous kind have been tolerated, and robbery of hard earnings winked at by those in authority.

The Supreme Court of the United States has recognized as constitutional the infamous constitution of Louisiana, and dodged a reference to the unconstitutional one of Mississippi.

A race of people who, denied the right of suffrage, outraged, butchered, with their rights ruthlessly trampled upon from one end of the South to the other, would kiss the hand that smites, and beg the privilege of dying for their oppressors, is degenerate indeed, and can but merit the contempt of the people in whose cause they enlist.

Again, we voice the cry, one that we have repeatedly uttered during the past ten years: A man who is not good enough to vote for a government is not good enough to fight for it.

We do not profess to be able to keep colored men from enlisting. We are not trying to do so. We are stating the facts and they can act to suit themselves.

The flag of race prejudice has been raised. Colored companies have been barred from white regiments, and the talk is to enlist them in separate regiments and brigades.

If this be true, we insist they be commanded by colored officers.

We do not propose to be insulted and have those who insult us profit by our bravery.

In the South today exists a system of oppression as barbarous as that which is alleged to exist in Cuba, and yet those in authority at Washington could declare war, spend one hundred million of dollars, muster in one hundred and twenty-five thousand troops, and offer to spend a million of dollars to feed foreigners while more than a hundred thousand people are starving in this country.

No, we do not like it, and we would be slaves indeed were we to be silent in the face of such rank injustice.

We are not a candidate for public office. Our duty is to advocate the cause of the people we represent, and about here they, with us, are saying, Mr. Editor, "No officers; no fight!"

Richmond *Planet,* May 28, 1898

No Officers, No Fight!

Governor J. Hoge Tyler has asked for permission to muster in two colored battalions in this state and the request has been granted. The *Dispatch's* news columns are responsible for the following:

> The question as to whether the negro companies will be allowed to retain their present colored officers was at once raised when it was known yesterday that the negro troops would be mustered in. There are

four regiments of colored troops in the regular army but all the commissioned officers are white men. It is not known whether the President will accept colored officers, or whether the white officers of the regular and volunteer armies would be willing to receive them.

And again:

Alabama furnished several colored companies as a portion of her quota, but the Governor of that State removed the negro officers and put white men in their places. This raised a great uproar among the men, and it seems probable they will not volunteer. It is stated by one of the men that they would have been perfectly willing to accept white officers had they only been permitted to choose them. The Governor of Alabama appointed them without any election.

The following telegraphic report is an answer to the above:

Mobile, Ala., May 31.—The Gilmer Rifles, Mobile's colored company, held a meeting tonight and refused to volunteer under Captain Robert Gage, appointed by the Governor of Alabama. They adopted resolutions and petitioned the Governor to allow them to select their own officers, as has been done by the white companies.

The *Dispatch* continues:

So far as could be ascertained, it is the sentiment among officers here that the company and battalion commanders of the negroes should be white men, but that the rank and file of the companies should at least choose the former. It is not known what the Governor will decide in the matter, but it is to be believed he favors white officers, whether by election or otherwise cannot be known.

Well, the Governor will have an opportunity to let it be known what he favors. And again: "There is no reflection on the colored officers, but it is believed that the companies could be handled much more effectively by white officers. . . ."

The above requires no reply. The fact that the present efficient corps of officers measure up to that standard is too well known for comment.

The *Dispatch* very kindly remarks:

Major Johnson, who commands the First Battalion, is the ranking major in the Virginia service, and has been for some time, his commission bearing the date of June 20, 1892. The last annual report of the Adjutant-General, discussing the First Colored Battalion, says: "The major commanding is thoroughly competent."

We cannot get the colored officers to talk. They are as "dumb as oysters" . . . but they know the spirit of the men sufficiently well to state that they have no desire to, and will not, volunteer to fight Spain unless they are commanded by the present corps of officers.

Their present efficiency is due to the untiring efforts of their major . . . J. B. Johnson, and they will insist that he occupy the position which he has capably filled for so many years with credit to his command and honor to the state.

*   *   *

"No Officers, No Fight! Position Defended"

The Washington, D.C. *Post* in its issue of May 26th lectures the Richmond, Va. *Daily Times* for paying any attention to the attitude of Afro-American journals, and then proceeds to do exactly what it advises the *Times* not to do.

It says:

> We observe with regret and pain a disposition on the part of certain newspapers—among them the Richmond *Times*—to criticize the colored man and brother on account of his attitude to the government at this time. It is objected that he is too self-assertive, that he wants too much, that his demands are in excess of his deserts. Much of this criticism has been provoked by utterances of so-called "Afro-American" organs from one of which, published at Richmond, Va. we quote by way of illustration.

Then follows an extract from our editorial column relative to the enlisting of colored men under colored officers. The *Post* says:

> Of course this is the most ridiculous nonsense. The question is whether it represents the sentiment of intelligent and respectable colored men. If it does we are sincerely sorry for them; but we do not believe it does. We are rather inclined to think that it is merely the frothing of some would-be "leader" who hopes by protests and vociferation to center attention upon himself. However that may be, the truth of the matter is that the article we have quoted is merely a stupid and ignorant outburst which well-disposed white people will not construe to the injury of their fellow colored citizens.

This is a very charitable view for our contemporary to take. As to the stupidity of the article in question we pause to remark that it is a matter of the *Post*'s opinion, which really concerns no one but the *Post* and the *Planet*. And again:

> All this talk about "insults" and "striking back" is nothing more than childish rant, and proves, if it proves anything at all, that the negro could not do himself greater harm than by listening to it. The trouble is that there are a lot of self-appointed colored leaders, whose only qualification consists in their bumptiousness and whose only possible achievement is mischief. The race in general can make no greater mistake than that of accepting their statements and following their advice. Nobody cares three straws whether they go into the army or stay out of it. Nobody wants them at all unless they are ready to obey orders and accept discipline. The war will go right along whether the colored warriors join the army or stay at home, and if we send a million fighting men to the front, there will still remain several other millions to preserve order at home and attend to any "trouble" the disgruntled colored leaders may see fit to make.

We would have presumed that this was a deliverance in the columns of a journal published in Mississippi, Louisiana or Texas.

Our view is that the editor-in-chief was studying war news and that the office-boy had been entrusted with the task of writing "a line or two upon some questions."

Certain it is that such language is unbecoming a non-partisan journal and at variance with every rule of decorum which governs the editorial department of great metropolitan journals.

But enough—our point is to emphasize the statement which is a fair one that if colored men are good enough to fight as privates they should be good enough to fight as officers.

That whenever color is allowed to bar one from military service rather than capability that the rights guaranteed in the Constitution of the United States are abridged.

If no one cares three straws as to whether we go into the army or stay out of it, we are prepared to consult our own wishes, and stay out of it.

We were not called for during 1861-5 until the front part of the United States Army became "too hot for comfort" and we expect that experiment to be repeated in this war with Spain.

We presume that the *Post*'s editor was overburdened and anxious as to the whereabouts of the Spanish Admiral Cervera or was suffering from an acute attack of dyspepsia.

Had he been better informed he would have known that all the colored people hereabouts are demanding has been already granted by the Democratic state officials. . . .

Why, my dear sir, J. B. Johnson, colored, Afro-American or Negro of this city, as you like it please, is Major of the First Battalion, Virginia Volunteers. He the ranking major of the state in point of service without regard to race or color.

W. H. Johnson, colored, of Petersburg, Va., is Major of the 2nd Battalion Virginia Volunteers.

By a system of military jugglery it is proposed to unsettle all of this and to transfer these commands to white officers, so that others will reap the honor and benefits of these capable officers' efforts.

These colored officers were honored by Virginia's democratic officials. Richmond City has given the First Battalion a magnificent armoury building at the cost of ten thousand dollars, and it was done under a resolution of John Mitchell, Jr., a Negro and a Republican, who was at that time a member of the Board of Aldermen and not a "would-be self-appointed leader."

Now, if the matter is left to the Governor, J. Hoge Tyler, there will be no question as to the result. The colored officers would be mustered in with their commands in their entirety. We venture too the assertion that if a Negro regiment is formed in this state, Major J. B. Johnson will be given command of it by the official referred to.

As the Washington *Post* seems to think that they are not needed now, they are perfectly content to remain at home with their families.

It may be, sir, that this will be a sea-fight with only a handful of troops engaged, but conservative army officials see ahead the need of just double the number of troops as have been mustered into the service.

We pause to remark that whether we have war or peace, it will take numerous drafts for the mustering officer to find his way into the private office of the editor of the *Post* in order to serve notice upon him that he is wanted at the front.

The *Post* concludes:

> What our colored friends need is a little common sense, with a dash of modesty to make it palatable. We are well enough disposed regarding them, but we are getting just a trifle tired of their Editor and spokesmen with their ridiculous bombast and their stupid airs. They persistently claim that they want to be respected. Why don't they do something to deserve respect?

Yes, we thought you were tired, and so is the government. What you need is a little more common sense and a little less race prejudice.

We did not bring on this war, and are content to watch the outcome of it.

Certain it is that we will for once do something to deserve respect. We will sit on the limb of the tree of inaction until you whip Spain or find out that you are to be whipped by her.

Should the contest wax warm and help is badly needed, we will then become the much-wanted quantity and requests now scornfully denied will be readily granted.

Those white men who are itching for a fight can have it. For our part, war is a serious business and death a long rest to the weary.

We are ready to help the government, to rally to its defense, but the barnacles must be removed from the ship of state and the Negro-haters stowed away in the rubbish before we are ready to do and die and to carry aloft the standard of the nation led by the bravest Afro-American officers the world has ever seen.

Let our test be thorough this time, Mr. Editor. Let our commanding officers be of our own hue.

For the present, sir, the flag of our racial characteristics is flying and emblazoned upon it in resplendent letters are the words, "No officers; no fight!"

Richmond *Planet,* June 4, 1898

MORE ABOUT COLORED OFFICERS

[From a letter of J. W. Cromwell:]

Mr. Editor: Permit me to congratulate the *Planet* on its outspoken, straightforward and very manly position respecting colored enlistments and the mean article in the Washington *Post* entitled, "Colored Compatriots."

Anyone who read between the lines will discern that the administration will appoint no colored commissioned officers above the grade of lieutenant. . . . That of the 125,000 volunteers, less than 2,000 are colored is not a mere coincidence. . .

The purpose of the administration is reconciliation between the sections at the expense, if need be, of the very men who made the nomination of McKinley possible and his election sure.

Thirty-five years ago under the shadow of the Dred Scott decision, the negro was enlisted with nothing but a non-commissioned officer's position before him to stimulate the deeds of daring. To-day a citizen in contemplation of law and with the record of his soldiers on the plains, he should at least not be placed below the status of those who wore the gray, when to wear the blue alone was loyalty to the nation.

Simple respect forbids any other course than that there should be no great enthusiasm to enlist even for the freedom of Cuba, in a service which proposes to insult us in advance by saying, "Thus far shall you come and no further. . . ."

Massachusetts to-day, as in the time of Governor John A. Andrews, blazes the way for Company L of her historic "Sixth" with her commissioned company and battalion officers. Ohio, it is true, has a colored major in charge of a battalion, but as a West Pointer of nine years standing a commission could not be refused former Lieutenant Charles Young. It is a current rumor that this colored battalion is to be recruited under the second call to full regimental strength, in which event Major Young will be promoted to a colonelcy. Governor Bushnell and Senator Foraker, who do not always train with McKinley and Hanna, will see to this. . . .

Fitzhugh Lee might whisper into the ears of Governor J. Hoge Tyler a significant message that would cause Virginia to do at least as well as North Carolina, Ohio or Massachusetts. . . .

The District of Columbia Colored Military contingent were left entirely in the cold. The quota under the first call was increased to a regiment, and the demand will be under the 75,000 proclamation.

It is now proposed to recruit two companies of the four regiments of maneuvers allotted to our race here in the District. The colonels have been appointed, the captains also—all white. One of the latter, a policeman, called on R. H. Terrell, Esq., to tender him a position as 1st lieutenant for the honor of getting a company of men together. A more insulting proposition cannot be imagined, especially when the white "Tom, Dick, and Harrys" have been commissioned paymasters, quartermasters and adjutants without number.

Among the colored men here who received medals of honor from the United States for heroic conduct on the field of battle during the Civil War, there reside here Sergeant Major C. A. Fleetwood and Sergeant Major Milton M. Holland. Yet we must still be humble and keep our place.

With the progress of the war and its delay, I trust these matters will be righted. . . .

Richmond *Planet,* June 11, 1898

" 'No Officers, No Fight' in Iowa"

A message just received from the war department states that they will not accept the colored Captain of our colored company. We answered back that we positively refused to go under a white captain. We are glad that our people made this stand because if they need us or at least wanted our service they would permit us to have colored officers.

Iowa State Bystander, June 17, 1898

"No Officers, No Soldiers"

If negroes cannot have their own officers in the service of their country then the country needs not their services. It is an insult to tell us that we are incapable of holding the rank of an officer—no officers, no soldiers is our motto and we are loyal too.

Kansas City *American Citizen,* June 17, 1898

"John E. Bruce Supports 'No Officers, No Fight!' "

[From a letter of John E. Bruce to the editor:]

I most heartily commend the courage and consistency which characterize your editorial utterance under the question of the recognition of Negroes as officers over Negro troops in the pending war with Spain. . . . Your slogan, "No officers, no fight" is a good one and will find a response in the breast of every Negro who has a spark of manhood in his anatomy. . . .

Richmond *Planet,* June 18, 1898

"Kansas Permits Negro Officers"

Governor Leedy is proving to be our ideal governor and has decided to have two colored battalions of soldiers . . . he . . . puts colored officers over the colored soldiers. . . . We have had all manner of things to endure, but the action of the authorities in refusing the negro a chance to die for a country that does not protect him was most humiliating. . .

Kansas City *American Citizen,* June 24, 1898

"Louisiana Volunteers Get Negro Officers"

[From a letter by Ed Barnes, New Orleans, dated June 18, 1898:]

The colored people held a mass meeting on the 22nd of April last, with more than 5,000 people in attendance and adopted resolutions tendering their services to the Government for the common defense of the nation. [1,500 men enrolled, 10 companies were organized, and officers were selected.]

With the passage of the "Immune Volunteer" bill, the leading colored men . . . appealed to the authorities for recognition. . . . The authorities said only white captains were to be in charge.

To go in under such conditions would necessarily bar the officers chosen by the companies, especially the captains. . . .

A meeting of the black regiment with the public was held on June 7 and the decision was that Negro companies should have Negro officers.

In the personnel of the regular army officers lurks the rankest and most deep-seated prejudice to the colored soldier's promotion . . . and the War Department lends support to such a policy.

*   *   *

"McKINLEY SHOULD PERMIT NEGRO OFFICERS"

When [you made] your several calls for men to enlist . . . our black citizens, feeling secure that with a Republican administration, the Republican amendments to the Constitution of the United States would be jealously executed, came promptly to the front. Few of the State Governors availed themselves of their offers [Negro volunteers] but as a rule promptly turned them down. . . .

Ten regiments of so-called "immunes" were placed absolutely at your personal disposal, Mr. President and . . . from you came the ruling discriminating against us . . . that no colored man should be given a position higher than a lieutenant in the six regiments set aside for negroes. Possibly a captain or two may have slipped through, but only as the exception to prove the rule. . . . We are told you positively deny the existence of such a rule, but the War Department officials just as positively assert that it exists. . . .

The mistake was made when a self-constituted committee without a constituency offered you the services of nine millions of negroes for the war. . . . Throw down the bars, open up the positions and promotions, and the negro will flow into the army as a flood. Keep up the color line you have established and they will trickle in as now. . .

Washington *Bee,* June 25, 1898

"PRESIDENT McKINLEY AND GOVERNOR BLACK OF NEW YORK EXCORIATED FOR NOT PERMITTING NEGRO OFFICERS"

[From the New York *Herald:*]

One of the most sensational public meetings ever held by the Afro-Americans of New York was the afternoon session Friday of the

New England Baptist Convention at the Berean Baptist Church of Brooklyn. The Convention is composed of prominent colored men.

The excoriation of President McKinley's administration and denunciation of Governor Black because of their refusal to accord what the Constitution termed "proper recognition" to the colored volunteers of the country, created great excitement in the church. . . . One woman, with tears in her eyes, begged the Convention to let her voice the sentiments of the women.

"Just for one minute. For God's sake, hear us!" she cried.

When the Rev. A. Gordon of Philadelphia declared that he hoped and was hoping that the American arms would not be victorious until justice had been accorded to the Negro soldiers, there was vociferous applause.

W. Bishop Johnson of Washington, D.C., editor of the National Baptist Magazine, precipitated the discussion by a report he submitted on the state of the country, in which he said that the reporting committee viewed with alarm the administration's attitude toward the Afro-Americans in its refusal to give Negro officers to Negro regiments.

He declared that the Convention should go on record denouncing the Administration's attitude, and he urged the appointment of a committee to go to Washington to present to the President the sentiments of the Convention. . . .

Addresses were delivered by Dr. J. Anderson Taylor of Washington, Rev. A. W. Adams of Boston, E. E. Anderson of Virginia, W. S. Holland of Rhode Island, and Dr. D. W. Wisher of New York in which the administration was severely denounced. Some of the speakers declared that the administration was not doing justice to those who had been brave and loyal in the rebellion, while it had placed in high position those who had rebelled against the nation.

On motion the Convention went on record as denouncing Governor Black for his refusal to accept a colored regiment of volunteers which was offered during the week by a delegation of colored ministers. The Convention telegraphed congratulations to the Governors of Virginia, North Carolina, and Massachusetts for giving colored officers to colored regiments.

Richmond *Planet,* June 25, 1898

"Kansas Gets Negro Officers"

Now that Gov. Leedy has decided to accept two battalions of colored infantry, Capt. Levi Holt of this city will no doubt have a chance to prove his patriotism.

Mr. Nelson Marshal is endeavoring to raise a company in Coffeyville to "fight against Spain."

Lawyer George Fitzpatrick delivered an interesting lecture to a fair-sized audience at the A.M.E. Church Friday night on the subject of

"War." He urged that notwithstanding the flag fails in many instances to protect the Negro, he should be loyal to the stars and stripes and especially so since colored troops have been allowed their own officers in Kansas. That war is always for gain and a blessing in disguise. He hoped to see a hearty response of the colored men to the present call. After the lecture, W. H. Fuller of the *American* was called upon and made some patriotic and enthusiastic remarks.

*   *   *

[The following is a letter which appeared in the *American*, addressed to Rev. K. P. Bond:]

Topeka, Kan., June 22

Dear Sir and Brother: The governor of this state has called for two battalions of colored volunteers for the United States army, and has agreed to give all colored officers, both field and line. Our John M. Brown and James Beck have been commissioned majors already. I hope you will preach on this subject Sunday and encourage our colored people to enlist, for this is the greatest thing for colored people since the emancipation proclamation of Abraham Lincoln.

I am yours,
J. R. Ransom

American (Coffeyville, Kansas), June 25, 1898

" 'NO OFFICERS, NO FIGHT' IN MISSOURI"

The Negroes of Missouri made a brave stand when they refused to enlist under white officers.

Parsons *Weekly Blade,* July 2, 1898

"NO OFFICERS, NO FIGHT!"

There is no American citizen upon this continent who possesses any more patriotism than what we do. But if we had the power we would not permit one negro battalion or company or regiment to assist in helping to fight against Spain unless they are officered from top to bottom by members of our own race.

Salt Lake City *Broad Ax,* July 2, 1898

"NEGRO VOLUNTEERS IN KANSAS"

[From the *Weekly Call*, Topeka, Kansas:]

Young colored men now have a splendid opportunity to enlist and show that they deserve the confidence Governor Leedy has placed in them in calling out two battalions of negro troops, officered by colored men. It is a compliment to the military genius of our race; negroes universally express for it a very high appreciation.

*   *   *

"GOVERNOR BLACK OF NEW YORK REFUSES NEGRO TROOPS"

[From the *Weekly Triumph*, New York:]

A special committee composed of Messrs. C. A. Dorsey, T. M. Stewart, T. Thomas Fortune, S. R. Scott, James Garner, and Bishop A. Walters called on Governor Black the 13th inst. with a view of persuading him to create another regiment in order to give the colored patriots a chance, but he refuses on petty excuses. The committee, however, will hold a public meeting at St. Mark's next Wednesday evening to consider the condition of affairs. Rev. Dr. Brooks, Bishop W. B. Derrick, T. M. Stewart, and Bishop A. Walters will address the audience. All welcome.

*   *   *

"NEGRO OFFICERS IN KANSAS"

[From the *Rising Sun*, Smithville, Texas:]

Governor Leedy has tendered a lieutenant-colonelcy to Maj. Chas. Young of Ohio. John M. Brown of Topeka and James Beck of Manhattan have been appointed majors and our own John M. Waller has been made captain of the Kansas City, Kan., company. Gov. Leedy is all right.

Indianapolis *Freeman,* July 16, 1898

"NEGRO VOLUNTEERS IN KANSAS"

The colored people of this city are overflowing with patriotic devotion for the cause of humanity. Last night's meeting was held in Judge Pott's court, the object of which was to raise another company for the army. . . .

Kansas City *American Citizen,* July 16, 1898

"MCKINLEY ASSAILED FOR NOT PERMITTING NEGRO OFFICERS"

[From the Richmond *Planet:*]

The New York *Age* declares that President McKinley has established "a dead line behind which Afro-Americans cannot go into the volunteer army" and cited in support of this contention an extract from a letter written by Congressman George H. White, of North Carolina, to Mr. T. Thomas Fortune, who on May 18th made an offer to the President to raise an Afro-American regiment. It was to be in command of Afro-American officers. The extract is as follows:

> I have seen the President twice since I wrote you, and opinion is that neither you nor any other colored man will be appointed to a place in the immune regiments above the rank of lieutenant. I called his attention to your case specifically, and from all that he said I have reached the conclusion here given.

This is "cheek" with "gall" thrown in free of charge. The Negro-haters of the nation seem to be in full swing at the White House. It should not be forgotten that the military authorities of Indiana gave as their excuse for not appointing Afro-American officers that it was contrary to the wishes of the war department. . . .

For our part we see no good to accrue from forcing ourselves on the war department, other than to place it on record. If President McKinley and his advisers are against us, we should be pleased to have the constantly accumulating evidences of that fact for future reference. We have tens of thousands of white friends in this country, and we do not have to go wandering into other states than our own to find them.

*   *   *

"CONGRESS DOES NOT CALL UP 25,000 BLACK TROOPS"

Congress adjourned without doing anything with the bill providing for 25,000 Afro-American troops, asked for by Secretary of War Alger. As we expected. We regarded the whole thing as a "jolly" for our people of the entire country, from the very beginning.

Cleveland *Gazette,* July 16, 1898

"NO OFFICERS, NO FIGHT!"

The very best method for the negro to adopt in order to secure their just rights as soldiers is for every negro who is now engaged in fighting Spain to throw down their arms and refuse to pick them up again until members of our race are selected to officer them from head to foot.

Salt Lake City *Broad Ax,* July 23, 1898

"WHY ARE THEY UNPATRIOTIC?"

[From the Omaha *World-Herald:*]

"Those negroes of St. Joseph who refuse to enter the volunteer army to fight against Spain because the superior officers are white men are not brave nor loyal and are not deserving of the right of citizenship.—St. Joseph *News.*"

Indeed! And why are they unpatriotic if they refuse to enlist **under** white officers? Would it be difficult to find enough colored men to officer a regiment? Are there no negroes fully as capable of being assistant adjutant-generals with the rank of colonels as the pampered society pets who have been appointed to staff positions because their fathers happened to be good soldiers or mediocre Congressmen?

The St. Joseph *News* is unjust to the colored men. There is probably not a disloyal negro in America. They proved their loyalty thirty-five years ago, and any veteran of the late war will bear out the assertion that a Union soldier was never betrayed or allowed to go hungry by a negro.

Indianapolis *Freeman,* July 23, 1898

"No Officers, No Fight!"

No Negro officers, no Negro volunteers.—St. Louis *American Eagle.*

Remember the slogan, Afro-American officers for Afro-American regiments.—St. Paul *Appeal.*

Negro officers for Negro soldiers should be the slogan of every Negro in America.—*Evangelist.*

Negro officers for Negro troops.—Norfolk *Daily Recorder.*

It is the unanimous verdict of the colored press—that no officer, no men.—Savannah *Tribune.*

If we get no general we do no fighting. You may call it disloyalty or anything you please.—Washington *Bee.*

Cleveland *Gazette,* July 30, 1898

"No Officers, No Fight!"

[From the *Florida Evangelist*, Jacksonville, Florida:]

Every one of the hundreds of Negro newspapers of America, and every leading and influential Negro leader in the United States are agreed that the Negro soldiers in the United States army must be commanded by Negro officers. And they are urging their race throughout America to refuse to enlist in the army unless they are placed under Negro officers, and for once the black men of this country are a unit and are following their leaders.

Cleveland *Gazette,* August 6, 1898

"Colonel Lee Returns to the Regular Army"

[From the *Tribune*, Savannah, Georgia:]

It is reported that Colonel Lee has given up his rank as colonel of the colored immune regiment and returned to the regular army. The colonel finds it a very hard matter securing recruits among the colored men and we suppose that is the reason of his recent step. The reason why the colored men refused to enlist is not because of a lack of patriotism, but because they were not allowed to select their own officers, or in fact were told they were not fit to command companies. The colored men came to the conclusion that if they were not able to secure commissions as captains, etc. that they will stay out until their ability is duly recognized.

Richmond Planet, August 6, 1898

IV

CIVIL RIGHTS, PATRIOTISM AND THE SPANISH-AMERICAN WAR

Black patriotism during the Spanish-American War was restrained, critical, and often bitter. Many felt that the main enemy of the Negro was not Spain but southern lynchers, and at least one paper, the Milwaukee *Wisconsin Weekly Advocate*, compared the war to the "unjust" Mexican war of 1846-1848.

After war was declared, a committee of three prominent black Republicans, ex-lieutenant governor of Louisiana, P.B.S. Pinchback; James Lewis, editor of the *Republican Courier* of New Orleans; and Judson Lyons, Register of the Treasury, visited President McKinley and offered the services of 9,000,000 Negroes in support of the war. This offer was severely criticized in the black press, especially in the Washington *Bee* and the Richmond *Planet,* which maintained that Pinchback and his "pie-counter crowd" spoke only for themselves. The *Planet* urged black men not to volunteer if they did not get black officers, but to concentrate on making money during the war to enhance their economic status.

Throughout the war the cardinal emphasis in the black press was on the anomaly of protecting the citizens of Cuba, and not protecting American citizens in the South.

"NEGRO'S MAIN ENEMY IS SOUTHERN LYNCHERS"

[From the *Enterprise,* Omaha, Nebraska:]

The negro still insists that his chief kick is not on the Spaniards but on those fellows who shoot and burn and hang and otherwise kill our fellows in the South. Every negro who bubbles over with patriotic enthusiasm for bleeding Cuba and forgets about the unatoned blood of Baker, Loftin, and hundreds of others is a fool and a chump. Every conservative black man in this country must say no to the whites in the language of the Son of Man: "First pick the mote from thine own eye, then thou canst see clearly to pluck the beam from thy brother's eye."

Salt Lake City *Broad Ax,* April 30, 1898

"WHITE AMERICA'S CRUELTY EQUALS SPAIN'S"

The American white man's rule in dealing with the American Negro . . . in times of peace and prosperity [relegates] him to the rear, deprives him of his rights as an American citizen, cuts off his opportunities of existence, outrages colored women, burns down his home over his wife and children. . . . More than 500 colored men and women have been murdered by the American white people in the past 25 years and now they . . . have the audacity to talk about the cruelty of Spain toward the Cubans. There is no half-civilized nation on earth that needs a good hard war more than the United States, and it is high time if there is any such being as an omnipotent just God, for Him to rise and show His hand in behalf of the American Negro.

Iowa State Bystander, May 6, 1898

"CIVIL RIGHTS AND PATRIOTISM"

[From the *Bee,* Washington, D.C.:]

"The committee of colored residents of this city, purporting to represent every state and territory in the United States, called upon President McKinley last Wednesday morning and offered the services of 9,000,000 Negroes for Cuban independence and to assure the President that these Negroes are loyal to the flag.

Every Negro who is an American citizen is pledged to support the Constitution of the United States; by virtue of that pledge he stands ready to fight to sustain the Constitution. What the *Bee* contends is that the American Negro needs protection himself, and he does not hesitate to fight this enemy or offer his life for his country if his government will guarantee protection to him. We have had enough of a few colored men who have no constituency whatever, arrogating to themselves to speak for the millions of loyal negroes in the United States."

The *World,* of Indianapolis, Ind., commenting on the above says:

> It struck us precisely as it did editor Chase of the *Bee* and we heartily second his cry of disgust. The 9,000,000 colored citizens do not need anyone to pledge them. They can do that for themselves. It takes a good deal of cheek for a little coterie of politicians seeking notoriety to claim that they have 9,000,000 colored people in their pockets which they carry around for advertising purposes. The whole performance is disgusting and every Negro newspaper in the country should resent their impudent obtrusiveness.

The *American* would like to know when that committee will be ready to present the government with the services of 9,000,000 negroes. The negroes of this country want it understood that when the time comes they will march to the front like the true American citizen.

* * *

"No Negro Volunteers in Coffeyville"

[From the Coffeyville *Journal* (white):]

"The Kansas negroes are not spoiling for a fight. It is said not one Atchison or Topeka negro even offered to volunteer."

No, not noticeably so. But then, Jim Crow cars and southern hostility are not very great inducements. The Kansas negroes are loyal and patriotic but that is no reason why they should not have some sense, some pride, and some manhood.

* * *

"Temper Patriotism With Wisdom and Pride"

Half the negroes who are moving heaven and earth in order to enter this contest against Spain are not troubled with any considerable amount of wisdom or pride. It is all right to be patriotic. . . . But the spectacle of patriotic negroes being transported in Jim Crow cars to defend their country, leaving their brothers at the mercy of mobs, their demands on their behalf unheeded or laughed to scorn, almost fighting their way to the common enemy through the hostile ranks of their own fellow citizens, is one, we believe, for which history has no parallel. We shall never question the patriotism of the negro for, wonderful as it may seem under the circumstances, he is patriotic. We do not think, however, that a little horse sense minus weapons, is what most of these clamorous patriots need. The fact that civilization could spare not a few of them without any noticeable setback is no reason why they should publicly declare it. A few grains of self-respect added to the necessary amount of pride as a people would also materially assist this class of Afro-Americans in the matter of deciding how to act in a great emergency.

Coffeyville *American,* May 7, 1898

"Spanish-American War Unjust"

Lowell's poems, especially the immortal "Biglow Papers," furnish an inexhaustible text for Americans who hate any war that is not a righteous one. The Mexican war was not a just one; it was forced upon Mexico deliberately by a slaveholders' conspiracy, and it richly merited the scathing satire with which Lowell exposed the cant and false pretenses that covered the nakedness of a land-grabbing raid:

T'aint eppyletts an' feathers
Make the thing a grain more right;
T'aint a-follerin' your bell-wethers
Will excuse ye in His sight;
Ef you take a sword an' drow it,
An' go stick a feller thru,
Guv-ment ain't to answer fer it,
God will send the bill to you.

And here is a verse that seems to have been written in a spirit of prophecy to suit the conditions of 1898:

Take them editors thet's crowin'
Like a cockerel three months old,
D'ont ketch any on 'em goin',
Though they be so blasted bold;
Ain' they a prime lot o' fellers?
'Fore they thin on't they will sprout
(Like a peach that's got the yellers),
With the meanness bustin' out.

The inspired poet, in using the "yellers" as an expression of contempt, builded better than he knew for a crisis half a century later than the Mexican War.

* * *

"MILWAUKEE NEGROES TO RAISE A COMPANY OF VOLUNTEERS"

[A meeting at the A.M.E. Church in Milwaukee sponsored by the Afro-American League passed the following resolutions:]

Resolved, that we the Afro-Americans of the city of Milwaukee in meeting assembled fully appreciate the needs of the hour and approve of the wise, broad, human, course of Congress and the President in their efforts to secure the liberty of the people of Cuba, for which the brave patriots have struggled against odds for the past three years and more, and for which cause the greatest soldier of our race gave up his life—Gen. Antonio Maceo—therefore be it

Resolved, that we, though small in number, tender our services to the governor and promise to raise a company of volunteers to assist in repelling the enemy and avenging the lives of the 266 brave young sailors, of whom 35 were Afro-Americans, and the loss of our splendid battleship Maine.

Resolved, that we deeply sympathize with the unfortunate inhabitants of Cuba, many of whom are members of our own race, in their enthrallment, that we ourselves from experience know the benefits of emancipation and civilization, and that if secured will be the means of uplifting them to a higher plane of life. Inspired by this belief and the love of patriotic devotion to our country, for which we have been ever characterized, we cheerfully tender our aid and offer our lives, if necessary, for the maintenance of the honor and integrity and purposes of our common country.

Wisconsin Weekly Advocate (Milwaukee, Wisc.), May 7, 1898

"AFRO-AMERICAN MILITARY ORGANIZATION BARRED"

The Ninth Battalion of Illinois, I.N.G., seems to be the only Afro-American military organization that has been able to get under the cover of the President's call for 125,000 volunteers. In every state in the Union our military organizations have been barred. In the south they are told to enlist in the regular army and thus get "in it." The "color line" won't down in this country even in the face of war, it seems. It was so in 1861. If this war lasts long enough, the Afro-American will be, too, welcome, just as he was in 1863.

Cleveland *Gazette,* May 7, 1898

"SOME LOS ANGELES NEGROES DON'T ENLIST"

The Negroes of Los Angeles are losing no time in proving their bravery and patriotism. They are enlisting every day. There has been a colored company formed under the influence of Dr. George D. Taylor. All honor and praise to the Negroes . . . showing a kind disposition to return good for evil, showing his respect for the soldiers, both black and white who fought for his freedom; his willingness to help free his brother in black over in Cuba. . . . [but] 'Tis true . . . we have a number of Negroes who cry down the flag, cry down the governor. . . .

Indianapolis *Freeman,* May 7, 1898

"NEGROES SHOULD BE PATRIOTIC DESPITE MISTREATMENT"

[The *Bee* quotes from a speech of lawyer Thomas L. Jones:]

The question is being asked what part, if any, should the negro of this country take in the Spanish-American war. By some it is argued that in view of the treatment he receives at the hands of this government in permitting discriminating laws to be passed by state legislatures against him and refusing to use the Federal Government for the suppression of lynch law and mob violence in the state, he should be neutral in this contest; that until these evils are remedied he should not go down into the valley of death in defense of the government and a flag that hangs upon the citadel of liberty, a flag that has thus far unfurled its stripes but concealed the promise of its stars.

Standing in this august presence here in the capital of the nation as it were in the presence of the commander-in-chief of the army and navy, let the edict go forth to the American people that we as Afro-Americans are the representatives of a race whose devotion to and patriotism for their country knows no bounds and whose chief aim in this war, now as in all national struggles through which the country has gone on its pathway to glory, is to save this country, perpetuate the republic, and to place our civilization and national honor on the firm but solid foundation of liberty, religion, morality, and law.

This is our country and our government. Here we will live and here we will die. We have purchased our right to citizenship and all its immunities by our blood sacrificed by God himself and . . . we treasure in our memory the historic battle fields of Shiloh, of Fort Pillow, of Lookout Mountain. . . .

The Spanish American War will mark a new era for the Negro in our national history. . . . This is a fight for humanity and for liberty and as Americans let there be no division among us, and when the war is over, Cuba is saved, the wrongs perpetrated upon us avenged and our national honor vindicated, all of the sister nations . . . will applaud your deed and the American people be compelled to accord you that honor and distinction which shall be due to all of her loyal sons. . . .

Washington *Bee,* May 7, 1898

"AMERICAN PREJUDICE"

What sensible objection can there be to the enlistment of colored troops into the army of this government? Any attempt to give an intelligent reason for such national discrimination against the most loyal citizens of the nation would prove as insipid and futile as Cain's excuse was for killing Abel. A nation that cannot separate itself far enough from its prejudice to respect and protect the inherent rights and patriotic devotion of all its citizens is unworthy of eternal life.

* * *

"TOPEKA WHITES DON'T WANT NEGRO SOLDIERS"

The Negroes of Topeka are trying hard to impress upon the patriotic soldiers of Kansas who have assembled at our State Capitol for the purpose of being sworn into U.S. service that grabbing colored men women and children and tossing them up in blankets and then running them out of camp will increase the hospital lists and the death rate for the army. Liberty or death is our motto.

* * *

"FOR AMERICAN PROTECTION OF CUBA"

Shall we fight and take Cuba and then set her free or shall we hold it as conquered territory subject to the territorial laws of this country? In either case does she not come under the protection of the United States, and a part of the same?

Kansas City *American Citizen,* May 13, 1898

"Support the War For Cuban Independence"

[It is disconcerting to] hear or read the unpatriotic utterances of the presumptuous individuals who dare to pretend that they speak the sentiments of the race when they denounce America and disclaim any concern for the flag. . . . If there are 7,000,000 here who disclaim any respect or love for the flag, then, indeed, they are a dangerous element . . . when leading newspapers and pulpits allow such terrible expressions to be sent forth with their sanction then we are made to feel great fear as to the ultimate consequences.

The Negro has failed to respond to the influences of American civilization if his heart does not beat in sympathy with the sentiment of brotherly love that has led America to go to the rescue of the down-trodden people of bleeding Cuba.

All that is said of the injustices done us here is true, but not a single mob was ever composed of men who were swayed by the sentiments that have called the present great army to war. The same feelings that now lead America to reach out her arm to the oppressed of Cuba will one day lead her to rescue the Negro of America from his oppression. . . . We should denounce the base prejudice that denies our rights as men, but we should be the first among those who are led on to the noble deeds of the lofty sentiment that demands the freedom of Cuba. All the bishops of the great A.M.E. Church stand forth as patriots. . . .

*   *   *

"Lay Aside All Differences in the Present War"

F.Z.S. Peregrins of Buffalo, N.Y. has an excellent article in the Buffalo *Evening Times* of the 3rd inst. relating to the stand the race should take in the present strife with Spain. He feels that all differences should be laid aside and only the common cause should be kept in mind at this time. His views are in keeping with those of the advanced thinkers of the race.

Indianapolis *Freeman,* May 14, 1898

"Economic Power, Not Humiliating Military Service"

The latest information comes that even in Pennsylvania the colored militia has been notified that it is not wanted.

It seems that the Grey Invincibles belong to the first brigade and went into camp with the other militia.

They wanted to enlist in a body, but this was not permitted. They were told they could so enroll themselves provided they would consent to go to one of the frontier posts and hold the Indians in check.

And yet there are people who tell about patriotism, when men of our race are thus humiliated and insulted.

We think it is time for colored men to stop surrendering their self-respect by offering their services to either state or national governments.

When they are wanted, they will be wanted badly and will be called for.

For our part, the victories of peace are even more glorious than war.

Let us lay down the rifle for the government and secure money for ourselves.

Industrial and mercantile pursuits are open to us. Let us buy land and accumulate money.

When we own a goodly portion of this earth and a large proportion of what is on top of it, we shall be among the first called for both in war and peace. No officers; no fight.

Richmond *Planet,* May 14, 1898

"REPORT ON BLACK TROOP ENLISTMENT"

[George T. Robinson, Captain, 1st C. C.T.V., reports on black troop enlistment:]

So far as I know, only four states have recognized colored patriots in responding to the President's call for volunteers. South Carolina's battery of artillery, which she will furnish, is composed of blacks. North Carolina will offer a battalion of blacks as a part of her quota. Maryland's black troops are in camp same as the whites. Alabama's black troops were moved into camp with the whites to be tendered to the President, while the 9th battalion of Illinois has been recruited to a full regiment and is held in readiness to be offered when the next call is made. Eight or ten volunteer colored companies have organized in this state [Tennessee] which Gov. Taylor promises to "attend to" as soon as he gets the first brigade off his hands. Our time will come before this cruel war is over. I desire all colored men who have raised volunteer companies in the state to drop me a card, giving names of commissioned officers and number of men.

*   *   *

"RESTRAINED PATRIOTISM"

We see there is some talk of the President making a call for 50,000 more troops and these to be colored men. We are neither laughing or crying at this twaddle. Since our contemptible rejection by the highest authority in the land, our patriotic lamp, which was then full of ambition, zeal, and devotion, has exploded, and a spirit of supreme disgust overwhelms it.

Kansas City *American Citizen,* May 20, 1898

"To Raise Ten Colored Regiments"

Tuesday, ex-Gov. P.B.S. Pinchback of La., Col. Jas. Lewis, and Capt. Judson Lyons, of Ga., now Register of the Treasury Department, held a long interview with President McKinley and Gen. Alger, in regard to mustering in ten colored regiments from the South, to be officered by colored men; they also urged the appointment of Capt. Thomas Kelly as one of the officers from La. These ten regiments to be raised are to be immunes for the special purpose of sending them to Cuba at once.

*   *   *

"Loyalty Will Be Rewarded"

The love of our country, its flag, and its laws should enthuse and stimulate each of us to that higher degree of patriotism. . . . Yet you hear big able-bodied colored men say, "I will not go to war, I have no country to fight for, I have not been given my rights." True, we may not enjoy the full blessing of our rights and there are many injustices done the race... Now in regard to us having no country to fight for, it is folly to think and absurd to speak it because this is our country by adaptation and by importation as well the whites. . . . Our forefathers labored, tilled, fought, bled, and died to perpetuate this country and leave a heritage to us. Let us be men and show loyalty and we shall be rewarded.

Iowa State Bystander, May 20, 1898

"Indianapolis Negroes Enlisting"

The colored men of the city are enlisting very rapidly. It is the proper thing to do. Other states are sending their hundreds and thousands of men to the field. The negroes of this state cannot afford to be less loyal and enthusiastic. The Maine needs remembering. Her cargo was generously sprinkled with negro seamen. Many of these are sinking with the keel of that noble vessel in the mud of the Cuban seas.

Indianapolis *Freeman,* May 21, 1898

"War Department to Give Some Regiments to Negroes"

A delegation of colored men consisting of Hon. Judson W. Lyons, ex-Gov. P.B.S. Pinchback, Col. James Lewis, and Capt. Thomas S. Kelly, called on the Secretary of War Tuesday morning to advocate the enlistment of colored regiments . . . which was made possible by the passage of the "immune bill." The Secretary informed them . . . it was the intention . . . to give five or possibly six regiments to the colored people.

*   *   *

Capt. T. S. Kelly, who is being urged for colonel, is one of the best known military officers in the United States. He was the first man to organize and equip a colored regiment in this city [Washington, D.C.] known as the Capital City Guard. . . . Among the others . . . are ex-Senator Demas, who has organized 1,500 colored immunes in Louisiana. . . . Other officers are Major Charles R. Douglass, son of the late Frederick Douglass, Major C. A. Fleetwood and Col. M. M. Holland. . . .

*   *   *

"COLORED PATRIOTS READY"

If reports are true the President will issue a call for 20,000 colored volunteers in the near future. As the invitation will come from so high and respectable authority as that of Mr. McKinley, it is to be presumed that colored soldiers are now or are soon to be in evidence. We have been and are opposed to forever pushing ourselves forward when not wanted, but when it is shown that the country wants us and will treat us like men, there is no honest, patriotic man in the race who will not do his utmost for the stars and stripes. Now that we are to be called let us respond quickly and in order.

*   *   *

"NEGROES SHOULD SUPPORT THE GOVERNMENT"

"Should the negro take part in the Spanish-American trouble?" was the subject of a well-written paper read by Miss Nannie H. Burroughs before the Congressional Lyceum Sunday afternoon last . . . the essayist observed that the negro is a citizen and as such, notwithstanding the fact that in certain sections of the country he was lynched and denied the exercise of the rights to which he is entitled, he could not justly sulk in his tent when his country called him to duty. Messrs. Frisby, Davis, Wingard, Quisenbury, Henderson, Mrs. Hicks and others who discussed the paper . . . patriotically and heartily commended Miss Burroughs. . .

Washington *Bee,* May 21, 1898

"BLACK SOLDIERS CAN BE AN ARMY OF OCCUPATION"

[From the Kansas City *World:*]

"If the President needs more troops, he should call for 50,000 Negro volunteers. . . . The black brother was crowded out in the recent enlistment because of the anxiety of the white man to get to the front. Next time give the Negro a chance. If it should become necessary to maintain large garrisons after the war to hold the Philippines, Puerto Rico and Cuba . . . the black man would make an ideal soldier for such work."

*   *   *

"Negro Volunteers Refused"

The American white people have virtually turned a cold shoulder to the black Americans: "Before this year is over somebody is going to be glad to enlist even the services of a yaller dog." But the Negro doesn't stop for insults when it comes to patriotism. Though one man is turned down, another one steps up and asks for the same thing. One prominent Negro after another has organized troopers and tendered their services to the government only to be refused, but others are going right on over the same ground. Some of them will get through the gates by and by. There are other days coming when the sun will shine in our favor. There never was a war that ended in a day, and this won't end none too soon.

Parsons *Weekly Blade,* May 21, 1898

"Colored Volunteers Meet"

At a meeting at the Second M.E. Church, Wednesday evening . . . short patriotic speeches were made by Rev. Parks, W. A. Ray, John Elias, Messrs. E. Moreland, Hill, and L. D. Fuller telling why the negro should be ready to defend the stars and stripes.

* * *

"Praise for McKinley's Peaceable Policy"*

[From the *Express*, Dallas, Texas:]

In all the threatened hostility which has pervaded the very atmosphere between Spain and the United States the past two years, thoughtful and observing men have had a great opportunity to estimate the forces which really run a country. The loud-mouthed, light brain jingo on the rostrum and the limitless and inconsequential space writers on the great newspapers have spent their awful fury trying to bring about organized warfare; but up till now, have not succeeded in getting a single blamed gun fired. While all this row-raising and pyrotechnics have been going on among the wards and underlings of the nation, the representatives of wealth, letters, arms, and enterprise—the men who must maintain the history, glory, and triumph of our institutions—have simply stood on the side of peace, and gone on keeping the even tenor of their way. McKinley has shown himself a statesman of foresight and conservatism; and unimpassioned history will not fail to give him a place among the nation's greatest statesmen and diplomats."

Coffeyville *American,* May 21, 1898

*This obviously was written before war was declared.—Ed.

"Is America Any Better Than Spain"

[From a letter to H. C. Smith, editor of the *Gazette*, written by George W. Prioleau, chaplain, Ninth Cavalry, Port Tampa, Florida:]

"The prejudice against the Negro soldier and the Negro was great, but it was of heavenly origin to what it is in this part of Florida. . . . Here, the Negro is not allowed to purchase over the same counter in some stores that the white man purchases over. The southerners have made their laws and the Negroes know and obey them. They never stop to ask a white man a question. He (the Negro) never thinks of disobeying. You talk about freedom, liberty, etc. Why, sir! the Negro of this country is a freeman and yet a slave. Talk about fighting and freeing poor Cuba, and of Spain's brutality; of Cuba's murdered thousands, and starving reconcentradoes. *Is America Any Better Than Spain*? Has she not subjects in her very midst who are murdered daily without a trial of judge or jury? Has she not subjects in her borders whose children are half-fed and half-clothed because their father's skin is black and cannot labor side by side in her factories, etc. etc. with the white man? Yet the Negro is loyal to his country's flag. O! he is a *Noble Creature* loyal and true. Toussaint L'Ouverture said to his son while waiting in the prison in France for his last hour to come: 'My son, forget that France murdered your father.' Here was the forgiving spirit of the martyr, equal to that of the apostle Stephen. The Negro of America is the same today. Forgetting that he is ostracised, his race considered as dumb driven cattle, yet, as loyal and true men, he answers the call to arms and with blinding tears and sobs, he goes forth; he sings 'My Country, 'Tis of Thee, Sweet Land of Liberty,' and though the word 'Liberty' chokes him he chokes it and finishes the stanza of 'Of Thee I Sing.'

The four Negro regiments are going to help free Cuba and they will return to their homes, some of them, muster out and begin again to fight the battle of American prejudice. . ."

Cleveland *Gazette,* May 21, 1898

"Afro-American Volunteer Organizations"

Under President McKinley's second call for 75,000 volunteers and 10,000 "immunes" there ought to be mustered into the service a regiment or two of Afro-Americans.

The Ninth Battalion (three companies) of Ohio, and Company L, Sixth Infantry, of Boston, Mass. are the only two Afro-American *volunteer* organizations now in the service of the country. Thus it will be seen that Ohio is in the lead as usual. They got in under the President's first call for 125,000 volunteers too.

Richmond *Planet,* May 28, 1898

"Negroes to Get Military Opportunity"

[From the *Journal*, Indianapolis, Indiana:]

It is said the President has decided that if another call for volunteers is issued it shall include a call for 25,000 colored troops. Out of the 125,000 troops responding to the first call, there are only four colored companies. The President thinks the colored citizens have not quite been fairly treated and proposes, if the opportunity occurs, to give them a better chance.

* * *

"Negroes Loath To Enlist In Indiana"

[From the *Recorder*, Indianapolis, Indiana:]

At the President's call for volunteers the colored people of this city, with much beating of drums and flow of oratory, opened a recruiting office and announced that a regiment was to be speedily enlisted. To-day, about one month from that date, the drums have ceased to beat and oratory is only allowed to escape in fitful bursts, and only 150 men in this city [Indianapolis] have enrolled their names. Governor Mount's action in mustering out the colored troops of the state service has caused them to stand aloof from the enlistment idea. While we heartily condemn the governor for this action, we believe it the duty of every loyal American to enlist. Governor Mount is not personally conducting this war; he is merely an atom in the great machinery of government. It is starved and oppressed Cuba and Governor Mount that we are to fight. It is a serious reflection upon our loyalty and patriotism to be unable to raise a colored regiment in this city.

* * *

"Negroes Not to Get Military Opportunity"

[From the *World*, Indianapolis, Indiana:]

As there is no likelihood of a second call, as the administration itself admits, there is not much point to this belated promise as to what will be done for the colored people. They should have had their chance under the first call, like all others. Of the 125,000 men called for, at least ten or twenty thousand should have been apportioned to the colored citizens. President McKinley is a little late with his sympathy.

Coffeyville *American*, May 28, 1898

"Negro Soldiers Under White Officers Criticized"

In our last week's paper we discussed the attitude of two Southern governors in respect to the offer of colored militia organizations in their respective states to enlist in response to the President's call for 125,000 volunteers. . . . It was seen that both of those governors—Tyler of Virginia and Atchinson of Georgia—refused to accept colored soldiers as a part of the quotas of their respective states, the evident motive of their action being their unwillingness to appoint colored officers to command these troops. The colored men, although ready and eager to join other patriotic citizens in the service of Uncle Sam, indignantly declined to place themselves in the humiliating and contemptible attitude of allowing these two former devotees of the "Lost Cause" to appoint men to command them whose interest in the Negro does not extend beyond the point of his serving their schemes of self-aggrandizement. . . .

But it seems that the colored men of Alabama—or at least a part of them—lack the manhood of their brethren of Georgia and Virginia. A dispatch from Mobile, Ala., tells us of the presence there of a battalion of Negro troops under white officers.

We have heard nothing of the question of enlistment of colored soldiers in Alabama before—whether they had any militia organizations in the state or not, or whether any objection was raised against the appointment of white officers over them.

Afro-American Sentinel, May 28, 1898

"NEGROES WILLING TO SERVE THE COUNTRY WHEN THE COUNTRY SERVES THEM"

[From the *Daily Times* (white):]

"Up to this time the negroes have shown no great display of patriotism. They have not tried to enlist and efforts made in different sections to raise regiments composed of negroes have failed entirely because of their apparent unwillingness to serve their country.

"President McKinley, it is said, proposes a practical test of negro patriotism.

"In his second call for volunteers to be issued soon it is said that he will ask for a specific number of negro troops—probably 20,000."

We desire to inform our esteemed contemporary that the negroes are patriotic and loyal enough to this government and are willing and ready to fight when they are wanted. These self-constituted negro leaders do more to embarass the manhood and independence of the negro than anything that he may do. . . .

A man would be a very big fool to show patriotism for a government that says she does not want a people—not even to die in defence of a righteous cause on account of color or previous condition. There has not been any great disposition on the part of any State, with the exception of Massachusetts and North Carolina, to encourage the enlistment of Negro troops. . . .

If we are citizens we want to be treated as such. The negro is willing and ready to serve his country when that country can serve and protect him.

Washington Bee, May 28, 1898

"Sink All Differences Until The War is Over"

We rather hold the idea that since there are to be separate companies of colored men in the army, that they should be officered by colored men. The government will not deny this concession, but on the other hand, the colored men must concede that the government has no choice but in separating the companies. The war is on; it must be prosecuted with vigor. . . . The situation regarding the races is well known and needs no rehearsing at this time. It is the proper thing to sink from view all differences on the well-known score until the war is over. It is extremely unpolitic as well as unpatriotic to strike back in a time so disadvantageous. . . . The fault [of prejudice] does not lie with the government, except from a moral standpoint; the people are stronger than the laws and there must be a further revolution of sentiment in order to receive further concessions. . . . It is very likely that those who would at this time take advantage of the government by counselling inactivity on account of the prejudice and so forth are largely responsible for many of the ills of the race.

However, all feeling of opposition is dying out, and even if maintained the government will succeed, and opposition for the mere sake of opposition is no virtue, nor a panacea for existing ills.

Indianapolis Freeman, May 28, 1898

"Negroes Should not Serve Until Civil Rights Are Protected"

[From a letter of Robert P. Jackson, Chicago, Ill.:]

"Mr. Editor: . . . I noticed an article in the Chicago *Journal* of May 18 which stated that President McKinley is going to make a test of Negro patriotism in his second call for volunteers as he will ask for a specific number of Negro troops. . . . But up to this time the Negroes of the South have shown no great display of patriotism, they have not tried to enlist, indeed, efforts made in the different sections to raise colored regiments have failed entirely because of their unwillingness to serve their country before they are accorded the rights and privileges of an American citizen. . . . What protection do the Negroes of the South receive from this government? Look at the number of Negroes that have been lynched since McKinley has been our President. . . .

"The government did not offer to protect the 25th colored infantry while en route to Tampa and when they were on their way to fight to save their country's honor, they were forced to ride in Jim Crow cars. Yet you think the Negro should be patriotic. . ."

Kansas State Ledger, June 4, 1898

"MAJOR CHARLES YOUNG ONLY NEGRO OFFICER"

[From an article by W. W. Scott in the Huntington, West Virginia, *Daily Herald*:]

"First Lieut. Chas. Young, who since his graduation has been detailed at Wilberforce University, Ohio, was commissioned a few days ago major of the Ninth Battalion of the Colored Ohio Volunteer Infantry. He is the only Negro army officer. The leading Negro journals, notably the Indianapolis *Freeman* (Ind.), *Colored American* (D.C.) and New York *Age*, speak in no uncertain tones."

Indianapolis Freeman, June 4, 1898

"COUNTRY SHOULD CARE FOR SUFFERING HUMANITY AT HOME"

We are natives of this country, we have no other country. We have purchased our right here at tremendous sacrifice, and a nation that makes such big pretenses for caring for suffering humanity should see to it that we are secure in our rights to live under its protection.

Though we are fighting the Spaniards on the one hand, the hot-headed murderers have not ceased to butcher the poor negroes without judge or jury. How much longer shall this inhuman practice go on before the strong hand of the government puts a stop to it?

*　*　*

"ANNEX CUBA"

If we come out victorious in this fight and destroy the Spanish fleet and take the island of Cuba, why not then annex it to this country as a permanent possession? "Unto the victor belong the spoils" is an old proverb that has governed the nations of the world in all ages. Why should it not hold good now?

Kansas City American Citizen, June 10, 1898

"A HINT OF FUTURE CRISIS"

We are at a place in our existence as a race when the Negro is standing on the brink of a mighty uncertainty. He is patriotic, full of fire and anxious to fight for his country whether his country protects him in his rights or not. Yet, he is being ignored and insulted at every opportunity presented. These insults to his manhood, coupled with the fact that the merciless slaying of Negroes goes merrily on, are trying the very soul of the Negro, and too, in a crucible over the hottest fire. If he stands the test, good; but if the worm turns, woe unto the United States of America, for with the enemy on the outside and a deadly [foe] on the inside, hell and pandemonium will reign supreme. We pray that time will never be; but a change must soon come, one way or the other.

* * *

"Uncle Sam Ignores Lynchings"

The lynching mill has started up again after a short suspense and is grinding out one, two, and three victims per day. Louisiana, to keep in the lead of her competitors in this bloody damnable work, took occasion to burn a Negro at the stake, a sight so horribly sickening and revolting that the perpetrators thereof couldn't stand the scene. Texas strung up two or three; Maryland, one; Missouri, two; and Arkansas, one. . . . This is a splendid home record for a great nation engaged in a war with another nation, because cruelty is laid at the door of the other fellow —good record, sure. Now, while Uncle Sam can find time to shoot Spaniards for their cruelty to Cubans, he ought to take a little of the time and make a thorough search among the persecuted part of the Americans about his own door mat. Take a peep, anyway.

Parsons *Weekly Blade*, June 11, 1898

"Afro-American League Meeting Should Be Called and Held in New York"

Why should we wait until the war is over before we call a meeting of the Afro-American League? This is a white man's war with which the negro has nothing to do, so we are informed. We don't want any negro league called in Washington to enable office-holders and cowardly negroes to control it. New York is the place to hold such a convention and it should be held soon. Delays are dangerous. Pay no attention to trimmers and apologists.

Washington *Bee*, June 11, 1898

"McKinley Seems to Prolong the War for Political Reasons"

Tuesday, June 14th, the Nebraska State Building was dedicated and thrown open to the public and . . . Bryan was one of the principal speakers . . . he sounded a note of warning by saying that "if this contest degenerates into a war of conquest we will find it difficult to deny the charge that we have added hypocrisy to greed." We do not pretend to be competent to criticise the actions of those who are engaged in conducting the war against Spain, but it does seem to us that President McKinley and his associates are determined to prolong the war for no other purpose but to carry the elections this fall and to reward the sons of millionaires with good fat positions in the army. The only way for the President . . . to dispel the idea from the minds of the people that the contest has not degenerated into a war of conquest is to invade Cuba and strike one grand blow for liberty and thus bring the war to an end.

Salt Lake City *Broad Ax,* June 18, 1898

"INDIANA GOVERNOR CAN COMMISSION NEGRO OFFICERS"

Simple justice has been done the colored companies of this state that are likely to be called to the front. [Secretary of War] Alger has notified the governor that any companies organized in the state may be officered by colored men, the governor having the power to commission them. Really there has been no necessity for this delay, for as long as white companies refuse colored men as officers, just so long should colored men resent the imposition.

Indianapolis *Freeman,* June 25, 1898

"WAIT UNTIL THEY WANT US BADLY"

[The Richmond Va. *Saturday Enquirer,* in its issue of June 11 said:]

"If the Negroes want to go to war let them do it as their brethren do in the United States army, viz.: Under white officers."

We do not want to go to war. It is the white folks in Washington and those in this city who keep calling for us to go. It says:

"The fact is that decent white men, for the honor of their country and themselves, want to see this war and others that may come fought by white soldiers, mongrel ideas to the contrary notwithstanding."

And so do "decent colored men" want to see the same thing. Let them all enlist. We'll form the "home guard" and protect your "belongings" until you return. The *Enquirer* says:

"Ben Butler's idea of Negro soldiers acted well for the business of bounty-jumping and jobbers like his own, but this is a time of different motives and of sincere and honest principles."

Of course it is! Join the army! Rally around the flag! Endure the mosquitoes and hot weather! Face the Spanish bullets and machetes, and go "shouting home" to—, if life ends.

It is a noble thing, sir, to die for one's country. You go and do that noble thing and we'll do as you suggest in the following lines:

"The westward coursing star of empire should not have a black spot on it. Let the inferior race of Africa, Manila, or Cuba be confident to bask in the protection of their patrons and be careful to show that they deserve it."

The time is up. Recruits are needed. On to Cuba, Mr. Editor, on to Cuba!

Colored folks, let us wait until they want us. It is only a little warm in Cuba now. It will be red hot after a while. Wait until they want us, colored men, wait until they want us badly.

Afro-American Sentinel, June 25, 1898

"The Negro an Instrument of Empire?"

The London *Spectator* says that "nothing stops the Americans from raising the Negro force to 20,000 men and with them holding the Philippines, Hawaii and Puerto Rico, paying them out of local revenues. With such a garrison those islands would be as safe as drawing rooms and as full of business as Broadway or Strand, instead of remaining a source of weakness to the Union; the Negro can be turned by wise and lenient management into an instrument of empire."

Is the war with Spain to solve more than one of our national problems? Is the field of our conquest so fittingly adapted to the colored people as a place of military residence and practical usefulness that these citizens are to become a "source of empire" instead of remaining a source of weakness to the Union? The *Spectator* reaches into the future with a vigorous advisory spirit, and at most there is much to command consideration in what it says. As for the colored man, there is room for him to become a more useful factor in our national make-up, and in the eyes of himself and his country.

* * *

"Black Soldiers Should Be Sent to the South"

[From the *Appeal*, St. Paul, Minn.:]

Lynching goes on in the South. A regiment of black soldiers should be sent South to avenge the wrongs of their brothers in the past thirty years.

Iowa State Bystander, July 1, 1898

"Indiana's Negro Volunteers"

The colored companies of this city and the people generally are to be congratulated on the successful outcome of their contentions. The companies will figure in the war very much according to their own election. The *Freeman* has always contended that in view of present conditions that separate companies officered by colored men was right and proper. It also maintains that if a little more forethought had been employed a regiment officered completely by colored men could have as easily been received as these two companies. . . .

These who now go must sustain the tradition of the race and help to neutralize the crowning disgrace of the century—intense racial discrimination—by deeds of prowess that will command the respect of the world.

Indianapolis *Freeman,* July 2, 1898

"THE UNITED STATES CAN PROTECT CUBANS BUT NOT AMERICANS AT HOME"

It would seem that the war with Spain would tend to allay race prejudice and bring closer together the races in the South.

It has had an opposite tendency, for the number of lynchings has been steadily on the increase. . . .

Does it not appear ludicrous for the United States government to be waging a war in the interest of humanity and to bring about the cessation of Spanish outrages in Cuba, when it has such a record at home?

It can protect Spanish subjects in Cuba. It cannot protect American citizens at home.

It should not be forgotten that Postmaster F. J. Baker was murdered. The government which could spend and is spending more than a million dollars per day in the interest of a people of another clime would not appropriate the sum of twenty-five thousand dollars for the maimed family of this devoted colored officer. It is a sad commentary upon the justice of this country. . . .

Afro-American Sentinel, July 9, 1898

"THE NEGRO WILL FIGHT IF TREATED AS A MAN"

The call to arms has been willingly answered by Negroes where they have been treated as men among men and recognized as American citizens, and we don't blame those who responded not to the call where these principles were not recognized.

Parsons *Weekly Blade,* July 9, 1898

"THE WAR MAY BRING CONCESSIONS TO THE NEGRO"

It may be doubtful leadership to pledge the loyalty of the race from the very fact that the necessity of such a pledge carries with it the assumption that the loyalty is or has been doubted. There has been no disposition to jeopardize the interest of this country in reverting to the wrongs endured by negroes in this country. The weight of war on the general country does not make the burdens of the race more tolerable, and if they should refuse to engage in the struggle the burden will not in any degree lessen. It is highly probable that out of the nation's necessity will spring the race's opportunity and from between the dragon teeth of cruel war may be wrung concessions that years of sulking could never bring about. At least it is the negro's business to be on the safe side.

Cuba . . . is largely composed of negroes or mixed races, more so than this country. [It is an] inspiring spectacle to witness the majesty of this mighty government stepping in and defending those half-negro Cuban concentradoes . . . struggling for . . . independence. Some such sentiments as these may have actuated the Pinchback committee that called on the government and tendered the support of the race. They saw the awful consequences of internal dissensions when the enemy was at the gate. The motives we can well imagine were pure, lofty, and patriotic.

Wisconsin Weekly Advocate, July 9, 1898

"THE SOUTH NEEDS LIBERATING, NOT CUBA"

We say again . . . that one Negro possessing even ordinary courage and a good repeating rifle would be a full match for a generation of those low-strung, drunken scoundrels whose daily and nightly depredations have rendered the Southern section of this Union the most forbidding portion of Christendom. . . .

The conduct of the colored man, Parks, of Batesville, S.C., is most commendable. A gang of these cutthroats attacked him the night of June the 3rd. Parks was charged with setting fire to his employer's barn . . . he was much handier with the gun . . . and the black man escaped unhurt . . . but they avenged themselves by fatally shooting the little 8-year old boy of the colored man.

And yet we are engaged in a bloody and expensive war for the liberation of the poor Cubans from Spanish outrages! Bah!

Afro-American Sentinel, July 16, 1898

"UNITED STATES AND SPAIN BOTH REPREHENSIBLE"

A German professor, commenting upon this country's interference in Cuban-Spanish affairs, some weeks ago said that "a country where lynch law survives is unfit to play the judge of other countries." This is a home thrust, and yet, "two wrongs don't make a right." Spain's treatment of the Cubans was inhuman. This country's failure to stamp out or even make any effort to stamp out lynching is almost, if not quite as reprehensible. When this affair with Spain is over, some country or countries ought to step in and compel our government to stop lynching and not only accord but see that all of its citizens enjoy all their rights in every part of the country without question. But they won't.

Cleveland *Gazette,* July 16, 1898

"IF GIVEN EQUAL OPPORTUNITY THE NEGRO WILL FIGHT"

We believe it is the right and duty of the colored man to take up arms in the defense of his country and for the maintenance of those American institutions which have conspired to construct the greatest republic in history. . . . We believe that the conditions of color and condition are by far too flimsy a matter to enter into the discussion as to the rights and duties of an American citizen to strike a blow for his native land.

Again, we sincerely believe that the colored man, if given equal opportunity with his white brother, will gladly and warmly respond to the call for volunteers. We believe that a full regiment of colored troops can be raised in Wisconsin . . . we would be glad to see our statement tested by a call for a colored regiment.

Wisconsin Weekly Advocate, July 16, 1898

"WHITE PAPER SUPPORTS PROPORTIONAL REPRESENTATION OF THE NEGRO IN THE ARMY

[From the New York *Globe:*]

The colored man, barred from so many avenues of making a living in civil life, owing to popular prejudice, finds he is discriminated against in the making up of the army and he protests against such treatment. In the regular army of 27,000 there are only 2,000 of his color. In the summoning of 200,000 more to crush Spain the colored men have considerable less than 2,000. The quota of the southern states, something like 50,000, was made up of white men, as the colored were not accepted.

Of the 72,000,000 inhabitants of the republic, 9,000,000 are colored. If the latter had their proportion in the call for troops they would have contributed 25,000. There are special reasons why colored men should be freely enlisted in these allotments. They are accustomed to hot weather in the South and in a summer campaign in Cuba would be able to stand the climate better than the white men of the North. . . .

This . . . expresses the merits of the colored people while it outlines a just and equitable policy for the government [to follow]. . . .

Now there is a bill before Congress directing the President to provide auxiliary volunteers for the occupation and defense of any islands that may come under our control to be composed exclusively of colored men. This will give those now discriminated against a chance to prove their patriotism. They should be allowed to enroll until 25,000 are mustered in. . . .

*   *   *

"DISAPPOINTMENT OVER CONGRESS'S REFUSAL
TO CALL UP 25,000 NEGROES"

The failure of Congress to pass the bill authorizing the enlistment of 25,000 colored troops was a grievous mistake. In the first place it was an indication of the unwisdom of allowing race prejudice to enter into the consideration of the proper defenses of the nation. President McKinley recommended the measure. . . .

Had the country seen the wisdom of the President's recommendation, must less loss of life would have been the result for the reason that there are thousands of colored people who reside in the Gulf States, who are practically immune from the attacks of yellow fever. . . .

Wisconsin Weekly Advocate, July 16, 1898

MCKINLEY'S GOD

[From a letter to the *Planet* by J. Thomas Hewin, dated July 9, 1898, Boston, Mass:]

Long before this article appears in the columns of your paper, the readers of the *Planet* will have acted upon President McKinley's proclamation, asking them to thank God for the recent victories over Spain. I will say that such an act is a relic of barbarism.

A Recognition of God's Power

He says in his proclamation that God holds nations in the hollow of his hands. True, too, we have been taught from our childhood up, that there was a just God who presided over the destinies of nations. I lay down the proposition that the justice or injustice of God has nothing to do with the affairs of nations. It is a case which depends for its existence on the survival of the fittest. For example, when the Spanish admirals took command of their ships they called together the captains and their crews and bowed before God, and swore by Him that liveth, that they would never return to Spain again, until they came back with the honor of Spain.

The Pope's Promise

. . . Yet, in spite of all, this Spain has been overwhelmingly defeated.

Now, does it not follow by a parity of reasoning that Spain has the same right to charge God with slothfulness toward her as President McKinley has to ask the American nation to praise Him for their victories? Now one of the reasons why civilization cannot be advanced any more rapidly in Africa is because the natives can see God in a bush, stick, river, sun, moon, and stars.

The Bible is very plain in its definition of God. It says God is love. But President McKinley has the heathen idea. He can see God in the murder of thousands of men; in the sinking of ships; in sending men into another country's territory to put down the same hellish butchery prevailing at home.

For nineteen hundred years we have been waiting for Christianity to bring men together in a more friendly relation, yet the world to-day is a little more than a hell to the human race.

The Butchery of the Negro

When I see a Negro taken from the hands of a sheriff within seven and a half miles of the national capital and lynched, and the same government which is today spending millions to protect citizens of another nation, refuses to protect its own, I say the Negro owes God nothing.

They tell us Free Trade is ruinous to this country; that free silver is ruinous; that mormonism is worst of all; nay more, there is an evil more threatening to the safety of this American republic than all of these combined—it is orthodoxism.

The institution of slavery was founded, built and rested upon the Bible.

The words of Whittier are in point, when he refers to John Calvin, who went around teaching the colonists that Negro slavery was justified by the Bible.

Calvin and Slavery

He made his ships to fly along the Atlantic coast; blown by winds of the Holy Ghost. Calvin was a great advocator of Negro slavery.

Whatever success may attend the American Army or Navy is not due to any individual effort on the part of President McKinley, because he and Thomas B. Reed were opposed to the recognition of Cuba, first and last, because so large a part of her population was colored.

Will Never Bow

I will never bow my knees to McKinley's God nor the God who has the big hollow in His hand, until my race is protected at home.

Only a few days have passed since a U.S. Senator in his debate on the annexation of Hawaii said that he opposed its becoming part of the Union, because so many Negroes were there; and that he did not believe a Negro was as good as a white man because God painted him black.

Now here is another man who has the heathen idea of God. He sees Him in the color of a man's skin. Any person who has an intelligent conception of God loves his fellow men. The Bible says that love worketh no ill to his neighbor.

Again, how can a man love God whom he hath not seen, and hateth his brother whom he has seen? Let the people of the United States who have expended $210,000,000 in property to worship God and yet treat the Negro as they would a beast, answer these questions. . . .

Speaking to Conservatives

I am not speaking to gain the smiles of the masses. I am speaking to the conservative thinking element of Afro-Americans. The Constitution and the Declaration of Independence of the United States were written by a man who did not believe in a God; yet he says, "all men are by nature free and equal." Thanks to his name for that. If the orthodox demons who compose our Congress had the Constitution and Declaration of Independence to revise, that statement would not appear.

Let us proceed unmoved, and leave McKinley's God out of the question.

Richmond Planet, July 16, 1898

"For Cuban Independence"

The war with Spain will cost your Uncle Sam something like a billion dollars. But the American people never hesitate at cost when honor, credit, and humanity is at stake.

It is said that the United States wants an indemnity of $240,000,000 from the Spaniards and the Independence of the Island of Cuba. Reasonable enough. . . .

Tribune (Wichita, Kansas), July 23, 1898

"Protest Against the Exclusion of Negro Officers"

[A meeting of the Ohio A.M.E. Sunday School Institute Conference passed the following resolution:]

That any government or military policy that excludes colored soldiers in this war from the higher ranks of commissioned officers is wrong and the discrimination should be at once abated; and be it the sense and sentiment of this convention that every colored regiment of volunteers in the Spanish American war be fully officered by soldiers of our race.

That inasmuch as it has been charged by the press of this country that colored soldiers have been transported in so-called "Jim Crow" cars, we do protest against and deprecate such treatment of soldiers of our race.

*   *   *

"War Department Opposes Negro Officers"

We don't ever expect to see at the front an Afro-American battalion, brigade or regiment with Afro-American officers, if a white battalion, brigade or regiment is to be there also. The war department is determined that white and "colored" officers shall not "mess" and mingle together on a plane of equality. This is its main reason for opposing so strenuously the appointment of Afro-American commissioned officers.

Cleveland Gazette, July 23, 1898

"AMERICAN COLONIZATION"

It's going to be hard to stop the policy of territorial aggrandizement. When once it has been fairly inaugurated it will be pursued to the limit. We might as well settle down to the fact that America has outgrown the Monroe Doctrine and started in the competitive colonial scheme.

Kansas State Ledger, July 23, 1898

"ATTEMPT TO DRAFT NEGROES IN MISSOURI"

Over in Missouri the Negro would not volunteer his services to Uncle Sam because his manhood was not recognized by Gov. Stephens and he had to be drafted into service. A bold stand, if it didn't work.

Parsons *Weekly Blade,* July 23, 1898

"CHARLES GANO BAYLOR ON CUBA AND IMPERIALISM"

[From a letter to the *Planet* by Charles Gano Baylor, dated July 23, 1898, Providence, R.I.:]

The splendid letter of J. Thomas Hewin, of Boston, to the Richmond *Planet,* published in your edition of the 9th of July, is one of the most important contributions to the literature of the war between Papal-ruled Spain and Papal-ruled Imperial America, yet published. . . .

That Cuban Proclamation

Concurrent with General Garcia's manly resenting of Gen. Shafter's proceedings in Cuba (under instructions from Washington) and the President's Cuban Proclamation (under prompting from Archbishop Ireland) the subject raised cannot be suppressed by all the irresponsible powers of presidential military dictatorship at Washington, even when combined with Jesuitism and supported by a venal press cowering basely under the lash of Papal censorship and the Catholic boycott.

No better place to raise this issue and fight it to the end than Richmond, Virginia; no better journal for the work than the leading Afro-American paper of the United States, The Richmond *Planet.* That mysterious thing called the "Hand of Providence" is evidently in this matter, as it has been in so many other affairs in humanity's struggle for freedom against despotism, superstition, and priestcraft.

A Rigid Examination Demanded

The issue thus raised involves of necessity a rigid examination into the character of the American government. The time has come to institute that examination. The United States under this issue will be placed at the bar of the civilized world.

Is our government really a Republic or a Plutocracy? Is America after all a sham sailing under false colors?

This issue also involves the Republican Papal coalition, an epoch-making event in history as much as the reformation under Luther, the Protestant succession in England, the Declaration of American Independence, or the French Revolution.

A Foul Coalition

If the foul and damnable coalition known as Hanna Irelandism is allowed to stand, liberty in the New World is at an end and the struggle for liberty here must be at once transferred to Cuba and Canada. Free Cuba and the Republic of Canada being the counterpoise to the Papal Imperialism, which with sword in hand controls every function of the American Government, Federal, state, and municipal as it commands all the educational and journalistic forces of the country.

A Question Answered

What are the facts?

The central and important fact in this whole matter is that the revolution in Cuba was, from the beginning, an Afro-Cuban Socialist up-rising against Spanish tyranny, capitalistic greed and priestly rule and rapacity, the church being the mainstay and prop of the entire infernation.

It was a struggle, which from the first, aroused a universal revolutionary sympathy, nowhere more powerfully than in Spain itself. The Afro-Cuban revolt in Cuba drew to its side lovers of liberty all over the world. In the United States it penetrated all grades of society, arousing the masses, and alarming the Plutocracy. It divided parties and shook the fabric of Jesuitism to its foundation.

The War Has Degenerated

The present war which has taken the place of that holy cause, has from one cause or another degenerated finally in a bloody farce, the chief object of which is to put down that revolution in its socialistic aspect and fasten the chains of Hanna, Irelandism, and color-line barbarism and race despotism in the name of stable government, on the necks of those brave Afro-Cubans after all their sufferings and heroic sacrifices for personal liberty and political independence and progress.

A Reference to Maceo

Maceo, the great Afro-Cuban military leader, was a full-blooded Negro. General Gomez is an Afro-Cuban—a quadroon. Nearly all the leaders and fighters in the Cuban army of liberation are men, who, if in South Carolina, Mississippi, or Louisiana, would be made to ride in the "Jim Crow Cars" and would be refused the right to occupy a private residence on Beacon St. in Boston. You see the proposed Afro-Cuban

Republic was too close to our own Cuba and Armenia at the south to suit either the northern or southern plutocrats.

Why Colored Troops Were Not Sent Earlier

Too close to a smouldering volcano of brutal oppression, and consequently of revolutionary discontent. Proximity dangerous. And this is why Afro-American troops from the United States (immunes as well as fighters) to the number of 100,000 men were not promptly thrown into Cuba at the outbreak of the war, to join forces with Afro-Cuban Revolutionists there.

The fraternization of such forces was bound to follow this joint occupation of the Island, and the Afro-American invaders would also have remained on the island, and helped to govern it after the war of liberation was over.

Calling Loudly Now

However, General Shafter is already calling aloud for colored troops and his call is destined to become louder and louder.

Yellow jack is on the side of the cause of humanity this time. In the meanwhile Garcia and Gomez may assert their self-respect and make the Cuban army of liberation the nucleus of one of the most startling and dramatic incidents in human history.

And this is just what Hewin's letter to the *Planet* is leading up to. In my opinion nothing can avert this "dramatic incident" with such intellects as Hewin's aroused and on the alert. . . .

A Timely Comparison

It is important to remember that the Cuban leaders were fighting for the practical realization in Cuba of those sublime liberty ideals proclaimed by the British-American colonists of 1776 to a world in chains at the foot of kings, parliaments, autocratic judges, nobles, soldiers, and priests.

Those sublime liberty ideals were overthrown by the Federal Imperial, Slave compact of 1789, the cornerstone of which was the recognition of the principles of the right to property in man side by side with judicial absolutism (taught in all the public schools as the "Divine Constitution") and which the Anti-Slavery man and woman of America forty years ago spat upon, defied, and declared truly to be [wrong]. . . .

That Covenant With Satan

"A Covenant with Satan and a League with Death, Aye a League with Death," as the white wage slave of the North, (a la Hazleton, Pa.) [is] also finding out as well as the United States postmaster in South Carolina murdered in cold blood, whose sole offense was that he was a Negro.

To restore the liberty ideals of 1776 and avoid the imperialism (protected and guarded by Parliamentarism) which in the United States has wrecked those liberties, was from the first the declared purpose of the

Afro-Cuban leaders. They proposed to advance along the line of progress. Such an Afro-Cuban-created Insular Switzerland as this at our very doors, was not to be tolerated by the Hannas and Dingleys, Pullmans, Wanamakers, Carnegies, Rockefellers of America any more than by the confederate white aristocracy of the South.

A Confiscation of Church Property

Besides, the Afro-Cubans proposed to confiscate the church property and other fabulous wealth robbed from the Cubans through centuries of priestly rule and intolerable oppression. That is why Archbishop Ireland (and who made McKinley President) has been so active at Washington, as the confidential correspondent of Cardinal Rampolla at Rome, in this entire Cuban business.

This activity has extended down to the late Cuban Proclamation of the President. Let the intelligent reader turn to that extraordinary document, the terms of which are in defiance of the will of Congress as embodied in the joint concurrent resolution which forced the secret hand of this same intriguing Jesuit and Ecclesiastic (Archbishop Ireland) and his ally at Rome, Cardinal Rampolla.

Mr. McKinley's Proclamation

Read the proclamation carefully, for it is destined to become historic. Do not miss that passage which must have been written by Archbishop Ireland himself, in which the American President is made to speak to "law and order"—"the sacredness of private and church property" and of property consecrated and dedicated to the arts and sciences.

Pope blessed Weyler. "Arts and sciences" in Cuba is rich. It is on a par with Negro-baiting civilization in South Carolina and Texas.

How White Scoundrels Commit Crimes

As to our own Cuba, any white scoundrel who wants to commit a secret crime in the South can do so with comparative immunity and impunity. All he has to do is burn a piece of cork and blacken his face and then go ahead. Rape, murder, arson—it is immaterial which.

He can, after the crime, lead a mob and seize the first Negro who comes along and charge him with the crime. After the black scapegoat is done for, announces that "he confessed." Then call a meeting of the best citizens to deplore the sad event. Follow this up by an editorial paragraph in the Boston *Herald,* that the editors are not surprised at the southern mode of dealing with "black fiends" and the performance is complete.

A Harlot's Privilege

Any professional white harlot at the South can make a local heroine of herself and regain social recognition by accusing what is called a "black fiend" with assault, and some innocent and helpless Negro is forthwith burned alive, the harlot applying the torch. And all this upon the unsupported accusation of a woman whose oath would not be taken by an intelligent unbiased jury in any ordinary action of law. On such law, the victim also "confesses," there is "deep regret" from the "best citizens" and such northern papers as the Boston *Herald* are promptly on hand to apologize for and condone the crime.

To Keep The South Solid

It is perfectly well known that what is known as the "Nigger Racket" is a systematic game in southern politics to keep the South "solid" for Tammany Hall, which is only another name for "Holy Pope" in American affairs. So it is all along the line.

Speaking of gods in this connection, it only remains to say that McKinley's God "besting" Spain's God at Manila and Santiago simply serves to bring out in strong relief the fact that according to strict orthodox superstition, the "faithful" of the Roman Catholic gang can plausibly claim that the Pope's God "bested" them both, for Cardinal Rampolla is on top in Europe, and his co-ecclesiastic close friend and political ally, Archbishop Ireland, is on top in the United States.

Must Be Answered

The question which must be answered in the face of such facts at such a time as this is, Shall the Liberty Cause in Cuba be thus betrayed and sacrificed without a determined resistance by liberty men and women everywhere? Shall Hanna-Irelandism linked to color-line barbarism be allowed to be placed on the necks of the brave Revolutionists of Cuba, and the Philippine Islands in the name of and by the power and authority of Imperialized Pope-ruled America?

Europe is Watching

In a word, is this the first step in a New American Imperialism which Europe is watching so intently?

That is the question. It is a question which submerges all others. If yes, then Americans, white as well as black, must prepare for the same yoke at home.

Do I then underestimate the importance of the issue raised by Mr. Hewin's letter to the Richmond *Planet*?

Do I underestimate the tremendous responsibility which has thus suddenly been laid at the feet of its editor? . . . I ask the question because the American Negro cannot become the ally of Imperialism without enslaving his own race. Before you answer the question, remember Crispus Attucks, that brave Negro who led what was called the "Boston Riot" against the king's authority backed by the King's soldiers.

The Effect of Attucks' Courage

It was this daring revolutionary act of a Negro in the streets of Boston which lighted the fires of the Revolution of 1776 and made Patrick Henry of Virginia exclaim "Give me Liberty or give me Death!" . . .

A Martin Luther Wanted

There is a Divine power in individual unsupported human courage from the poor friendless monk, Martin Luther, facing the whole power of Rome when Rome was supreme over the world, down to John Brown facing the whole power of a slave-ruled America. . . . As a starter of the discussion, I propose that we shall organize at once an Afro-American Military Colonization of Cuba to unite forces with the Cuban Revolutionists and that Generals Garcia and Gomez be informed of our purpose.

Another Proposition

I also propose that all who are in full sympathy with the liberty ideals of the Cuban people (the principles of 1776) be invited to join in the movement.

I would not confine the movement to the United States. I would make it international and invite the liberty men and women of all nations to unite forces with us in the conquest, control and perfect such a regeneration of Cuba as to make its reinslavement by the Hannaites of plutocratic America in alliance with papal ecclesiasticism . . . impossible.

Both to be Faced

If need be, all should be prepared to face both the Spanish and American Imperialists.

The demand for our action is imperative. Immediately on the breaking out of the war . . . that political ecclesiastic [Archbishop Ireland] organized a literary war bureau with headquarters at Washington City. He employed correspondents and scribblers whose chief duty was to vilify the Cuban and Philippine insurgents.

Severe on the Cubans

The Afro-Cubans especially were the favorite targets for these journalistic Hessians. They were described as a lazy, thieving, plundering, worthless, murdering mob who needed to be kept down with a strong hand. . . .

So successful has this intrigue and propaganda of his been managed that finally the semi-official statement is given out from the State Department at Washington that the United States will soon be compelled to occupy the same position towards the Cuban Revolutionists that Spain has occupied for the last two years.

Can Sink No Lower

There you have it. Can national dishonor sink lower than that? . . .

Its Importance Apparent

The timeliness and importance of this Afro-American military colonization of Cuba must be apparent to all. Cuba will either become politically independent or exist under some sort of a joint protectorate or become absorbed in the United States as a State or territory. In either case, the Liberty struggle will be renewed on the island. As long as such men as Gomez and Garcia live this may be relied on.

No Place Found

If Cuba becomes a state of the American union, then no better place could be found in which to assert and establish the principles of free government by the Sovereignty Referendum against delegated legislative and judicial despotism under parliamentarism. This liberty ideal is perfected and materialized in Cuba, is destined to become the one all-embracing liberty issue around which Americans everywhere will have to fight finally for their own freedom rights, for imperialism is here.

A Prediction for the Future

Freedom under Sovereignty Referendum government, being once firmly established in Cuba, will then be asserted in S.C., Mississippi, and Louisiana where liberty now "lies bleeding" under the heel of a ferocious white minority rule race despotism. The issue is already up in the west, and is destined to spread.

Now friends, let us all get together and show the imperialists, the money sharks, and the clericals that the sacred cause of humanity can never be permanently be put down (because the unconquerable self-respect and self-assertion of the human mind cannot be put down) and that the liberty ideals of 1776 are still a potential force in the world's affairs.

Brave Men Yet Willing

There are ideals for the maintenance of which brave men are yet willing to pledge their lives, their fortunes and their sacred honors, and keep the pledge as did our heroic Revolutionary forefathers.

Richmond *Planet,* July 30, 1898

LIBERTY-LOVING ARKANSAS DEMOCRATS LYNCH NEGRO

[From the *Appeal*, St. Paul, Minnesota:]

The Arkansas democrats held a convention last week and passed resolutions endorsing the war "now being waged to assist an oppressed people struggling for liberty." After the adjournment of the convention some of the delegates returned to their homes and assisted in the lynching of an Afro-American who was charged with stealing a pig.

*   *   *

"WAR DEPARTMENT BOWS TO SOUTHERN PREJUDICE"

[Clarissa Olds Keeler (white) in a letter to the *Planet* says:]

"Dear Sir: In looking over the last number of the *Planet* I was much interested in what I read on one of its pages. The extracts from the

Cleveland *Gazette* express my opinion exactly. 'The closer the north and south get as a result of the war the harder it will be for the Afro-American.' I have watched the progress of the war very carefully and have not failed to see that the 'union of the two sections will be at the expense of the colored brother.' I have shuddered when I thought of what the end would be. But then, God reigns."

The treatment of the Afro-American who wanted to enlist and was not permitted to enlist; and the treatment of both Afro-American regulars and volunteers is all the direct result of the closer relations of the north and south. The War Department does not allow anything to be done for the Afro-American that will antagonize the prejudice of the south. The closer the north and south get the greater the care that will be exercised to not do so and consequently the harder it will be for our people, north and south.

Richmond Planet, August 6, 1898

MR. BAYLOR SPEAKS AGAIN

[From a letter by Charles Gano Baylor dated August 4, 1898, Providence, R.I.:]

As the war with Spain has imparted a tremendous impulse to the final solution of the race problem at the South and as the solution of that problem involves potentially the cause of liberty in the United States, I think the time opportune to place before the white wage slaves of the North through the Richmond *Planet* the facts which they will find in this letter.

The Capitalistic Trust

There is now forming in the United States a capitalistic trust the colossal proportions of which will overtop all the other trusts combined in this land of trusts.

This new trust is the American Cotton Manufacturers National Association. Its formation has already begun. It will be composed of two distinct divisions. One division will represent the South, the other the North. The southern division will produce all the lower grades of goods including yarn.

The Northern Division

The northern division of the trust will produce the higher and finer class of goods. The foundation stone of the trust will be cheap labor and long hours at the South. This cheap southern labor with long hours is to be established through maintaining Negro serfdom at the South.

It Will Do This

Cheap Negro serf-labor at the South, on the farm, in the mines and in the mills will drag poor southern white labor to its level. Nothing can prevent this, Caucasian or no Caucasian. Southern wages of both the

Negro serf and the poor white being thus established on the basis of long hours and low wages will, under the trust and the national industrial policy of government bounties to monopoly, drag white labor at the North down to their level. This is inevitable.

A Hope Expressed

I wish every reader and friend of the Richmond *Planet* to get these simple, yet tremendous economic facts before the white wage slaves of the North. Show them that the Negro serf labor at the South, under social, political and educational Race despotism, must react with terrible power on northern white labor.

The Remedy

Free South Carolina, free Mississippi, free Louisiana and a national uniform tariff labor day engrafted by Congress on the industrial policy of the nation, to take the place of government bounties to monopolies. Government bounties to monopoly is not protection to labor. It is a direct corrupt and corrupting partnership between monopoly and government under which defenseless labor is left to such "Protection" as this same government bounty enriched monopoly may extend to it, labor finally paying the bounty as labor finally paying every other bill from the President's salary down.

A Timely Warning

Let no white wage slave at the North make any mistake in this matter. The cause of the black proletariat of the South is the cause of the white wage slave of the North. They must stand together. I would urge our colored friends all over the North to join hands with their white labor comrades in Labor Unions in the Socialist Labor Party and everywhere else. Get together. Unite your forces to compel the government at Washington to place free South Carolina, free Mississippi, and free Louisiana side by side with free Cuba and free Philippine Islands.

The Demand of Labor

Demand with this a uniform national eight-hour labor day to be engrafted on the tariff legislation of this country.

By the power of united labor, North and South, we can before next winter closes secure liberty for South Carolina, Mississippi, and Louisiana, and the eight-hour tariff labor day with political and economic justice at home thus established.

Then give us a mighty navy and America, a republic of fact as well as in the name resting on the love and happiness and welfare of the masses (the true source of her power), can defy the world in arms.

Richmond *Planet,* August 13, 1898

V

CIVIL RIGHTS, THE WAR'S END, AND CUBA

The Spanish-American War ended on August 12, 1898 and the Treaty of Paris was signed on December 10 of that year, giving the United States possession of the Philippine Islands and Puerto Rico. The disposition of Cuba, freed by the treaty from Spanish rule, was yet to be determined. Only a few scattered issues of black newspapers exist for this period, and they show that sentiments were divided on the question of Cuba. The Richmond *Planet*, Cleveland *Gazette*, Washington *Bee*, and others desired Cuba to be an independent nation, whereas the St. Joseph (Missouri) *Radical* and the Coffeyville (Kansas) *American* welcomed expansion because they believed the new possessions (including Cuba) would benefit the blacks economically and socially.

Whatever their opinions on Cuba and expansion, however, the black newspapers kept up their drive for full citizenship in the United States. The *Planet* printed excerpts from nine other black weeklies criticizing President McKinley's annual message, which dealt with foreign policy but did not contain a single word on lynchings and terror at home.

"THE UNITED STATES TREATS SPAIN GENEROUSLY"

Spain has at last yielded and accepted our terms of peace offered by the President. Never before in the history of war has the conqueror ever treated the conquered more generously, no money indemnity is asked from an exhausted and impoverished people and no humiliation pressed upon them other than that which is entailed upon defeat in battle.

So far as the exaction of territory is concerned it is nothing but what the world foresaw at the beginning of this war. When the Spanish government dismissed our Minister at Madrid it placed its American possessions in the scale. The war was entered upon . . . to give independence to Cuba and as a corollary to that followed Puerto Rico possession. There could be no other outcome. . . .

[N]ow . . . the American people must address themselves to the solution of this problem. . . . Some believe that all the Cubans needed was a chance to assert themselves free from Spanish tyranny and that they would set up a government of their own and others doubt their ability of self-government, and there are others who say if we go too far we will have to pay the Cuban debt, but as a matter of fact there is no Cuban debt; Spain has contracted certain indebtedness for which she has pledged the revenues of Cuba but that indebtedness was not contracted by, nor with the consent of the Cubans nor for their benefit and it would be criminal injustice to compel the people of Cuba to pay any part of that debt. The American people and Congress will back the administration in seeing that these people are treated fairly. . . .

Iowa State Bystander, August 12, 1898

"REMEMBER POSTMASTER BAKER'S MURDER"

[From the *Standard*, Lexington, Kentucky:]

" 'Remember the Maine' is the white man's watch-word. 'Remember the murder of postmaster Baker at Lake City' should be the Negro's."

*   *   *

"THE NEGRO'S STATUS UNCHANGED BY THE WAR"

Col. Marshall, of Eighth Illinois Volunteers, the Afro-American regiment doing garrison duty at San Luis, Cuba, writes to a Chicago paper that the Eighth is enjoying good health, and that regardless of the efforts of the southerner editing the Santiago *Times* to disgrace the regiment, its officers and men are conducting themselves as soldiers and gentlemen, as representatives of the race and army should.

In the new territory now being annexed to the United States the Afro-American will very likely receive about the same treatment accorded him wherever the American flag waves. It was thought that the very active and prominent part taken in the recent struggle in Cuba would insure him at least a semblance of fairness, but the shameful way the war department has treated him or caused him to be treated throughout this war, seems to remove all doubt as to what is to be his portion. And yet there is still hope, for in the face of the utterances of that scurrilous sheet, The Santiago *Times*, Col. Marshall has been appointed governor of San Luis, which is indeed an honor and a progressive step.

Cleveland *Gazette,* August 17, 1898

" 'THANKS' TO SECRETARY ALGER"

Now let the band play and Afro-Americans go down on their knees in thanks to the mighty Secretary of War [Alger]—he has stated that "colored cooks *may* be enlisted for white regiments," as a result of an act of Congress. This is rubbing it in with a vengeance. That "color-line" war department makes us sick; and a Michigander presides over it too. . . .

*   *   *

"Gloomy Outlook for the Dark-Skinned Cubans"

The Cubans are reported to be dissatisfied with the terms of the protocol as signed by representatives of the United States and Spain.

There is evidence steadily accumulating that their army will decline to recognize them despite the hurried declarations of the Cuban junta at New York to the contrary.

It is the same old story. The capitalists of the United States and France and Spain will settle the matter and the misguided followers of Gen. Gomez and Gen. Garcia will find that their last condition will be as wretched as the first.

They have been used to accomplish a purpose and their usefulness is at an end.

The wealthy Spaniards upon the island of Cuba will surely control its destiny. The white men of this country will surely combine with them in insuring this control.

The dark-skinned inhabitants of the island will be the victims of race prejudice, and this combined with Spanish contempt will make their wretched lives miserable.

It is indeed a gloomy outlook with not a ray of light visible upon the horizon of their future.

Richmond *Planet,* August 20, 1898

"The Suffering Here Not Looked After"

Protocol is today the suspension of hostilities for a while, say the powers that be.

It is said the United States began the war on a humanitarian basis to relieve suffering and downtrodden humanity in Cuba. The question naturally rises, why was she not zealous for such in her own midst? Has she not suffering, downtrodden humanity within her own domain?

Are not lynchings and brutal outrages often evaded in the U.S.? The Constitution of the United States says decidedly that no person shall be deprived of life, liberty or property without due process of law.

The Cost of the War

The war with Spain has cost the nation nearly a billion of dollars, simply, it is said, to put down cruelty and oppressions in Cuba. Why spend so much money to put down such enacted by Spain and spend not a cent to put down lynching, cruelty and outrages in the United States.

Two hundred and fifty thousand men called out as U.S. troops to put down cruelty in Cuba and to assist the oppressed Cubans, but not a corporal's guard called out to put down lynching, or call to an account men for violating the Federal Constitution in depriving men, women, and children, simply because they are black, of life, liberty, and happiness without due process of law.

Money to spend, tears to shed, homes, parents, children and wives to leave, and go forth and face the enemy outside of the United States and shed blood or lay down life for persons who never saw the United States while there are thousands, yea millions in the United States, native to the manner born, who certainly need the help of the strong, but yet that help is not given.

*   *   *

"ACQUISITION OF TERRITORY REAL CAUSE OF THE WAR"

Is not the acquiring of territory more the real cause of the war than the relief of suffering humanity?

Chickens, they say, come home to roost. Do unto others as you wish to be done by. The U.S. has been zealously applying the Monroe Doctrine of the Atlantic Ocean. It will be funny if they apply the Monroe Doctrine upon her, saying unto the U.S., you are opposed to European powers acquiring territory on the Western Continent, equally so are we opposed to any western power acquiring territory on the Eastern Continent.

Richmond *Planet,* August 27, 1898

"AGAINST CUBAN ANNEXATION AND BOOKER T. WASHINGTON"

It is hoped that Cuba will not be annexed to the United States. Under Spanish rule the negro is treated, to a great extent, as a man, although the Spanish laws may be severe and oppressive. The moment an attempt is made to establish American prejudice on the Island of Cuba, that moment there will be trouble.

The negro Cuban will not tolerate it, neither will he submit to American prejudice and her discriminating customs. There is a great deal of difference between the Cuban and the American negro. The former is brave, bold, and intelligent, while the latter is intelligent but submissive. If Mr. Booker T. Washington is the great race benefactor, as our wild-goose journals would have the American people believe he is, he will tender his resignation to the board of trustees of Tuskegee Institute at once and pack up his duds and sail. Mr. Washington can be spared with ease, as the American negro has no time for apologists and trimmers.

Washington *Bee,* August 27, 1898

"Hope For Freedom and Justice For All Men"

[From the Committee on Address of the Western Negro Press Association:]

It congratulates the country upon the speedy and happy end of the war with Spain and expresses the hope that the Government will have wisdom to deal wisely with the new conditions confronting us as the legacy of this war, to the end that freedom and justice for all men may be the recognized policy of the United States.

Afro-American Sentinel, August 27, 1898

"Bishop Turner Against Negro's Enlistment"

[From an article by Bishop Henry M. Turner in *The Voice of Missions* (Atlanta, Georgia), an A.M.E. Church organ:]

"If these white people can get to Heaven with all their devilment toward my race, then hell is good enough for me."—Col. W. A. Pledger [Editor, Atlanta *Age.*]

The above were the remarks uttered by Col. Pledger when we read to him the following from a letter written by our Superintendent of Missions, Rev. H. C. C. Astwood, dated Santiago, Aug. 30th, 1898. The paragraph referred to runs as follows:

> The color line is being fastly drawn by our whites here, and the Cubans abused as Negroes. It has been found out at last, as I used to tell them in the United States, the majority of Cubans were Negroes; now that this fact has dawned upon the white brother, there is no longer a desire to have Cuban independence, but they must be crushed out. The political situation is alarming, and if President McKinley is not careful he will have a terrible job upon his hands.

When we returned from South Africa and stated through *The Voice of Missions* that had we been in the country when the war broke out, we would have done all in our power to have prevented the enlistment of colored men as soldiers to fight Spain, we were set down as a crank. But knowing the Spaniards as we do, having been through the entire kingdom, we knew they were far better friends to our race than the United States will ever be. We said all the time that all the deviltry of this country would be carried into Cuba the moment the United States got there.

Cleveland *Gazette,* October 8, 1898

"For Expansion"

The St. Joseph (Mo.) *Radical* believes in imperial America. "Negro editors should encourage the expansion idea," it says, "since it means the opening up of avenues for employment of members of the race. Every Negro should be thinking along this line, because the effects of this war are far-reaching, and no man can read the future. . . ."

Wisconsin Weekly Advocate, October 14, 1898

"ANTI-ANNEXATIONIST SENTIMENT GROWING"

The aim of this nation to suppress cruelty in Cuba, give aid and comfort to the ignored Cubans, it seems will not prove to be as salutary as was thought. A leading journal on the question of annexing Cuba says:

> "Already an opposition to annexation is being manifested by the cane-sugar growers of Louisiana and Mississippi, and those interested in the nascent industry of producing beet sugar. Both of these classes feel that they cannot compete against the sugar of Cuba if admitted free of duty, as it would have to be if Cuba were a state of the Union. There are signs also of disposition on the part of the organized working men to oppose expansion, feeling that it will lead to a large increase in the supply of labor, especially of the cheaper sort. If a notion of this sort should take root among the working men, it might have a very strong influence upon the course of Congress. The whole question of the future relations of Cuba to the United States may yet become a very lively issue in the national politics."

Many will find, from the President down, that suppressing the cruelty of lynching in the United States would have been cheaper and less vexatious than suppressing cruelty in Cuba.

Lynching, depriving persons of life, liberty, property, without due process of law, is as damnable a flagrant outrageous cruelty as ever enacted by Spain from the Spanish Inquisition down. As it regards the Philippine Islands, it is not every person that can play Philopens. Some of the people of the Philippine Islands strongly speak of applying the Monroe Doctrine. They declare that they will suffer death before a foreign power shall have a part or all of the islands.

Richmond Planet, October 22, 1898

"FOR EXPANSION"

Of all men the negro should favor territorial expansion. The retention of Uncle Sam's newly-acquired possessions furnishes a brighter outlook for the negro climatically, industrially and socially than any other class of American citizens.

Coffeyville *American,* October 29, 1898

"Negro Soldiers Mutiny"

Knoxville, Tenn., Nov. 2—The recent appointment of nine white officers in the Sixth Virginia (colored) Regiment today occasioned a mutiny among men of that regiment.

The officers in question were mustered in a few days ago and since that time there has existed considerable feeling among the colored troops, as they much prefer to be in command of men of their own class.

The feeling has grown until it gave evidence of being most extensive and for a time this morning grave fears of most serious trouble were entertained by the colonel commanding the regiment, and also by the division commander.

This morning at the first drill call, the men of the companies to which the white officers were assigned refused to obey orders and commands emanating from their white officers.

The trouble was at first thought to be of no consequence, but the officers were soon convinced that it was useless to attempt any fighting of this disposition at least for the time being.

The companies were therefore put in charge of colored officers, who conducted the first drills. Later the police call was sounded, and again the troops refused to be commanded by their white officers.

This time the matter was reported to Colonel R. C. Croxton, the white officer commanding the regiment. Col. Croxton in turn reported it to Col. J. A. Kuert, temporarily in command of the division.

The colored troops had grown so determined and so violent in their denunciation of the white officers that it was considered advisable to order other troops to the scene in the event of further trouble.

The Thirty-first Michigan Regiment and the Sixth Ohio Regiment were accordingly ordered to the scene.

Both were supplied with several rounds of ammunition and for a time it seemed like a genuine battle was to ensue here in Camp Poland.

Maj. Gen. John C. Bates arrived in division headquarters while the trouble was in order and he too was summoned to the Virginia camp.

In company with Colonel G. L. Brown of the Fourth Tennessee, and several staff officers, General Bates went to the camp, hoping by his presence to put an end to the difficulty.

Colonel Kuert had in the meantime addressed the men, telling them that their action was totally in violation of military law and order, and begged that they file any grievance they might have through the proper channel and assured them it would receive proper attention.

Major L. V. Caziarc, the assistant adjutant general stationed there, also addressed the men. He told them it was very unfortunate that they should indulge in such an escapade upon the initial day of Gen. Bates' presence in camp. He said the General would have a very unfavorable opinion of them in the event such an action was continued.

Major J. B. Johnson, a colored officer, was the next to speak and his speech seemed to have the desired effect inasmuch as he is a colored officer. He admonished the men to heed the commands of their white officers and also assured them that their complaints, if any they have, would be given proper consideration if filed in the proper manner.

Colonel Croxton, who is the commander of the regiment, was less solicitous in his remarks than the others. He told the men he was ready to assist them in securing a hearing of their complaints and would send a memorial to the Governor of Virginia if they desired.

He further added that they must obey their officers and if it was not done he would enforce the discipline empowered for such offenses.

This series of speeches seemed to satisfy the men and they returned to their duties.

The Michigan regiment was at that time standing under arms ready for an emergency, and had the mutiny been continued longer, this regiment would have been called upon to enforce obedience to order among the Virginia colored troops.

It is understood that the troops will prepare a memorial to Governor Tyler of Virginia asking him to remove the white officers and put colored ones in their places.

Richmond *Planet,* November 5, 1898

"CUBANS AND FILIPINOS WARY OF AMERICAN CONTROL"

No wonder the Cubans and Filipinos look with fear and distrust upon American occupation and control. The way we treat our own citizens in North Carolina and other southern states is positive proof that their doubts are well founded.

Washington *Bee,* November 5, 1898

"MCKINLEY'S MESSAGE"

The situation in Washington seems to be one of compromise, so far as the South is concerned, and people throughout this broad land seem puzzled to understand why so much consideration should be shown to a section, which, when an analysis of the vote of recent elections is made, did not furnish a Republican majority in any of the states of the late Confederacy.

And this too, despite the fact that some of the rankest Democrats from South Carolina, Georgia, Alabama, Mississippi, Louisiana, and Texas had been honored with positions of the highest rank in the volunteer army.

Southern Democrats have been and are as influential at the Executive Department of the government at Washington as are the northern Republicans. What is the meaning of all this?

To our mind it was a bid for the senatorial vote upon the treaty of peace and a pledge of Democratic support of the conduct of the war. The President does not rely upon his own party in the struggle, but has compromised in such a manner as to make it well-nigh impossible for him to speak out upon existing conditions which exist in this country "as he did of yore."

In compromising the southern Democrats, unfortunately, he is himself compromised.

No one who will bear in mind that he informed the committee of colored citizens from the meeting held at the Vermont Avenue Baptist Church, Washington, D.C., that this is a time for conservatism, will doubt the force of all that we have said upon the subject.

And yet such a suggestion seems ludicrous. Spain was the one to have used that language, for while we started out to free Cuba, and not to acquire territory, we have forced our late antagonist to give Puerto Rico, one of the Caroline Islands, and the Philippines, which embrace from fifteen hundred to two thousand smaller islands, while the Spaniards have been no doubt wondering whether or not the next proposition would be to annex the Canaries and Spain itself.

We already have Cuba, and the Lord only knows when our flag will come down in that blood-stained island. We believe it will come down, only to go up again.

This then would seem to us to be the situation in a nutshell. The only dark clouds upon the horizons of the political schemers at Washington are indignation meetings of citizens of color, which have been held in that section of the country, where a vote can be cast, and the election officers will count it as the voter casts it.

The rallies at Boston; Newport, R.I.; Providence, R.I.; Philadelphia, Pa.; Indianapolis, Ind.; Columbus, O.; Cincinnati, O.; St. Louis, Mo.; Washington, D.C.; and Pittsburgh, Pa., together with the presence of influential white sympathizers, tell their own story. The vote of the citizens of color will be an important factor in settling the next Presidential contest.

Mr. McKinley's managers have compromised with an element, which has been and is today shooting the life out of the brave Republican martyrs in the South and in this number white Republicans are included as well as colored ones.

The President is a man of stern convictions. Let us hope that he will call a halt on the part of the politicians and re-enthrone himself in the hearts of that patriotic constituency which has loved Republicanism throughout all of these years and given their best blood that its banners might wave in triumphant supremacy throughout the land.

*   *   *

"Disappointment In McKinley's Message to Congress"

[From the *Enterprise,* Omaha, Nebraska:]

We are sadly disappointed. Injuries almost unparalled have been inflicted upon the Negro race only a few days ago, yet the one whom we fondly hoped would champion our cause has passed us by without a word. . . .

President McKinley proclaimed himself deeply concerned in the welfare of the Cubans. Our Saviour branded those who said they loved God whom they have not seen and hated their brother whom they have seen as liars and hypocrites. . . .

The President's silence may be due to "policy," which is but another way of saying that his convictions of right are pretty weak, or are subservient to his political ambition. This view is strengthened by his action in the Baker case. If his intentions are right he is badly in need of moral stamina that turns them into actions. If Tom Reed was in the chair, with only one half the good intentions McKinley is credited with, something would drop.

*　　*　　*

[From the *Weekly Blade,* Parsons, Kansas:]

The much talked of and eagerly awaited message of President McKinley to Congress has gone forth and even Congress was surprised at the poor quality of such a lengthy official document. Like a balloon, it was full enough, but puncture it with a needle of common sense and it sinks into nothingness.

McKinley chased over all the world to find conditions to discuss, but could not see anything in the deplorable conditions of things around his own domain to attract his sympathetic vein of love for downtrodden and pressed-down humanity. It is a wonder he didn't discuss matters of the moon as to the feasibility of a revision of tariff rates on cheese.

*　　*　　*

[From the *Conservator,* Chicago, Ill.:]

The message is significantly silent on the recent outrages and lawlessness of the South—thousands upon thousands of people of this country had anxiously awaited the message expecting that the President would administer, at least, a merited rebuke to the lawless elements of the country. However, the President thought it proper not to say a single word in condemnation of these outrages; yet he may have another plan by which these evils are to be corrected. We hope so. At any rate we must wait—patience is necessary in these times of trouble and oppression.

*　　*　　*

[From the *Union,* Augusta, Ga.:]

The colored citizens of America had hoped that the President would have at least followed the proper example followed by President Grant and had said something about the recent slaughter of his fellow citizens in the Carolinas—that he would have said to the American people that he had at least a frown for such outlawing.

In this one particular the document is painfully weak and disappointing, especially so since the President has employed the army and navy to put down in the island of Cuba the inhuman treatment that was accorded the natives of that island by Spain.

* * *

[From the *Odd Fellows Journal*, Philadelphia, Pa.:]

The President has sent his annual message to Congress. It is able and comprehensive. It tells all about the victories that we have achieved by land and by sea for the sake of humanity—what has been done by our government by way of righting the wrongs of the oppressed of other lands, but he is as silent as the tomb about what ought to be done for the sake of humanity at home, what ought to be done to protect at home the people who have been fighting in defense of our flag abroad.

* * *

[From the *Christian Banner*, Philadelphia, Pa.:]

The President was dependent upon the South to aid him in the war with Spain and will still need their support to maintain the sovereignty of the United States over the newly-acquired territory. In order to have their support he must not interfere in any way with what they regard as their State rights; therefore, the Negro is sacrificed and left to a sad fate without any protection whatever. The President and his cabinet yields to the prejudiced demands of the South and allows not only inoffensive citizens to be brutally treated and murdered but the country's defenders also.

* * *

[From the *Colorado Statesman,* Denver, Colorado:]

We have not read the message thoroughly . . . but have read the heads and subheads of the various subjects discussed and found nothing concerning the oppressed and unfortunate sons and daughters of Ham.

Some people claim that there is no reason for special mention of this class of American citizens. Under ordinary circumstances there would not be, but the condition and experience of the Negro in this country are extraordinary, and something should have been said about his present and future citizenship in America.

The President mentions the killing of aliens, which has been proved justifiable under the law, but he has no suggestions to make about the infamy of killing Negroes, when there is no excuse in the majority of cases, except malicious murder. Evidently McKinley is aware that the Negro is entitled to actual citizenship in this country because he helped to make it what it is; both in war and peace. Yet, the President may know his business and the people with the most influence will have no criticism to make because the Chief Executive has apparently forgotten the existence of the Negro race.

* * *

[From the *Observer,* Xenia, Ohio:]

Millions of money, and hundreds for the lives oppressed in Cuba, but not one word or dollar for the oppressed in America. Was the President's silence on this subject "golden" or was it "consent"? We leave God to be the judge.

*   *   *

[From the *American Baptist,* Louisville, Kentucky:]

In speaking of Cuba, the President says it is our duty to give the people of that Island the needed aid and direction in forming a government of their own that should be stable, just, beneficent, without revenge and in accord with the enlightened principles prevailing in our own land. This is right and proper but charity should begin at home and the same principles be first firmly and permanently established in this country.

Richmond *Planet,* December 17, 1898

"CUBAN ANNEXATION"

Robert R. Porter, President McKinley's special commissioner to Cuba and Puerto Rico, has made the startling discovery that the Cubans are not capable of self-government, and declares the political situation to be rather complicated. It is to be regretted that Mr. Porter was not sent on his errand sooner, that he did not make his report to Congress before that honorable body declared war for the freedom and independence of Cuba. There is not much surprise over this discovery. The opinion as expressed by Mr. Porter has been rapidly gaining ground, and it will be but a short time before the complications in the Cuban situation will disappear. Annexation will accomplish this end.

Record, (Indianapolis, Indiana), January 14, 1899

"CIVILIZE AMERICA FIRST"

When Senator Mason, while speaking against the Expansion idea, asked the dignified senators if their method of civilizing the natives of the Philippine Islands was to send special instructors to teach them how to kill postmasters, their wives and children, if their complexion does not suit the populace, and if this country should send the untutored Filipino illustrated pictures showing the works of the mobs in Illinois, North Carolina and South Carolina, he brought before the eyes of the Americans conditions here at home which should engage their attention before they reach out and try to civilize a people ten thousand miles away. It is a question that has agitated the minds of ten million American Negroes, who look with fear and suspicion upon the motives of those most anxious to extend the strong arm of protection around a people not unlike the Negroes of this country, who are even yet denied the liberties of American citizenship.

Illinois Record (Bloomington, Illinois), January 14, 1899

"AGAINST ANNEXATION; AMERICAN HYPOCRISY SCORED"

[From the *Tribune,* Philadelphia, Pa.]

What can be more scandalously perfidious than our pretensions of engaging in war with Spain to free Cuba? One half of the Americans had rather see Cuba at the bottom of the sea than to see her an independent country. . . . Cuba will likely be less free now than ever before. Even if the island be permitted to enjoy a quasi independence for a while, it will be made to feel the pangs of treacherous intrigues before unknown. The Cuban soldiers that maintained the war with Spain for three years were brave and sturdy patriots until we found ourselves in a position to seize the island, when they suddenly became . . . a lot of ragtags too ignorant and indolent to govern themselves. . . . If these Cubans should be left in control the Americans will bend every energy and resort to all sorts of intrigues in an endeavor to prove to the world that the Cubans are incapable of self-government and unworthy of independence in order to justify further aggressions on our part. What have a large proportion of the American press and people not done in their endeavor to prove to the world that emancipation of the slaves was a mistake? What stone have they left unturned in their effort to prove that conferring citizenship upon the Negro was a crime. . . . No, there will be no rest for Cuba unless by alleging a desire to teach her people to permit themselves to be domineered by the Americans. They will find that their scourge will not be of scorpions. We will justify a seizure of Cuba by alleging a desire to teach her people self-government; we justify the taking of Hawaii on the score of an alleged desire to teach her people our religion and civilization; we have not hit upon a better excuse yet for seizing the Philippine archipelago than the alleged necessity for a coaling station. There does seem to be some justification for saying that the Anglo-Saxon begins with you by an appeal to heaven to witness his innocence and honesty and ends by 'stealing your spoons.'

Salt Lake City Broad Ax, January 14, 1899

"CIVILIZE AMERICA FIRST"

When this great government of the western continent can put itself in a position to govern the civilized barbarians right here at home, then it is time to stretch out in an attempt to govern semicivilized peoples thousands of miles over the rolling waves.

* * *

"OBJECT OF WAR WAS GREED FOR GAIN"

Some of the Cubans are foolish enough to believe that the United States interfered with the Spanish in humanity to the Cubans, but the majority of them now realize that the object was greed of gain, and they intend to see that McKinley's policy is not carried out.

Parsons *Weekly Blade,* January 21, 1899

"EXPANSION INTRODUCES RACE PREJUDICE"

One of the strongest arguments we can make against expansion is the introduction into the acquired territory of the great American race prejudice. Americans who wish to conduct business enterprises in Cuba will find, as in the following instance, that the Cubans are unlike the American Negroes and will not submit to such unjust discriminations.

> Havana, Feb. 14.—Holman's Washington cafe, in Central Park, has been ordered closed by Senor Federico Mora, a civil governor of Havana, because of the refusal of the proprietor to serve drinks to a mulatto, the Cuban General Ducasse. . .

Illinois Record, February 18, 1899

"A PUERTO RICAN OPPOSES AMERICAN OCCUPATION"

The January number of the *A.M.E. Church Review* contains an able article from a native Puerto Rican, Chas. H. Sheen, upon the subject "Puerto Rico Under the Stars and Stripes." After treating the subject in a most exhaustive manner, he earnestly opposed American occupation of that most fertile island. Mr. Sheen says: "The population of the island is supposed to be about 850,000, of which about 350,000 are said to be whites; the remaining 500,000 being what would be termed, in America, Negroes. These are a Creole race of partial African descent, of mixed blood, many as fair and as well-favored as the Castilian himself. The barbarous limitations of race prejudice, so common in this country of boasted higher civilization, are unknown in Puerto Rico. . . .

Coffeyville *American,* March 4, 1899

"GEN. GOMEZ BLIND TO AMERICAN INTENTIONS"

Gen. Maximo Gomez expresses explicit confidence in the promises of the Americans to withdraw from Cuba and leave the island "free and independent." The old general is still blind to the handwriting on the wall.

Indianapolis *Recorder,* March 4, 1899

"CUBA SHOULD BE FREE"

Cuba should be free! We do not like the delay upon the part of our government in securing to the people of that isle the great boon they contended for so many years, and at so great a sacrifice of life, money, and property.

Cleveland Gazette, March 10, 1899

"GIVE PUERTO RICO THE BENEFITS OF THE CONSTITUTION"

The Puerto Rican muddle is considered on all sides a serious predicament and especially since the Republicans are responsible for it. Hon. Benjamin Harrison, our ex-President, recognized the world over for his legal acumen, casts his weighty opinion against the side of the government and he is not alone.

Opinions of experts who are trying to justify the government's attitude are trying to read Puerto Rico out of the benefits of the Constitution. The masses of the country, however, insist that the Constitution is explicit on the matter, holding that the few intervening miles of water do not alienate any portion of the country, when once considered as a portion.

Puerto Rico has been received in the Union upon just such terms as all subsequent acquired territories have been received. It expected, and had a right to expect, that the same form of government should be allowed them as is permitted all other portions of the government in the same degree of advancement. It seems that discriminating duties and tariffs should not prevail against her although it be at the behests of tobacco, sugar, and other interests.

Indianapolis Freeman, March 10, 1899

"PUERTO RICANS HAD BETTER LIKE ANNEXATION"

The Puerto Ricans have profited by the lesson taught the Cubans and the Filipinos—they express themselves as being delighted with the idea of annexation.

Indianapolis Recorder, April 8, 1899

VI

CIVIL RIGHTS, THE PHILIPPINES, AND IMPERIALISM

The battle over ratification of the treaty ceding the Philippines to the United States, in January and February, 1899 brought forth two opposing views as to the justice and wisdom of annexing the Philippines and other former Spanish colonies. Opposition to the treaty was led by the Anti-Imperialist League and by such senators as Richard F. Pettigrew and George F. Hoar, and such bigots as Senator Ben Tillman of South Carolina, who was anti-imperialist for racist reasons.* The anti-imperialists vehemently opposed the annexation as a fundamental departure from the American principle of government by consent of the governed and the Declaration of Independence. They also held that the Filipinos were an inferior people, who had an unassimilable culture, and that it was a violation of the solemn declaration made by President McKinley in December, 1897 that forcible annexation, according to the American code of morality, was criminal aggression. To many, the war fought for suffering humanity in Cuba was now being turned into a war of aggression by the American government, in order to take over the land of the Filipinos, who had been fighting intermittently for their independence from Spain for some years.

The Phillippine-American War lasted from the outbreak of hostilities on February 5, 1899 to the spring of 1902. The years 1899 and 1900 were the high points of anti-imperialist agitation. Most of the black press was strongly anti-imperialist and emphasized the interconnection between the government's domestic and foreign policy in dealing with dark-skinned people. These newspapers argued that an imperialistic foreign policy boded no good for blacks, maintaining that it was concomitant with the passage of state and local Jim Crow laws, lynch terror, and the absence of federal protection of civil rights. Though forced to agree

*A recent book by Robert Beisner, *Twelve Against Empire,* studies the twelve most prominent anti-imperialists and indicates, briefly, their various degrees of racism.

with the anti-imperialist position of some congressmen, they continued to attack their racist reasons for opposing imperialism.

However, some black newspapers, in particular the Indianapolis *Freeman,* supported annexation, stressing, among other things, the great economic potential the islands held for the Negro. When in September, 1899, two black regiments were to be formed to fight in the Philippines, these papers proclaimed that allegiance to the United States must come before racial considerations.

"PHILIPPINES SHOULD BE FREE"

What has Germany got to do with the disposition of the Philippine Islands anyway? Spain has ruined them and we don't particularly need them. . . . Leave the islands to the inhabitants, a free and independent government, and if they want to establish a protectorate over them it is their business and [not] our own.

Parsons *Weekly Blade,* May 21, 1898

"THE PHILIPPINES: A NEW FIELD FOR THE NEGRO"

As the indications point to the permanent occupation of the Philippine Islands by the United States, it becomes a matter of great interest as to what are the possibilities of these islands.

Owing to the tropical character of the climate it will take considerable development and cultivation before white men can settle there comfortably, but an immediate field is offered to the negro race in the United States. Hardy, capable of resisting the injurious effects of a tropical climate, peculiarly fitted for a tropical land, we predict that once the Philippines are a part of the United States that here will be found a field where the negro can easily carve out a home for himself which will yield him a handsome return for his labors, and in developing the rich agricultural and mineral resources of these islands which last have been practically untouched as yet, he will not only not meet unfavorable competition from his white brothers, but on the contrary will find in him his greatest helper and support. If the United States is going to undertake to develop these wonderfully rich islands, it will be the negroes of the states who will have to do the most of it, and they can do it with benefit to the nation at large and profit to themselves. We hope to see the day when the aristocracy and wealth of Luzon, Mindanao and the other islands will be the educated, refined, self-made negroes of the states.

Wisconsin Weekly Advocate, May 21, 1898

"NEGROES CAN MAKE MONEY IN THE PHILIPPINES"

[From the *Enterprise,* Omaha, Nebraska]

"The Philippine Islands will offer an excellent opportunity for Negro colonization, not colonization for the purpose of getting out of this country but for the same purpose that white man colonizes, for the purpose of making money. . . .

"Most of the islands are unexplored and undeveloped, and here is where a grand opportunity presents itself to the Negro. A colony of enterprising American Negroes could make money there, and the chances are the stars and stripes would afford him more protection there than it does here at home. . . ."

Coffeyville *American,* May 28, 1898

"FOR ANNEXATION OF THE PHILIPPINES AND CUBA"

Unfriendly critics have asserted time and again that the sole purpose of the present war on the part of America was the acquiring of territory. Dewey's victory at Manila and the events that have followed that victory give credence to these assertions. While it is true that no such purpose actuated the administration in going to war with Spain, it is also none the less true that the victory of Manila opened the eyes of America to certain possibilities along this line that would never have been noticed or seriously considered under peaceful conditions. The Philippines an American colony! American military governor-general; American army of occupation! There is something grand in the very sound of it all. A something that stirs the blood of the military and fires the imagination of the commonest civilian. This thing means power and glory and fame. Of course it is the old, old demon of conquest that has led and is still leading nations to ruin. Still, who can deny but that such a condition of affairs would not be a distinct gain to humanity? Not only in the Philippines but in Cuba and in fact all other colonial possessions of Spain. . . . Yes, America should and will undoubtedly hold the Philippines. Further than that we shall see. It is a great temptation no doubt, but Americans are not fools. They have read and pondered the history of dead nations, followed the rise and fall of the world's civilizations and inquired into the why and wherefore of these things. The administration can be depended upon to wisely continue the traditional policy of profiting by the mistakes of other nations. To whatever extent the spirit of conquest may be developed as a result of this war we can rest assured that it will be firmly met and properly handled.

Coffeyville *American,* June 11, 1898

"For Philippine Annexation"

"While we are fighting to free Cuba would it be right to hand the Philippines back to Spanish tyranny and cruelty?"—Coffeyville *Daily Journal.*

My dear sir, this is not a question at all. It is all a matter of dollars and cents. Having poured out our money like water—having literally bought and paid for this speck of territory, would it be right or sensible to give it away? Realizing the advantages and benefits that will possible accrue to them as a result of holding these islands, would practical Americans ever consent to give them up? Hardly. In the case of the Philippines then, to be plain, the prime consideration is not one of tyranny or slavery but of territory. And this is right.

The nincompoops who oppose the Presidential war policy are not sleeping. No stone is being left unturned looking to the embarassment of the administration. Following the failure of every other attempt to break through the divinity that hedges a President comes the wild and unlooked for charge of imperialism. This, they allege, is a new as well as a dangerous thing in American annals. The imperialistic tendencies of the administration are a little short of high treason. Pshaw, now this is too bad. Why doesn't someone see after it?

When the Stars and Stripes are flying over the Philippines, Puerto Rico, Cuba, Hawaii and a few other island kingdoms out that way, it is just barely possible that the oily-tongued agitator will find a sufficient number of idle men who are willing to listen, while he sings in fury, strains of Bill McKinley, the imperialist. For the present we say, "Go to."

Coffeyville *American,* July 2, 1898

"Annexation Debated"

[From an account of a meeting of the Epworth League of St. John's Church called to debate the subject, "Should the United States retain the Philippine Islands?":]

Mr. Hall said the retention. . . . will afford an outlet to this vicious race prejudice here. . . . The same argument, he said, applied to Cuba, Puerto Rico, and other prospective conquests. By adding the care of looking after these new acquisitions to the dominant class of the country, they would have less time to devote to the oppression of the Negro. Besides this, it will offer opportunities for the acquirement of money and other property which will be superior to those which the Negro will generally meet with here. The Negro would gain politically, too. . . . for the government, which is unable or unwilling to protect him at home, would have no difficulty or hesitation about protecting him abroad.

Mr. Bell said that the proposition. . . . that the Negro would receive better protection from the Government in a foreign land than at home was unsupported by a single fact of history. . . . The truth is. . . . that we have now a large representation of that element of citizenship which, in proportion as it is augmented, the menace to free and legitimate government is increased. There are hundreds of thousands of persons that are enjoying all the rights and privileges of full-fledged citizenship here and yet have practically no knowledge or appreciation of the spirit and fundamental nature of our institutions. To increase this vast volume of ignorance and moral depravity among our present citizenship by the incorporation of the heterogeneous populations of those islands would seem to be a suicidal policy of government.

The negative had intended to add to these arguments the facts that the retention of these conquests would necessitate the maintenance of a standing army and navy. . . . Indeed, every feature of such a policy . . . would involve a radical departure from our lifelong theories and traditions of government. . . .

Afro-American Sentinel, July 23, 1898

"PHILIPPINES NOT DESIREABLE FOR ACQUISITION"

The Philippines are not very desireable for acquisition. The turbulent citizens, natives, half-breeds and Spaniards will in all probability always be restless and discontented with any form of government, no matter how modern or enlightened. . . .These people will never be able to understand the institutions of this country and hence will not appreciate them. They will be as ready to strike a benefactor as they would a foe, causing our country to put into practice methods which to the world would appear inhumane, but which in reality would be necessary for restraint or the suppression of revolting tendencies. . . . The Maine has been amply avenged, and our country cannot righten all the wrongs on earth. . . .

Indianapolis *Freeman,* July 30, 1898

"THE PHILIPPINES"

[Reprinted from the *World* (white), New York, N.Y. without comment:]

If, as Senator Hoar's speech foreshadowed and as later reports from Washington indicate, President McKinley is opposed to the conquest and permanent possession of the Philippines, he is guided by real wisdom and high courage. There are difficulties in the way of a complete conquest far greater than our easy-going optimists imagine.

The Singapore *Free Press* of June 8 contains a letter from H. W. Gray, an Englishman who has lived long in the islands and knows them as few Europeans do. He says that "the possession of Manila [does not mean] the possession of the Philippines. . . . The islands will be occupied in a military sense by the Americans with the assistance and good will of the Filipinos." But without this good will and aid he declares "neither the United States or any other nation could ever hope to take the Philippines except with an army of 200,000 men or more."

"The only possible solution of the Philippine question," according to Mr. Gray, "is an independent government under American protection." As a friend and counselor of Gen. Aguinaldo he had recommended this policy, and he has faith that it will be carried out.

Afro-American Sentinel, July 30, 1898

"For Philippine Annexation"

Why should we squabble about the Philippines? Why should we try to evade our responsibilities? Why should we shrink from the situation. . . .

Everyone understood that war and victory would bring new obligations as well as new responsibilities with this all before us . . . shall we now take the courage to meet all obligations incurred by the war? Can those people [Filipinos] expect any security for their life or property from the hands of Spanish officials; when Dewey destroyed the Spanish controller in the Philippines the natives welcomed the Americans as the forerunners of a new era. Since May 1st, they have been conducting a successful war against Spain.

Shall we now surrender these people to the mercy of the men against whom they have made war in our interest? We would say no a thousand times; the United States should free them from the oppressive rule that has held for three centuries and again our commercial interest in the Far East needs protection. How can we accomplish that end better than keeping these islands? It would open new markets for us, why cast aside such an opportunity that lies within our grasp to do our duty?

Iowa State Bystander, August 5, 1898

"Aguinaldo No Fool"

The Philippine insurgent chief, Aguinaldo, wants to do the right thing by the Americans for Dewey's goodness to him, but he doesn't propose to let those smart jays run a hog bluff over him, and we glory in his spunk.

Parsons *Weekly Blade,* August 13, 1898

"The Philippines"

Our Commissioners in Paris are still insisting on the possession of the Philippines. The government in the first place should never have asked Spain for these islands. We should have landed our land and naval forces and taken possession. Had England been in a fight with Spain and whipped her, she would never have appointed any commissioners. She would have given Spain to understand that she was whipped and must give up and if she failed to accede to her demands she would have run her into the sea. If the United States would cease demanding and act more, this Spanish-American war would be terminated.

Washington *Bee,* November 12, 1898

"U.S. ANNEXATION IS HIGHWAY ROBBERY"

Because Spain tried to whip some of her children, Uncle Sam steps in and takes the children under his arm for protection; and then steps a little further on and takes another part of the Spanish family and their land to pay for the trouble of taking the other set, and then steps around on the other side of the world and gobbles up another small kingdom for trading stock. All this highway robbery is done in the name of humanity and is done by a nation that shows by its actions at home that the principles of humanity are an unknown factor when the treatment of the American Negro is taken into consideration.

Parsons *Weekly Blade,* December 10, 1898

"FILIPINOS SHOULD HAVE REPUBLICAN FORM OF GOVERNMENT"

Now that the Philippines are about to be ours the alarmists of the Vest [a Missouri senator] ilk are beginning to spread the news that it won't do to guarantee the dark inhabitants a republican form of government. If the republican form is so well adapted to others, why not to them? It is the same old fear of "nigger dominance" albeit it is to be 8000 miles away. No wonder the howlers do not want to guarantee it at home.

Washington *Bee,* December 10, 1898

"SOUTHERN ANTI-EXPANSIONISTS HYPOCRITICAL"

To hear the southern anti-expansionists talk about the unwisdom of accepting the Philippines without the consent of the governed, one would think that they were the most ardent and honest supporters of republican government, wherein every citizen whether white or black is accorded the full and free exercise of the right of suffrage. . . . Of all the people who claim to be Americans the southern autocrat is the last person who should talk of the consent of the governed. He is even now in the presence of a class of citizens who by the organic law of the land are citizens in the fullest sense of the term. They form the most substantial and reliable portion of the southern population, producing about everything that is raised, deporting themselves in a quiet and law-abiding manner. In point of education, they have far outstripped the white southerner and have shown moral aptitude and demonstrated official integrity of a superior order. They are in the best sense entitled to recognition as a part of the governed. And yet they are treated as aliens and are denied that consideration which these southern hypocrites declare belong to the Philippines. It were better if the alarmists set about showing their patriotism and consistent interest in the theory and practice of republican government and proving themselves good citizens before they presume to stand as the sponsors and exponents of the most enlightened American citizenship. This opposition to expansion on the part of the South is in sad and ludicrous contrast with the expansion of slave territory upon which they insisted even to the dismemberment of the Union, if need be. The fact is that the South, finding itself about to be set adrift for want of an issue dependent entirely or for the most part upon their will, is now grasping at the straw of anti-expansion, in the hope that by advocating it they may continue their hold upon the democratic party. They have tried slavery, territorial expansion, fiat money, irredeemable silver and have failed. They are now howling about anti-expansion and will for the same reason which doomed the other issues come out of the same end of the horn. It may be all right to object to the acquisition of more territory upon reasonable grounds; but when the southern red-shirt acts in the dramatic role of anti-expansionists on the ground that antagonizes the well-defined policy of acting in harmony with the consent of the governed, it is time for the world to take a day off and have a hearty laugh.

Washington *Bee,* December 17, 1898

"FILIPINOS CONGRATULATED FOR RESISTANCE"

This great government of ours has run amuck of a snag in the game of snatch-grab in the Philippine question and the high ones in this country have concluded that a war in that country would result disastrously to U.S. and Co. Those people are to be congratulated for the stand taken for they only can imagine what sort of rap they are to get by letting themselves in America's grasp.

Parsons *Weekly Blade,* January 4, 1899

"TERRITORIAL EXPANSION WILL BE GOOD FOR THE NEGRO"

[From the New York *Age*:]

The Hon. John P. Green, chief of the United States Stamp Agency at Washington, has furnished the following very interesting synopsis of his recent address on "Expansion: What Is It?":

"Expansion in the past embraces the following . . . recent acquisitions [being] Hawaiian Republic, Puerto Rico, Philippines, Guam, Sulu Islands. Original domain, about 800,000 square miles; present domain, about 3,000,000 square miles.

"When our inventive genius, industry, etc. result in manufacturing in six months as much as we can consume in a year, we must necessarily find markets in which to dispose of the surplus. Herein lies to a great extent the secret of Great Britain's success: in India, Australia, New Zealand, Canada, Egypt, Cape Colony, China and many other sections of the earth, she buys from the producer at first cost and sells the great surplus manufactures of her furnaces, mills, and factories. The Philippines will be our great center of distribution. We are nearer them now, from our western coast than Europe. When a canal across the Isthmus is completed, we will be several days nearer than England.

"The dawn of a new civilization is just now breaking in the East, and in the near future the demands for our manufactures will be manifold greatly. If we do not hold onto what is now within our grasp, other nations will take them, and our producers and workers will be the sufferers thereby.

"Our 'colonial' trade will stimulate shipbuilding, railroad building, and car building; and this, in turn, will call for immense supplies of raw and manufactured materials, from steel plates and rails down to the finest fabrics. When the sources of supply are in full operation, then our farmers will have their day of prosperity; since the United States, when prosperous, furnishes the farmer his nearest and best market.

"The addition of so many dark and mixed races to our population will enlarge the scope of our usefulness and enhance our opportunities for attaining to spheres of usefulness, honor, and wealth, along commercial, artistic, scientific, political, and literary lines. I expect to live to see the day great generals, merchant princes, bankers, railway magnates and others belonging to our race will be in evidence in our new possessions. White people go out into the world in quest of land, money, and honorable places; they get them and hold them; why cannot we do likewise? It will give employment to many of our young men as soldiers, also, and create a demand for commissioned officers, now only in its inception.

"We own Puerto Rico by conquest; Hawaii by peaceful annexation; Guam by conquest; the Sulu Islands by treaty; and the Philippines by both conquest and purchase. Their present state of civilization is low. Our intentions towards them are good; and, inasmuch as ignorant and half-civilized people (like some children) do not always know what is for their welfare, we must constrain them for their own good. . . .

"The war now being waged in the Philippines is of the Filipinos' own seeking, and the olive branch is now, and has been from the first, extended to them. They can expect peace and live in peace and happiness or continue to fight and die.

"There are worse things than war. Gen. Sherman says: 'War is hell!' This is no fiction; it is true; but, there are things worse even than war. I refer to physical, intellectual, and moral slavery. We will give the Filipinos, for peace, physical, intellectual, and moral regeneration. We will give them that light which men in darkness most need."

World (Seattle,Washington), January 4, 1899

"IDA WELLS BARNETT AGAINST EXPANSION"

[From an account of the Washington D.C. meeting of the National Afro-American Council:]

Ida Wells-Barnett spoke on "Mob Violence and Anarchy, North and South." She said Negroes should oppose expansion until the government was able to protect the Negro at home.

Cleveland *Gazette,* January 7, 1899

"PHILLIPPINE SUBJUGATION WILL DESTROY AMERICA"

That gigantic bluff made by the McKinley administration may yet cost Uncle Sam some trouble. The leaders of the Philippine insurgents can't understand such tactics on the part of friends (?) and therefore cannot put any trust in anything now said and done. But just as sure as the force of arms is attempted to bring them under subjugation of the rule of America, that day will the United States unloose the chains that bind her to the brow of the hill and the momentum gathered in her downward flight will plunge her into [destruction—Ed.].

Parsons *Weekly Blade,* January 21, 1899

"IMPERIALISM ISSUE SHAKING UP THE PARTIES"

[From the *Tribune,* Philadelphia, Pa.:]

The opposition of the southern and western wings of the Democratic party to the policy of expansion, and the recent utterances of Mr. Croker in favor of such a policy, suggests the idea of a possible break all along the line of the old parties. With Senator Hoar leading the antis against the supposed Republican majority in the east, and Croker breaking away from what was supposed to be the Democratic stand in New York, it is not unlikely that by 1900 the old parties will be severely shaken up. For our part, we welcome an issue which is broad enough and plain enough to admit a division among all our people along the lines of intelligent individual opinion. Surely any of us who may follow such a man as

Senator Hoar, whatever may be our reasons, cannot be taunted as ingrates to the Republican party or as traitors to the race.

Indianapolis *Recorder,* January 21, 1899

"ANNEXATION QUESTIONED"

On sober second thought there appears to be a grain of wisdom in the Philippinos' refusal to come under the sheltering wing of a country which has repeatedly demonstrated its inability to protect the lives and property of its own citizens within a stone's throw of the seat of government.

Are those tender-hearted expansionists in the United States Congress really actuated by the desire to save the Filipinos from self-destruction or is it the worldly greed for gain? When one of the great Christian countries finds a strip of land it desires to possess, it is quickly seized with a commendable desire to spread the benign influence of civilization over the natives; and what a remarkably small number of natives are left after this process of civilizing has been completed! Why are the natives of good-for-nothing, God-forsaken lands liable to stumble along in blissful ignorance of this great "civilization"?

Indianapolis *Recorder,* January 28, 1899

"MCKINLEY LIBERATES OTHERS BUT NOT THE NEGRO"

It is a sad truth; nevertheless, it is true that we are compelled to endorse the action of the Afro-American Council in supplicating the foreign powers to lend their influence towards bringing about harmony between the negro and white races in this country. We have contributed our brawn and sinew to this Government to help overthrow the bonds of oppression and tyranny of Spain from off her colonies.

And now it seems we must implore the aid of some great nation to insure us protection for life and liberty in many localities in our own home. . . .

He [McKinley] has liberated some of the oppressed colonies of another nation and has left the colored man to wonder why he would allow the massacres of the last campaign to go unnoticed in his all-seeing message to Congress, and again we wonder if he prefers falling victim to southern patronage rather than protect the negro subjects of that section. Indeed he is wonderful in many ways.

Coffeyville *American,* January 28, 1899

"FORCIBLE ANNEXATION IS CRIMINAL"

[From the *Southern Republican,* New Orleans, La.:]

Pinchback, Jim Lewis and other negro political pap-seekers, who stood up in the recent meeting of the Afro-American Council in Washington and advocated putting the Cubans and Philippines under the yoke of American prejudice, ought to be read out of good society. If the Cubans and Filipinos themselves want annexation with the United States, well and good. But to force it on them would be criminal. Right here the *Southern Republicans* takes its stand. We believe in this immortal principle enunciated in the Declaration of Independence: all just powers of government are derived from the consent of the governed. We are opposed to "expansion." . . . We have been taught that it was un-American and it is surely un-republican.

Washington *Bee,* January 28, 1899

"NO CONTROL OF DISTANT ISLANDS
UNTIL THE CONSTITUTION IS ENFORCED"

When it was ascertained that the ruling powers of Spain had decided to accept the treaty of peace, immediately the question arose in the minds of the leading statesmen, politicians and those who take any interest in public affairs what should this government do with. . . . the Philippine . . . and other islands which came into possession of this government. . . .

A great many have assumed the position that it is un-Democratic, un-American, and not in harmony with the Monroe Doctrine for this government to absolutely assume control over these islands, that by doing so it would entail an expenditure of more than two hundred million dollars per annum. . . .

Some are of the opinion that it would be much better for this country to dispose of her new territorial acquisitions and only retain a small portion of them to be used for coaling stations, and that it would be very injudicious and unwise to imitate or follow after England and other European countries and adopt the theory or policy of expansion, or an imperialistic idea for form of government. . . .

We especially approve of the attitude of the eminent senator of South Carolina [McLaurin]. . . . for we are more than convinced that this country does not possess the right or at least it should not attempt to inaugurate a new governmental policy or system to control the people which inhabit those distant islands, until it is able to protect the rights of each and every citizen within the confines of the present government. For if it cannot do that, it should not attempt to legislate for people who are unaccustomed to our form of government and who detest mob and lynch law.

There is one proposition [of McLaurin's]. . . . we cannot endorse, namely that "an amendment to the Constitution should be adopted, placing all the inferior races in this country and the inhabitants of the Philippines beneath the plane of the white men, and that it is the divine right of the Caucasian or the whites to govern the negro races. That by pursuing such a course the negro or the race problem will be forever settled in this country."

We are therefore opposed to the policy of expansion or colonial system of government until this nation is able and willing to enforce all the laws of the land and wrap the strong arm of the government around each one of her citizens. . . .

Salt Lake City Broad Ax, January 28, 1899

"MAJORITY OF NEGROES ARE OPPOSED TO EXPANSION"

The speech of George H. White of North Carolina in the House of Representatives last week . . . showed that many of those inimical to the negro had been elected by theft, fraud, and assassination. While his speech was a master defense of the negro, the Bee doesn't agree with him on the expansion scheme. A majority of the negroes in this country are opposed to expansion. A government that is powerless to protect its own citizens should never attempt to seize other governments by invasion and throw around them an American protectorate, which is nothing more than political and physical oppression. Expansion is a fraud and the American negro has long since come to the conclusion that before any government attempts to throw the protecting arm around a foreign foe, it should first protect its own citizens. The defense of the negro by Mr. White was admirable, but he is wrong on expansion. The best evidence is, of the recent overthrow of the local government in his own state. . . . Mr. White is a man possessing every noble quality and above all he is a truthful man. He will do his race more good if he opposes expansion.

Washington Bee, February 4, 1899

EXPANSION OR NO EXPANSION

To expand or not to expand is the question that is uppermost in the minds of the American people. Whether 'tis better to enlarge our present bounds, serve humanity and thus glorify ourselves in the eyes of the world by so doing, or content ourselves with our present domain, heedless of the plaudits. . . .

The situation is an extremely awkward one. The opinion of the best-informed as to the outcome of proposed annexation is but an opinion still. There is absolutely no data from which to proceed. The very small experience of this country in dealing with such problems has thrown the nation at sea. . . .

But the condition seems fairly forced on the government. It intervened in the interest of Cuba at the behest of humanity. As an expedient of war these islands were wrested from their ancient tyrant, master and enemy, Spain. . . .

Further, there stand the other omnivorous nations of Europe, with whetted beaks and clasped talons, ready to banquet on the carcass . . . of

Spain. In the interest of peace . . . America holds the key to the situation. England says, no; keep all you get, thus casting in its mighty consent, which is not given out of its great love for America, but because it does not tend to lessen her European supremacy. Very likely her political sagacity would advise against the acquiring of such a warlike tributary as the Philippines. However, she prefers that they do not go to the rival powers. . . .

Thus America is forced to enjoy her new acquired possessions in the interest of peace as well as humanity. Yet notwithstanding those opposing forces that compel the situation, our country is not a unit on the annexation movement.

It seems that there is nothing left but to annex, as foreign to the idea of American solidarity as it may appear, and as contrary to the Monroe Doctrine as it is. However, the Monroe Doctrine was not divinely inspired, although it quite suited the day in which it was uttered. The country has not repudiated the doctrine; but it has in spite of itself been forced to take on new obligations—the fortunes of war. . . .

The Filipinos are possessed with much pride and independence of spirit and have some notions of government. They feel that they should try their hand in managing affairs.

Their pride is pardonable, but enlightened governments are not born in a day.

The bushman of today cannot be the legislator of tommorow. Hence, the utmost that our country could consistently do would be to give them the best form of government possible under the circumstances, void of all sentiment and when they can maintain that, that which insures domestic tranquillity, showing superiority to the rule of Spain, then the staying hand of America might be withdrawn.

Or under such wise laws and regulations as America would enforce, the chances are the hostility to American institutions would cease to exist and the consent of the governed, the groundwork of the American government, would not be violated.

Indianapolis *Freeman,* February 4, 1899

"Sen. J. L. Rawlins' Anti-Expansionism Supported"

United States Senator J. L. Rawlins has favored the *Broad Ax* with several publications of the government. . . . Wednesday, Senator Rawlins delivered his speech in relation to the Philippine Islands. It contains some good points against the policy of expansion, but his thrust at the inhabitants of those islands, the darker races which inhabit the other portions of the Far East, was uncalled for and their merits or demerits have nothing to do with the right or wrong of annexing the Philippine Islands.

Salt Lake City *Broad Ax,* February 5, 1899

"SEN. J. L. RAWLINS COMMENDED FOR VOTING AGAINST THE TREATY OF PARIS"

While we do not agree with all the conclusions of Senator J. L. Rawlins in his speech against the annexing of the Philippine Islands, we desire to commend Senator Rawlins for voting against the treaty of peace, and he is eminently right when he says "that the ratification means the sacrifice of many lives and the expenditure of many millions." The occurrences in the last few days in those islands indicate that Senator Rawlins was justifiable in opposing this wildcat scheme.

Salt Lake City *Broad Ax,* February 11, 1899

"NEGROES OPPOSED TO TREATY OF PARIS"

The ratification of the peace treaty was the logical outcome of an entanglement which was fast bringing the republic into disgrace and making of it a laughing-stock for foreign nations. While we were and still are opposed to the acquisition by this government of the Philippines and believe their annexation would be a public calamity, working disastrously both to the Filipinos and ourselves, yet the one and only potent reason for prompt ratification was the necessity for the establishment, according to the explicit terms of the treaty, of a legal claim to the archipelago; otherwise we would still be in a state of war with Spain. Those voting for ratification are not bound to a principle of permanent ownership by the government. On the contrary, it is a well-known fact that the permanent occupation of the Philippines by the United States will be vigorously opposed by many Senators who voted for ratification. The consensus of opinion among the negro citizens of this government was naturally opposed to a ratification of the treaty upon the ground that if they were denied their rights in this country, the same conditions would obtain in the Philippines when once the whites got control. With the latter might makes right and the worst white man is regarded as being better than the best black one.

Washington *Bee,* February 11, 1899

"AGAINST ANNEXATION"

[From the *American Baptist,* Louisville, Kentucky:]

The annexation of territory as a result of war with Spain is becoming a serious question for discussion and is not confined alone to the right of our government to acquire territory by purchase or conquest. The matter of the treatment of these people who belong to the dark-skinned races is a matter which concerns us. The conduct of men in the future can only be determined by observing their conduct in the past. Experience and not promises weighs more potently in these matters, and the treatment which

the Indians, the Chinese, and the Negroes have received at the hands of
the white Americans speaks in no uncertain tone—it would be deplorable
to have the inhabitants of the Philippine Islands treated as the Indians
have been treated or the people of Cuba or Puerto Rico ruled as the
Negroes of the South have been ruled. . . . This kind of civilization has
very little to commend it and it is doubtful whether it ought to be
extended to our newly-acquired territory. It is the plain duty of this
government to remedy our own scandalous abuses rather than to extend
the system under which they have arisen to other people.

Coffeyville *American,* February 11, 1899

"FILIPINOS WHO DEMAND INDEPENDENCE
ARE CALLED BARBARIANS"

As long as the impression prevailed in this country that the Filipinos
were fighting to throw off the Spanish yoke and seek American annex-
ation, they were called patriots and martyrs, but when they demanded
pure and unadulterated independence, they became a set of blood-thirsty
barbarians.

Indianapolis *Recorder,* February 11, 1899

"FILIPINOS SHOULD SUBMIT TO AMERICAN RULE"

It is often said that gratitude is paid by ingratitude. . . . the insurgents
of the Philippine Islands. . . . are now fighting the Americans for no cause
save that of gratitude and liberty that we have recently given them. How
unjust and ungrateful is Aguinaldo and his poor ignorant and deluded
followers. Had Mr. Aguinaldo been like Garcia of Santiago or Gomez of
Cuba, he would be revered, not only by his own people but all the
civilized nations. If he had the true interest of his country at heart and the
welfare of his people as a loyal patriot should, thousands of his
countrymen would have today been living and by now instead of sorry
ruin and destruction, the natives would have been settled down to the
peaceable pursuits of happiness as the other islands that have recently
come under our control. Aguinaldo should be apprehended and court
martialed as a traitor to his country; however, it is hoped that these brief
engagements that we have just had will be a good lesson for the natives
and they will kindly submit to American protection and rule.

Iowa State Bystander, February 17, 1899

"WAR FOR HUMANITY NOW GREED FOR GAIN"

The ratification of the peace treaty by the United States does not
necessarily mean American retention of the Philippines, but our with-

drawal from the islands is extremely improbable. The war begun for humanity is ending in a gratification of the greed for gain. The slaughter of 6,000 natives because they objected to our method of administering civilization is certainly not humanity. American occupation of the islands will undoubtedly be a gain to civilization, but civilization's gain will be the natives' loss. It is merely the dominating mastery of the Anglo-Saxon asserting itself; humanity—never!

Indianapolis *Recorder,* February 18, 1899

"Filipinos Being 'Civilized' by the American Army"

The Filipinos are sueing for peace; they prefer assimilation to annihilation. Uncle Sam will doubtless give them a dose of the same brand that has proven so effective with the North American Indians.

Indianapolis *Recorder,* March 4, 1899

"Military Government of the Filipinos"

In his instruction to the commission in regards to the Philippines the President says: "The temporary government of the islands is intrusted to the military authorities, and will so continue until Congress shall otherwise determine." At the present rate the military authorities will soon reduce the number of natives until their government will be an easy matter.

Indianapolis *Recorder,* March 11, 1899

"Is Negro Press Anti-Expansionism a Pressure Tactic?"

A fair percent of the Negro press is opposing the administration in its administrative policy in the Philippines. Will these have the courage to espouse the vote-dividing cause and support the democratic party and non-expansion? Or is the opposition just so much leverage to foist oneself for recognition by the administration?

Indianapolis *Freeman,* March 11, 1899

"Filipino Struggle Admired"

There is certainly no disposition to gloat over the success of the Filipinos, far from it, but the spirit of heroism, of patriotism in the interest of independence, which is manifested goes to show that all races under favorable or unfavorable conditions will make a desperate effort for freedom and independence. The history of the Philippines will attest the fact that all people who are oppressed will fight, and if need be, die for their liberty. While we are with this country in its contest for supremacy of the doctrines of humanity, we cannot but admire the bravery of people who, escaping from the tyranny of one nation, looks with doubt upon the friendship of a new protectorate. Moreover, there is some analogy between the struggle which is now going on among the colored people for constitutional liberty and that of a similar race in the orient and hence a bond of sympathy naturally springs up. We are for the flag pure and unstained.

Washington *Bee,* March 11, 1899

"THE NEGRO NEEDS FILIPINO BACKBONE"

[From the *Progress,* Omaha, Nebraska:]

That manifesto issued by the Filipino government sounds of the right stuff and has caused no end of uneasiness among Americans. The backbone displayed by these "ignorant, uncivilized" barbarians as termed by the Americans, is what the Negro of the United States needs. Take pattern, ye black sons of America!

Salt Lake City *Broad Ax,* March 11, 1899

"BAYONET-IMPOSED CIVILIZATION"

The Americans are determined to make the Filipinos accept civilization at the point of the bayonet. The officers in command of the American forces are old Indian fighters, who owe their success to the close adherence to the theory that "a dead Indian is the best Indian." They will employ the same methods in dealing with the Filipinos.

Indianapolis *Recorder,* March 18, 1899

"FILIPINO DEFEAT REGRETTED"

It will be unfortunate if the sequel of our war with Spain ends in our fighting and defeating those whom Spanish tyranny drove into insurrection, and yet present conditions are such that, if this alternative is presented, we must courageously face it, even though we may regret that some other means of adjusting difficulties has not been presented.

Salt Lake City *Broad Ax,* March 18, 1899

"OBJECT OF SPANISH-AMERICAN WAR WAS ACQUISITION OF TERRITORY BY UNLAWFUL MEANS"

But the [Filipino] natives do not relish the change of masters or rulers; consequently they feel justified in assuming a hostile **attitude** toward their new enemies, who are more formidable, powerful, and tyrannous than the Spaniards ever were. And we do not blame Aguinaldo and his forces for resisting every effort to be subjugated by the American troops or forces. For we must not lose sight of the fact that when the cry went up, "Remember the Maine," the administration organs, and every one of its mouthpieces, declared that this nation must not and should not engage in warfare with Spain for special aggrandizement or conquest, but the war should be waged for the betterment of those whose lives were being gradually crushed out by the iron heel of Spain.

The high-sounding words which were then uttered by the hypocritical and would-be patriots have proved to be nothing more than an empty sound. For the real principle or cause of the war has been entirely ignored, and the emissaries of this government have surpassed the Spaniards in committing acts of cruelty against the natives. . . . In short, this government has launched upon a career of murder and robbery; and every native who is shot down in cold blood, like common dogs, is conclusive proof that the only object in waging the war against Spain was to acquire new territory by unlawful means.

This policy is in keeping with the course which has been pursued by the stronger and Christian nations against the feebler and weaker races.

When the Pilgrim Fathers landed at Plymouth Rock, they came into contact with the law-abiding and peaceful Indians; and the blood-stained pages of history record their hellish plots. The Fathers robbed, plundered the Indians and outraged their wives and daughters and murdered them, so that they could acquire their land without compensating them for it. But this was done in the name of Christianity.

The same fate awaits Aguinaldo and his subjects if they permit themselves to be conquered. Let them remember the burning words of the immortal Patrick Henry, "Give me liberty, or give me death." With these words ever ringing in their ears, let them meet their fate like heroes and die rather than submit to be ruled over by those who are unfriendly to them. For if they do submit, the same treatment is in store for them which has been meted out to the negro for over two hundred and fifty years.

What right has this or any other nation to interfere with the inhabitants of those islands? What right has it to foully murder innocent women and children? Is this civilization? Are these foul crimes committed in the name of the religion of the cross and for the betterment of the natives? No! This war is simply being waged to satisfy the robbers, murderers, and unscrupulous monopolists who are ever crying for more blood! This country is not invested with any valid title to those islands; and her troops should not be permitted to trample upon the rights and the liberties of the Filipinos.

Salt Lake City *Broad Ax,* March 25, 1899

"The Reason For Annexation"

Though the United States has pretended to want to rid itself of its Negro population, still it is constantly reaching out and getting control of every island it can in which the Negro either predominates or is a tremendous factor. If the Negroes are such monsters, why keep increasing to your home ten millions more? In our opinion all this howl about the Negro being undesirable personnages in America is a gigantic lie, and recent acquisitions of Cuba, Puerto Rico, Hawaii, Ladrone, and the Philippine Islands by this country will bear us out in this supposition. It looks as though the Negro is considered a good thing to pick up the white man's burden and the white man does not forget to have him do it.

Coffeyville *American,* March 25, 1899

"Sen. William E. Mason's Anti-Imperialism Commended"

Our last article on the war in the Philippine Islands invoked much favorable and unfavorable comment. Some few behind our back expressed their regret "that there is not some law or way whereby we could be sent to prison for expressing such treasonable and unpatriotic sentiments." But such hot-heads and ignorant creatures are too indolent to keep up with the times. They are not acquainted with the fact that the New York *World*, which has the largest circulation of any paper in the world, says that "President McKinley has no right whatever to expend twenty million dollars in purchasing ten million Filipinos, which is nothing more or less than $2 per head for human beings."

Many other influential newspapers, eminent writers and statesmen are bitterly opposed to the present war policy. United States Senator Wm. E. Mason of Illinois said in a public lecture recently:

> "I know that when the Filipino is mowed down like grass it makes no difference to him, whether it is one of our bullets or a Spanish bullet. I believe Lincoln is right when he said, 'No man is good enough to govern another man without his consent.' Do you insist on killing them to prevent anarchy? Are we burning their homes to teach them good government? But we are told that we bought the right to govern from Spain. If we did we bought what we had no right to buy, and what Spain had no right to sell. You say we govern the Indian without his consent. Yes, and the negro. You know the result. Our treatment of the Indian shows our ignorance, and is a blot upon our fair name. The negro worse still. . . ."

Senator Mason is a true American and we are in accord with his ideas and sentiments. The war against the Filipinos is unjust, uncalled for, and absolutely wrong. When this country sent her troops to Cuba, she achieved one of the greatest military victories in the world and lost only a few men. But since the 4th day of February over one thousand of her bravest and noblest sons have been killed or wounded . . . in the far-off Philippines, thus showing that this country is doing that which it should not do, and it is fair to assume from the present outlook that many more lives will be sacrificed before peace will be restored in the Philippine Islands.

Salt Lake City *Broad Ax,* April 1, 1899

"NEGRO SOLDIERS NEEDED IN THE SOUTH NOT IN THE PHILIPPINES"

It is high time for the U.S. to begin to look after the interests of its own people and leave the semi-civilized people of Cuba, Puerto Rico and other countries attend to their own affairs. Something must be done to settle this trouble in the South. It is a very strange thing that this government cannot find time or means to stop some of the lynchings in that section of the country. The Negroes have always believed in this grand government of ours. We have always been the back-bone of the Republican party and it is to this source that we look for protection. Mississippi, Arkansas and Georgia have disgraced the fair name of America. Our people have been treated worse than dumb brutes, but there has been nothing said or done about it although we are asked to go across the water to fight for the freedom of a people whose interests are not in common with those of this country. We are asked to fight for a people, not for the good they have or might do for America, but for the almighty dollar, for commercial enterprises, coffee trusts, banana trusts, etc. It is our hope that when the gallant 9th and 10th Cav. and the 24th and 25th Infantry go out again to fight that it will be for the protection of American citizens who are unfortunate only because they are black.

Illinois Record, April 1, 1899

"CIVILIZATION SHOULD BEGIN AT HOME"

More troops for the Philippines. The civilization of the Filipinos is getting to be a pretty big job.

It is a sinful extravagance to waste our civilizing influence upon the unappreciative Filipinos when it is so badly needed right here in Arkansas. Charity should begin at home.

Indianapolis *Recorder,* April 1, 1899

"SUPPORT THE GOVERNMENT IN THE PHILIPPINES"

As we see it, it is not the policy of enlightened nations to repudiate the administrations that have been instructed by the people to carry out their designs. America to-day is in just such a situation. It is the business of the government to prosecute the war until it reaches the ends mapped out. It is a war for the preservation of the political integrity of the nation. That it is waged against the Philippines is no ground for racial indifference in America. Those people are defying the authority of our government whose purposes are not known to be hostile to their interests. They might have taken the word of a great and honorable nation. With them would have always resided the power to rebel in event they conceived the idea that they were duped or the victims of deception.

Indianapolis Freeman, April 3, 1899

"FILIPINOS MAY HAVE LEARNED FROM THE FATE OF NEGROES AND INDIANS"

"The Filipinos do not realize what prosperity is in store for them, when they stop their fighting and submit to this great freedom-loving people. They are evidently judging the Americans by the Spaniards, as the poor natives have known no other masters for the last seven or eight generations. We can hardly blame them for being tired of Spanish rule."—Provo *Inquirer*.

Mr. Inquirer, maybe the Filipinos have caught wind of the way the Indians and negroes have been Christianized and civilized by the boasted Christian nations and they want none of it in their minds, and that is the reason they are loathe to surrender their form of government and adopt a new form which promises them so much prosperity and freedom.

Salt Lake City Broad Ax, April 8, 1899

"NO REAL ENTHUSIASM FOR THE PHILIPPINE WAR"

[From the *Utah State Journal*:]

"There is absolutely no enthusiasm over this warfare among the people of the United States. And why should there be? The Filipinos are fighting for home, for lands, for country, for liberty. They may have mistaken the charitable and humane purposes of this government, and it may be that they would be far better off, even as free men, if they would lay down their arms and allow the United States to untangle the knot. At the same time, they do not think so, and they certainly have a right to their opinions, and the privilege of fighting for their belief.

"There is no disguising the fact that there is a great undercurrent of sympathy for these Filipinos among the people of the United States, people who were born in liberty's cradle and nursed at her altar, and who do not believe that liberty should be the heritage of one race or one people.

"Every true American hopes that the warfare in the Philippines will soon be stopped, and that the unfortunate people of those islands will emerge from the sea of bloodshed to a newer and a better freedom than they have ever before experienced.

"Meanwhile, however, the true American does not feel like throwing his hat wildly in the air because a lot of poor ignorant creatures, battling for what they believe to be their rights and their liberties, are being put to the sword like so many rats in a corner."

[The *Broad Ax* comments:]

It is true there is a lack of real genuine enthusiasm manifested by the people of this country over the result of the war in the Philippine Islands. It is enough to cause every true American who believes in freedom and liberty to bemoan the day he was born to observe the hypocrisy which the rulers of this government have indulged in for the purpose of annihilating and exterminating the poor and unfortunate Filipinos under the pretense of securing for them a superior or better form of government, for it is impossible to accomplish that result until the federal authorities enforce the established laws of the land to such an extent that its humblest citizen feels secure in the rights which he has been invested with. If that cannot be accomplished, then it is the height of folly and all buncombe to talk about guaranteeing to the Filipinos their civil rights, a political liberty and freedom.

It is enough to cause the devil to smile and each one of his imps to move up another seat on the mourner's bench to listen to such balderdash.

The Filipinos may in time be subjugated and compelled to wear the yoke of tyranny and oppression, but when that is finally accomplished we firmly believe it will be the beginning of the end of our democratic form of government.

* * *

"NO DESIRE TO GREET McKINLEY, THE IMPERIALIST"

[From the *Herald,* Brunswick, Ga.:]

President McKinley passed through Brunswick last Monday on his way to Jekyl Island. . . . We were not here to greet him nor did we care to. Why should we bother our heads about seeing the chief of a nation who sees his subjects butchered like hogs or shot down like mad dogs without his uttering a word of protest? Why should we break our necks trying to see a man who pretends to be a Christian yet gives orders to his soldiers to mow down by thousands our kinsmen in the Philippines. . . .

* * *

"BLACK TROOPS FIGHT IN AN UNRIGHTEOUS CAUSE"

[From the *Progress,* Omaha, Nebraska:]

The black man may be called upon to go to the Philippines, but not a man of them that meets death in such an affair can die feeling that he was fighting in a righteous cause or that he fought for a cause of humanity; but he will go to meet his Maker feeling that he was an accessory to a great land-grabbing scheme not of his own will.

Salt Lake City *Broad Ax,* April 15, 1899

"Aguinaldo, the Philippine Washington"

[From the *True Reformer,* Littletown, N.C.:]

When Washington and his army repudiated the arrogance of England and fought for the freedom and independence of their country, they were called patriots and heroes—and they were. But when Aguinaldo and his people take up arms and fight for their homes, their countrymen, and their freedom, they are called rebels by the imperialistic press of this country.

Indianapolis *Recorder,* April 22, 1899

"Supports McKinley"

Our government has a policy to pursue in the Philippines. The administration did not seek the situation. It was urged by the people who clamored for years for some action in behalf of Cuba. Mr. McKinley was fairly forced into a war which a number of fickle-minded ones are now arrayed against. The independence of the Philippines is no part of the American program. We have nothing more to urge against the heroism of Aguinaldo than we have against the heroism of Gen. Lee or "Stonewall" Jackson. These had to submit and in this submission lost quite as much as Aguinaldo will lose. They battled for independence but did Lee or Jackson get it? The consent of the governed is a very elastic affair to many. . . .

Indianapolis *Freeman,* April 22, 1899

"This War is Inhuman, Blood-Thirsty, Wrong"

Within the past week the Filipinos have succeeded in capturing a number of American sailors and so far their fate is unknown. Some think they will be inhumanly treated by what they call the savages who inhabit the Phillippines. But all who entertain these ideas fail to take into consideration the fact that the American soldiers have on many occasions gone out of their way for the purpose of subjecting the Filipinos, their wives and children to inhuman treatment, and we should not be surprised if the Filipinos should feel like retaliating whenever they have the opportunity of doing so.

While the war is raging in the Philippines we must not lose sight of the fact that the American people were led to believe that her soldiers were being sent on a mission of love and good will, and to carry the torch of liberty and freedom to those benighted savages who are sitting in the shadow of darkness.

But instead of pursuing this course or policy we find that the American soldiers have already killed over 6,000 of the natives—more than the Spaniards have killed in fifty years. This may be considered as an act of mercy, and a blessing to the Filipinos, for many contend that they are not human beings—not created in the image of the Creator (if there is a Creator). Therefore they are not entitled to receive any consideration from the hands of honest and highly civilized men.

This may be partially true, and the Filipinos may be unable to measure up with the standard of civilization which has been adopted by the people of this country who believe in mob and lynch law. But we want to say right here that it has been our good fortune to read the state papers which have been put forth by some of the great rulers of the most civilized nations and none of them have been couched in better language than the proclamation which was promulgated by Aguinaldo, and we beg all who doubt his ability as a statesman to re-read his utterances.

Our foreparents were born upon this continent and we believe in the institutions which have been founded by the framers of this government. But we are free to confess that our sympathies, which are as broad as the universe, are with the Filipinos, and it is perfectly clear to our mind that the war upon them is contrary and antagonistic to the fundamental principles of liberty and justice.

Thomas Jefferson exclaimed before expiring, "If there be one principle more deeply written than any other in the mind of every American, it is that we should have nothing to do with conquests." But the rulers of this country today have ignored and spat upon this principle, and the result is that they are willing to wade in human blood and gore up to their knees in order to fasten a new policy upon the people.

This war now being waged is unhuman, blood-thirsty, wrong and is conducted for conquest only, and not in the interest of humanity.

Salt Lake City *Broad Ax,* April 25, 1899

"AGAINST NEGROES FIGHTING IN THE PHILIPPINES"

It is rumored that a proposition is on foot to utilize negro troops in future military operations in the Philippines. We earnestly hope that such a proposition will not meet with favor. We are certainly opposed to pitting negro against negro. It has been a custom in the United States for white men to be put to the front in all battles and wars and the negro given no consideration until the brunt of the situation is reached, then the negro is called to do things up brown. When the battles are over, the victory won, the white men come marching home to be covered with glory—the negro marches home to be the subject of ridicule and fall the prey to southern hell hounds and civilized American cannibals. God forbid the sending of a single negro soldier from this country to kill their own kith and kin for fighting for the cause they believe to be right.

Kansas City *American Citizen,* April 28, 1899

"A GOVERNMENT THAT DOESN'T PROTECT ITS CITIZENS CAN'T EXPECT THEM TO PROTECT IT IN WARTIME"

The recent lynching in the Southland, especially in Georgia and the Carolinas, of colored people who are accused of a crime without a trial, evidence, or facts except the mere accusation, has become a stench upon our civilization and damnable curse on our vaunted humanity. The horrible death in which those Georgian fiends and hell hounds perpetrated last Monday in Newman, Ga., is the basest and most atrocious known to criminology in a civilized country. Is this civilization? Is this America's justice? Is this humanity? Are those white people insane? Has mercy fled from our land? Have the lips of the ministers and other Christian beings been closed? Were Americans fighting the Spaniards to free Cube from barbarous treatment of Spain; what thinks Spain of our barbarous treatment of our own citizens? Why are we now fighting the natives 10,000 miles away in the Philippine Islands, trying to force our flag and banner over them to civilize them? If the action of the Southern States is civilization, then away with such a government.

A nation that cannot or will not protect its citizens in time of peace has no right to ask its citizens to protect it in time of war. If these Southern brutes who are not fit to live or even dwell in hades are not punished and their frightful crimes stopped by our government, then we had better close the school house, burn the books, tear down the churches, and admit to the world that Anglo-Saxon civilization is a failure. . . .

Iowa State *Bystander,* April 28, 1899

"AMERICAN ARMS SHOULD SUCCEED ONLY IN A RIGHTEOUS CAUSE"

[From the *Freeman,* Indianapolis, Ind.:]

"We shall not forget that our government is engaging the eyes of the world in the Phillipines. Our troubles at home will not compel us to entertain feelings otherwise than for the success of the American arms abroad. Our country, first, last, and all the time even though it beggars us. We have no desire to see America humiliated, and it must not be if it takes every man in the country. The die is cast. Retreat is disgrace, even though victory may mean national turmoil. Let the Negroes consider well before casting sympathy abroad what it all means."

This may be the patriotic view of the situation, but owing to recent occurrences here at home we beg pardon for displaying a reasonable lukewarmness. The situation in the Philippines is not the only way in which "our government" is engaging the eyes of the world. American arms, like those of any other government, should only be successful when enlisted on the side of right. However, there is no occasion for anxiety. There will be no retreat. Uncle Sam wants the Philippines. He has just paid Spain $20,000,000 for them, and a few thousand natives will not be allowed to stand in the way of the purchase.

Indianapolis *Recorder,* May 7, 1899

"Opposed to American Forces in the Philippines"

Several editors in and out of Utah and some of our readers have taken us to task because we have not been an enthusiastic supporter of President McKinley and the war policy which he has pursued in the Philippine Islands. If the editors and those of our readers would stop and reflect they could not consistently condemn us for refusing to lend aid and comfort to the American forces who are now engaged in murdering the inoffensive and liberty-loving Filipinos.

The chief reasons why we are opposed to the war which is being waged upon the inhabitants of those islands are that whenever the soldiers send letters home to their relatives and parents they all breathe an utter contempt "for the niggers which they are engaged in slaying." Many of these letters have found their way into the columns of the press and without exception from the highest to the lowest the writers set forth in glowing colors "the number of niggers they have succeded in putting to the sword." Even the Hon. R. W. Young of this city was unable to rise above race prejudice when writing in connection with the war in the Philippines. . . . For it will be observed in persuing his letter that that gallant officer referred to the "niggers" as he called them in a sneering manner.

In view of these facts, no negro possessing any race pride can enter heartily into the prosecution of the war against the Filipinos, and all enlightened negroes must necessarily arrive at the conclusion that the war is being waged solely for greed and gold and not in the interest of suffering humanity. For if it were waged in the interest of the latter, the American soldiers would not turn up their noses and look down with scorn and contempt upon the Filipinos.

Salt Lake City *Broad Ax,* May 16, 1899

"Negroes Should Support the Administration"

The colored people of the city have done a very sensible thing in voting sympathy to the government in her struggle with the Filipinos. At Allen Chapel Church of this city [Indianapolis] a mass meeting was held last week as a means of giving expression of sympathy and confidence in the administration. Prominent speakers presented the situation and were generously applauded by an appreciative audience that was notable for its quality.

It goes without saying that the movement is in the right direction. Had the meeting been a failure, it would have been a travesty; a burlesque on Negro suffrage. It may be insisted again that the race may find exception to the government's policy or proposed policy in reducing these people to terms from other considerations than from a racial standpoint.

*   *   *

A "loyalist meeting" under the auspices of the Anacostia Club was held Wednesday night at Allen Chapel Church for the purpose of endorsing President McKinley's administration and the policy of the United States government during the Spanish-American war. Judge Lott was the presiding officer and addresses were made by Mr. Gurley Brewer, Prof. Wm. Lewis, and Mr. George L. Knox.

Indianapolis *Freeman,* June 3, 1899

"This Costly, Unnecessary and Wholly Illogical Conflict"

[From the *Colored American*, Washington, D.C.:]

It is amusing to note the efforts of the Indianapolis *Journal* to justify our government's policy in the Philippines by comparing the number of American soldiers lost in the present campaign with the number of Union men lost in certain battles of the Civil War. It has never occurred to this paper that the number of Filipinos slaughtered should be taken into account. The true merits of a case cannot be determined by looking at only one side. The mere fact that the American soldiers are enabled to deal such destruction into the ranks of the natives with such a comparatively small loss to themselves should suggest to the fair-minded an idea of the unjustness of the struggle. At the time Admiral Dewey gained his splendid victory in Manila Bay these islands were in a state of revolution; the natives were fighting to throw off the Spanish yoke that they might enjoy absolute independence. Our government has taken up the fight against the natives which it made impossible for the Spanish to continue. We understand the motives that prompt civilized countries to extend their boundaries to rich possessions, thus widening their influence; but the comparative ease with which the armies of one nation may annihilate the armies of another must certainly be regarded as an innovation in determining the justness of international quarrels.

The Filipino war continues and the American laborer is footing the lion's share of the bills. This costly, unnecessary, and wholly illogical conflict—from the standpoint of our old-time national doctrines—could be ended in a fortnight by just treating Aguinaldo and his collaborators for independence as we would have had George III treat us something better than a hundred years ago. There never will be peace until peace is negotiated on humane, just, and equitable lines.

Indianapolis *Recorder,* June 3, 1899

"MAY THE SOLDIER WHO SAYS 'NIGGER' GET KILLED"

[From the *Progress*, Omaha, Nebraska:]

Every soldier in the Philippines who uses the term "nigger" does so with hell-born contempt for the negro of the United States, and it is our one desire that he be cured of his fiendish malady by a Filipino bullet buried in the heart of such a wretch.

*   *   *

"BOTH SIDES OF THE PHILIPPINE QUESTION"

[From the *Journal*, Indianapolis, Indiana:]

A "loyalist meeting" under the auspices of the Anacostia Colored Republican Club, was held . . . for the purpose of endorsing President McKinley's administration and the policy of the United States government during the Spanish-American war. . . .

The first address was given by Gurley Brewer, who said, in part:

> There is no doubt that, as a whole, the colored people of the United States are among the most loyal citizens of the country, but it remains for the negroes of Indianapolis to be the first in a public way to do homage to the flag and to the President. So far as the Filipino question is concerned the natives in these far-away islands in the Pacific are now being offered the same boon that was offered the American negro in 1861—the opportunity to become the subjects of a great and good government. This is the greatest blessing that could possibly fall upon the people of the Philippines, as it was the greatest blessing that ever fell upon the negroes in America. The Filipinos are fighting against their saviors because they do not understand what a future this country has to offer them. The future that Lincoln offered the negroes is being fulfilled. . . .

The other speakers were George L. Knox and Prof. William Lewis. . . . A committee on resolutions was appointed consisting of Willis Kersey, Dr. S. A. Furniss, Robert Williams, Frank Oliver and William Abstrom, and at the close of the meeting a resolution was adopted expressing confidence in the United States government and belief in the high honor and just action of the army and navy in the Philippine Islands.

[From the *World,* Indianapolis, Indiana:]

The above described meeting was held by a lot of fool would-be negro leaders who held it to endorse the action of the administration toward the defenseless Filipinos. . . . While the leading negro bishops and preachers of the nation and the leading writers and thinkers are proclaiming against this barbarous action of our government, a set of men meet. . . . in Indianapolis. . . . [to approve McKinley's policy.] In other words, they rejoice that they were the first to make asses of themselves and discredit the whole race of 9,000,000 people. While the government soldiers in the Philippines are writing home "how they made the niggers run" and others "that they didn't enlist to fight niggers," a little coterie of so-called negro leaders and would-be statesmen meet here and submissively endorse the infamy. What will such statesmen as Thomas B. Reed, George F. Hoar and George S. Boutwell and [other] . . . friends of the colored race think of this subservient and lickspittle action of Indianapolis negroes? The *World* sincerely hopes that the news of the disgraceful affair will not reach these eminent men. We would have thought that these men would have met and have taken action in reference to what the federal government would do as to the lynching of four negroes in Mexico, of which the Indianapolis *Journal* remarked, "Truly Mexico is becoming Americanized." We are glad to say, however, that the ministers of our city took no active part in these infamous proceedings, but we are sorry to have seen the house of God desecrated for such a purpose. . . .

[The *Broad Ax* comments:]

Brother Manning [editor of the Indianapolis *World*], you have voiced our sentiments, and all we have to say is simply this, that if any negro, be he great or small, endorses the policy which the government is pursuing in the Philippine Islands, or who upholds President McKinley's administration in any shape or manner whatever, are nothing more nor less than enemies and traitors to the negro race.

Broad Ax (Chicago, Illinois), June 6, 1899

"Call the Boys Home"

It is time now to call a halt to the Filipino-American struggle for supremacy. The poor soldiers are committing suicide and dying from terrible fevers. It is indeed time for the United States to call the boys home, their crown and stars are made honorable. Call them home.

Kansas State Ledger, June 10, 1899

"Black Troops to Go to the Philippines"

The difference between a rebel and a patriot is so slight that we are eternally getting the two mixed up. Most fair-minded Americans admit that, taking away the glory of his cause, Washington was but a rebel; but there are mighty few who are broad enough to see Aguinaldo in any other light but a rebel.

The Negro troops who have been "going" to the Philippines for the past three or four months will probably be off in a few days, thanks to the wonderful recuperative powers of the Filipinos. While at the front they will undoubtedly cover themselves with glory, and that class of our race who delighted in aping the whites, will reap a full harvest of "Black Funstons," etc.

Indianapolis *Recorder,* June 17, 1899

"AFRO-AMERICANS! DON'T ENLIST!"

An Afro-American in the Philippines advises our people not to go there and he is right. He also says the Filipinos are "holding their own," and that it will be many years before the American soldiers will be able to put down the uprising.

*   *   *

Boston, Mass.—Mr. Stanley Ruffin, a leading local Afro-American, in a recent communication to the N.Y. *Age,* states his position on a live question as follows:

> I see by the papers that in all probability the President will be forced to call for volunteers to meet the demand from the Philippines. Should it not be the policy of the colored press and pulpit to discourage the enlistment of colored men? Would it not be a dignified and effective position for all colored men to take to declare boldly: "We shall not attempt or assist to uphold a country that cannot or does not protect us in life, liberty, and the pursuit of happiness. Even the rewards of merit and efficiency are denied us by limiting the offices which on account of the color of our skin we cannot hope to aspire to. We shall neither fight for such a country or with such an army." I believe that if such a policy could be brought about, something practical could be accomplished. I had intended some time ago to write more fully to you. . . . You will note, too, that in taking this position of opposition to the administration and the army, it does not take into account the individual opposition which every colored man should feel to the criminal subjugation of the Filipinos. In such a policy as this, the colored people could stand united. They have got something this government wants; and now they have a chance to make the government accept their terms.

> Cleveland *Gazette,* June 17, 1899

"PHILIPPINE QUESTION ANALYZED"

[From a dispatch to the *Gazette* from Washington, D.C.:]

The hunt and slaughter of the liberty-loving followers of Aguinaldo by the highly civilized and humane army of the United States in the Philippine Islands are the favorite topics of the press and people here. Spain was conquered and driven from the western hemisphere and Cuba freed for humanity's sake. A great Christian nation could not stand the indiscriminate slaughter of the poor reconcentrados in Cuba by the destroyers of the "Maine," but can stand the bloody and indiscriminate slaughter of the poor, illiterate Filipinos by the military and naval agencies of this enlightened "Christian" nation. What a contrast! What a spectacle! Why was not the militant army of Christ given an opportunity to civilize and subjugate those people if they are savages instead of pouring out their life-blood in streams like their own native rivers? Surely this was nor is not necessary, simple [as it could have been] to assert our rights there as a nation and a purchaser of the archipelago. Too much haste has been resorted to in the matter. More moderation could have been used there without damage to our interests. I do not claim that assaults should not be repelled. They should be, and the occupants should be taught *vi et armis* that they must respect proper authority. The duty of the American nation is to teach them the proper relations between landlord and tenant, peaceably if it can, forcibly if it must. All force in the premises should be only that which is absolutely necessary or compulsory and not that which is unnecessary and which is used for a pretext to shoot down human beings. Some people claim that the Filipinos are Negroes, and for that reason ought to be shot down. This kind of argument shows that same spirit of prejudice against color which has cost thousands of inoffensive colored people their lives, as at Hamburg, S.C., Danville, Va., and Wilmington, N.C. While these poor but industrious Malays in the Philippines are not Negroes, they may be closely allied to the Hamatic race. People ought to know that the American government would be justified in killing a Filipino only in the preservation of American rights in the island, and not on account of color. When will our own people become more fully enlightened. . . .

Now eight companies each of the Twenty-fourth and Twenty-fifth United States infantry, by a decision of the war department, are to go to the Philippines. Everybody knows that these boys will do their duty everywhere under the stripes and stars. . . .

Cleveland *Gazette,* June 24, 1899

"COLONIZATION AGAINST THE DECLARATION OF INDEPENDENCE"

Particularly at this while she [the United States] is busy on a hair-brained attempt to go into the colonizing business against its own Declaration of Independence and while she is making such frantic clamor of some kind of independence which she has up her sleeve for Cuba and the Filipinos, would it be extremely wise for the American negro to show up to the entire civilized world the class of liberty they enjoy here. . .

Washington *Bee,* June 24, 1899

"BLACK TROOPS SHOULD GO TO THE PHILIPPINES"

It is now said that colored troops are to be sent to the Philippines. The sooner the better. The Negroes must be taught that the enemy of the country is a common enemy and that the color of the face has nothing to do with it.

Indianapolis *Freeman,* July 1, 1899

"FILIPINOS ENTITLED TO INDEPENDENCE"

[From the *Christian Recorder*, Philadelphia, Pa.:]

In the fight of this country against Spain in Cuba or Puerto Rico there was an enlistment of universal sympathy on our side. Such is not and cannot be the case in our hostilities against the Filipinos. Those far-off foreigners are as much entitled to independence as Cubans or Americans and it is madness to suppose that they would resist Spain so long and fiercely and to yield to the United States who has no right than might on her side. Justice and humanity may yet prove powerful and triumphant weapons on the side of the people alleged to be "half devil and half child."

Indianapolis *Recorder,* July 1, 1899

"WHY NEGRO REGIMENTS ARE NOT BEING FORMED"

[A Washington dispatch in the Kansas City *Star* (white), in regard to the call of 10,000 volunteers, among other things has this to say:]

No negro volunteer regiments will be organized for service in the Philippines. Any negro enlisted will be assigned to vacancies in the present negro regiments of the regular army. The experiment of the War Department with some of negro volunteers during the Spanish war was not a happy one, and, in spite of reports which come from the Philippines to the effect that the negro is greatly feared by the Filipinos, the authorities are averse to running the risk of a repitition of the troubles of last year.

In this connection a story of an experience with a black regiment at Macon, Ga., during the encampment there last summer, is cited. The regiment, which was commanded by a white officer of the regular army, became very unruly while in camp one night, and except for the skillful handling of the white troops by the officers commanding the camp, a revolt would have taken place. The white troops took positions surrounding the blacks and a negro officer was made to see the foolhardiness of the action of his men. His troops were then disarmed and were very soon mustered out of the service.

Daily American Citizen (Kansas City, Kansas), July 2, 1899

"DOES NOT ADVISE NEGRO ENLISTMENT"

Again the war department has called on the colored regulars to go to Manila to fight the Filipinos and relieve the white soldiers who are there now fighting for—God only knows what—and now the department is asking for volunteers to the amount of 35,000 and the department will expect that the colored citizens will fill their pro ratio. In case some who may renew their confidence in him—will he be allowed colored officers this time? We will not advise the colored men to go, but if they insist on going we would urge on them to compel the war department to allow the same privilege as any other volunteer company. . . .

Iowa State Bystander, July 7, 1899

"AGAINST BLACKS FIGHTING FILIPINOS"

The following is a leading editorial from *The Christian Recorder* (of a recent date), organ of the A.M.E. Church, and published at Philadelphia, Rev. H. T. Johnson editor:

"The call of the war department for the enlistment of colored soldiers to embark for warfare against the Filipinos should be met with universal protest from Afro-American citizens everywhere. In the face of the treatment meted to him as a soldier and citizen, the invitation now offered the colored man to become a target for the enemy's bullet can only be taken in a serious vein by every intelligent and self-respecting Negro, however lightly others may regard the matter. . . .

"The Negro soldier has put himself in demand in every national struggle, both by his pluck and patriotism. To the last trench of Spanish hostilities he has retained the luster purchased from revolutionary times to the present. What has been his reward? Has honor, promotion, assured citizenship, or protection crowned his career at El Caney or San Juan heights? Ingratitude, discrimination, humiliation are the only trophies which, so far, he can thank his country's star for. . . .

"It would be difficult, however, for the Negro to fight to deprive others of the things so dear to himself, even if he were spurred on by the hope of future rewards, and the assurance of future good treatment. He knows that the people of the Philippines are struggling for freedom; that they are in their own land; that they are foreign members of his own racial household; that he will get no thanks for being killed himself, or for killing others; that he is only needed because his white comrade cannot stand the fearful odds which daily task his ranks."

Cleveland *Gazette,* July 8, 1899

"REGRETS BLACK MAN MUST FIGHT IN THE PHILIPPINES"

[From the *Progress*, Omaha, Nebraska:]

Since it is the inevitable that black American soldiers must bear arms against a people of their own hue, and these people, too, for the right of self-government and the principles upon which the foundations of freedom, liberty, and happiness are built, then, if it is a decree of adverse fate, let them fight, if for nothing more than to show their calumniators in the country of their birth that they are not cowards. For the black man there is no glory in war, nothing save carnage, death, injustice, and—at last, unrelenting jibes, sneers, and calumny. No; there is no honor, and but slight reward; and since the brave black soldier must fight in this unholy war in the Philippines, let him fight like he can, in such furious onslaughts that nothing but the walls of hell can withstand him; and prove, to those vile creatures who would rob him of his glory and prowess, the soldier that he is, the most courageous, the most enduring, and the finest soldier the world has known.

Kansas City *American Citizen,* July 14, 1899

"SUICIDAL TO OPPOSE PHILIPPINE POLICY ON GROUNDS OF COLOR"

To oppose the government in the Philippine war on the issue of color is suicidal. It is to be regretted that there are among the race those who so express themselves. There are other good opinions for a difference of opinion on the matter.

Indianapolis *Freeman,* July 15, 1899

"SUPPORTS *Christian Recorder*"

[In a special dispatch from Washington, D.C. James W. Poe wrote:]

The Christian Recorder . . . is eminently right in coming out in a plain, straightforward, and truthful manner concerning the status of the Afro-American soldier in the Philippines. Three decades ago he fought for his own freedom in this country, now he goes to aid in keeping in slavery a people closely allied to himself. A Christian nation has forced him. This same Christian nation, or the major part of it, regards the Negro and all peoples allied to him as "big burley savages." . . .

*   *   *

"MOST INTELLIGENT AFRO-AMERICANS ANTI-EXPANSIONIST"

Our papers seem to agree that Afro-Americans should *not* enlist for service in the Philippines, principally because the President has not treated us right in the matter of the appointment of our soldier-heroes of the Spanish-American War as commissioned officers, and they are right. Intelligent Afro-Americans are, as a rule, anti-expansionists, largely because they feel that the American people generally, and the present administration particularly, lack the breadth of mind that would enable them to govern properly colored people abroad when those here at home are so sadly neglected, ignored, mistreated, and lynched in defiance of all law, order, and civilization.

Cleveland *Gazette,* July 15, 1899

"Negroes Against McKinley's Philippine Policy"

The report that colored men of Boston will begin to organize throughout the country against the imperialistic policy of the administration is significant.

The accompanying statement, that it is to be supplemented by an attempt to furnish arms and men to the alleged insurgents in the Philippine Islands, is a shrewd effort to throw the movement into disrepute from the start. No sane man would advocate or countenance such a policy. Our duty is to exert whatever influence we can bring to bear upon the political parties now contending for supremacy, reinforced by an effort to arouse the public to a realization of the dangers which now threaten the republic. The colored men are loyal and patriotic.

The sentiment against President McKinley's policy in the Philippine Islands is practically unanimous throughout the country, so far as the citizens of color are concerned.

This opinion is based upon private letters which we have received upon that subject and the attitude of the Afro-American press generally.

Those race journals which are not condemning him are painfully silent.

It is evident that if the feeling which exists among colored people in the southern states against Mr. McKinley as a political leader is shared by the colored people of the northern states, they will either vote against him or remain away from the polls.

There are enough parties in this country now offering for our votes to enable us to cast them intelligently, and without a sacrifice of principle.

The Democratic party's policy in the southern states has been of such a character in dealing with the citizen of color to make it well-nigh impossible for him to rally under its banners.

In the northern and western states, however, this feeling does not exist and colored men do not have many scruples in deciding to vote for [that] political organization.

The policy of the national administration in dealing with the Filipinos is the same as that of the Democratic state administrations in dealing with the colored people in the southern states.

It would be well to state here that the colored people of North and South Carolina would have secured just as much protection against red-handed Democratic murderers had a Democrat been in the White House as they got at the hands of a Republican, who occupied that edifice from the kitchen to the front door.

Mr. McKinley was not in favor of a war of conquest, yet he is engaged in a war of conquest.

Mr. McKinley was not in favor of subjugating the Filipinos, yet he is subjugating the Filipinos.

Mr. McKinley was not in favor of acquiring the Philippine Islands from Spain, yet he has acquired the Philippine Islands from Spain.

Mr. McKinley was not in favor of a large standing army, yet he asked for a large standing army.

Mr. McKinley was not in favor of barring Negro officers from the army, yet he has barred every Negro Officer from the regular army and Major Charles Young (col'd) has been "salted down" and laid away at Wilberforce College, O., for use possibly in the other world. He'll have no fighting to do as an officer "this side of the Jordan."

Mr. McKinley was said to be opposed to the color-line, yet he has recognized and encouraged the color-line.

Mr. McKinley was said to be in favor of arbitration and sent delegates to the Peace Conference at The Hague, yet when Austria proposed arbitration of the Hungarian subjects in Pennsylvania, he rejected it. It is needless to refer to a similar proposition from the kingdom of Spain.

Mr. McKinley was in favor of bimetalism and opposed to a single standard, and yet it is openly announced and practically conceded that he is about to offer for a second presidential term upon a single gold standard platform.

Mr. McKinley was said to be for Secretary Alger, now it is said that he is against him.

Mr. McKinley is said to be in favor of colored people, yet every moment which has of late been reserved seems to have been against their interests.

Verily it seems that which he professes to be in favor of, he is against, and that which he is said to be against, in but a little while he is in favor of.

It seems that he is a good man in the hands of shifting politicians, whose only guiding star seems to be the financial benefits accruing to themselves.

Under this arrangement, principles are disregarded and the most solemn pledges cast aside.

We are free; we have the right to express our opinions. With us Mr. McKinley has been the embodiment of great principles. We have borne and forborne, paused and hesitated before expressing such a caustic opinion, but in the light of the facts before us—"God helping, we cannot do otherwise."

*   *   *

"UNFORTUNATE AND UNWARRANTED WAR"

The publication of the "Round Robin" by newspaper correspondents at Manila, Philippine Islands, cannot tend otherwise than to add to the embarassments of the administration.

That the facts relative to the unfortunate and unwarranted war were being suppressed many suspected, and a few knew.

That the newspaper representatives should be forced to combine and issue such a protest as the one which has just been given to the public is evidence that the dangerous conditions have become more dangerous.

It places Gen. Otis in a most unfavorable attitude and virtually accuses him of a suppression of facts and a distortion of truth which borders on falsehood, even if it is not characterized by a much plainer designation.

It is evident that this disclosure will do good and we may now look for the arrival of truth even though he has been a long time "pulling on his boots."

Richmond *Planet,* July 22, 1899

"Negro Anti-Expansionism in Boston"

[Judson] Lyons, [John P.] Green, and [Henry P.] Cheatham . . . rushed to President McKinley on Monday to deny one of the silliest news fakes ever sprung on the daily press of this country by that peculiar organization known as the Associated Press. They grabbed at this flimsy excuse for a visit, in order to assure the President that "the effort of certain colored men to array the colored race against the administration, etc. would amount to little." They said what they hoped; that is all. The President only had, and in a large measure at least still has it in his power to do that which is necessary to allay the growing feeling against him. Ever since the Wilmington, N.C. massacre and the issuance of his last message to Congress, the dissatisfaction has steadily increased, particularly among intelligent Afro-Americans who thoroughly understand the President's attitude toward the race and also know too well Lyons, Green, and Cheatham, whose eagerness to toady to the administration seems to exceed their loyalty to the race. These "pie-counter" leaders (?), self-constituted and white man made, have been the bane of the race ever since the war. God deliver us from them as soon as possible.

* * *

Special to the *Gazette*—Washington, D.C.—What does the "pie-counter crowd," who called on the President the other day and assured him that there is little or nothing in the recent "colored" anti-expansion movement in Boston, know about the masses of our people? The President later may have the very pleasant surprise of knowing that "These gentlemen" do not control so many voters . . . Lyons, Green, and Cheatham's assurances amount to nothing in this instance. . . .

James W. Poe

Cleveland *Gazette,* July 22, 1899

"Not the Negro's Duty to Fight the Filipino"

It is true that some few men of the Tenth and several other regiments were temporarily promoted, that is, in the volunteer regiments. But is it not a fact that they have lost their commissions by the mustering out of their regiments? Does not this prove that President McKinley takes no stock in Negro soldiers and that he is endeavoring to rid the Republican party of the responsibility. . . . In spite of these cold facts, the Hon. T. T. Allain and several other supposed leaders of the Negro race have assumed the responsibility of voicing the sentiments of the ten million Negroes respecting the attitude of the administration in dealing with the Filipinos. They have assured the President that the Negroes are willing to enlist and eager to assist in helping establish a new form of government in those Islands.

Why should any Negro who possesses any sense be swayed by sentimental foolishness? Does he not remember the treatment his brothers received from the hands of President McKinley as soldiers; why should he be willing to further assist to uphold the hands of those who delight in humiliating him? Why should we desire to sustain an administration which looks upon him as an inferior creature in every respect and only fit to fight its battles? Ah no! My brethren, do not permit yourselves to be carried away with the idea that it is your duty to fight the Filipinos. Do not permit yourselves to be further disgraced and humiliated by sounding the praise of President McKinley. For he has proven himself an enemy and a traitor to the Negro race.

Chicago *Broad Ax,* July 22, 1899

[From the *Pioneer Press,* Martinsburg, W. Va.:]

Sycophants . . . Lyons, Cheatham, Green . . . are waxing fat at the crib and it is their bounden duty to say sweet things and "jolly" the President along. But we will vouchsafe one thing, i.e., McKinley will be renominated on an expansion platform and defeated largely by Negro votes, Messrs. Lyons, Cheatham, and Co., to the contrary, notwithstanding. . . .

Cleveland *Gazette,* July 29, 1899

"OPPOSITION TO PHILIPPINE ENSLAVEMENT IS NOT TREASON"

For the past thirty-five years all those who have affiliated with the Grand Old Party of Plutocracy, which is controlled by Rothschilds, Morgan, and the other members of the Lombard and Wall Street cortes, have persistently maintained that the war was waged against the Southern people for the express purpose of liberating the slaves. But at the present time the leaders and the rank and file of the Republican party are branding every person as a traitor to his country who is not in favor of enslaving the Filipinos.

Chicago *Broad Ax,* July 29, 1899

"Blacks Should Not Enlist"

[From the *Progress,* Omaha, Nebraska:]

It is the consensus of opinion with the majority of Negroes who are opposed to the present treatment of the Negro in the United States that any black man who enlists to fight the Filipinos is perfectly satisfied with the abuse heaped upon him in this country.

Chicago *Broad Ax,* August 7, 1899

"No Encouragement to Enlist"

[From the *Star of Zion,* Charlotte, N.C.:]

Mr. Lyons does not know how many black volunteers the President can get. . . . There is no encouragement for black men to "volunteer" to enlist and fight for a government that seems powerless to protect them "in life, liberty, and the pursuit of happiness."

Cleveland *Gazette,* August 12, 1899

"The Philippine War a Blot on the Nation's Escutcheon"

[From the *Odd Fellows Journal,* Philadelphia, Pa.:]

Aguinaldo, the Filipino chief, has sent a strong appeal to the Powers asking their recognition of the independence of his government. The American press may ridicule and caricature the same Aguinaldo as much as they please, but it is beginning to dawn upon a great many people that he is very much of a general and no mean statesman. This war in the Far East will forever remain a blot on the escutcheon of our nation and condemn the present administration in the eyes of posterity as nothing else ever could have done.

Indianapolis *Recorder,* August 19, 1899

"Bishop Gaines' Pro-Administration Position Attacked"

[From a letter by J. L. Edmonds of South Pasadena, California, Aug. 10, 1899 commenting on a speech of Bishop W. J. Gaines delivered July 31 in Los Angeles:]

The good bishop, the pious representative of the meek and lowly Nazarene, with a commission from the God of peace, the gospel of love, of justice, of the equality of men, of the eternal worth of the immortal soul, not only endorsed the wholesale slaughter of the brave Filipinos for daring to defend their homes against the invasion of a foreign foe, but said if the administration cannot complete its bloody work with white soldiers, he himself, though an old man, was willing and ready to go over and help finish the job. The fatherhood of God and the brotherhood of man, the Golden Rule, he throws down at one fell swoop at the foot of mammon. Looking back at the rugged path over which we have plodded, strewn with the wrecks of our deflowered virgins, by the wholesale raping of whom the skin of the Ethiopian has been changed, a path covered with sundered family ties and broken hearts, walled in with the bones of sixty thousand men, women, and children murdered in recent years by that popular American institution known as mob law, all of this done in the name and to preserve American civilization as a blessing to mankind. In view of all these facts, I hardly thought that there was an intelligent Afro-American in this country that would voluntarily aid in forcing these unfortunate conditions upon any people that God has made.

Richmond *Planet,* August 26, 1899

"OF THE TWO GREAT POLITICAL EVILS, CHOOSE THE REPUBLICAN PARTY"

[From a speech of W. Calvin Chase on Emancipation Day at Frederick, Md.:]

He [the Negro] is asked to change his position and affiliate with that party which kills him and approves lynching, and leave the party which gives moral and political protection. He is asked to denounce the President of the United States because he has been silent upon the question of lynching and join the party of blood and tyranny, oppression and barbarism. He is asked to oppose expansion because the inhabitants of the islands which have become recent possessions of the United States are Negroes. The President should not be condemned nor should he be defeated for renomination, because he is only carrying out the behests of Congress in which all parties affiliated. He was first opposed to the war with Spain, but now that she is defeated and her possessions have become the property of the United States, the hand of the administration should be upheld. . . . The President, to an extent, is being criticized by his enemies for political reasons. The very men who are denouncing him were the men who directed him to use the sea and land forces to destroy one of the most barbarous nations known to the civilized world. . . . The Democratic party, under Republican rule, was making an issue out of the President's seeming inactivity in recognizing the belligerency of Cuba. The ultimatum was that Congress had to declare war and the President was given authority to direct it. Now that the Nation's foes having been defeated, now that human beings under Spanish oppression have been freed . . . the President is confronted by another issue growing out of the war . . . anti-imperialism and anti-expansion—and the Negroes are now being asked to favor the issue that has been inaugurated by the foes of good government, human liberty and human rights. You are asked to aid your enemies to relinquish those possessions which have been rightly and justly won by our American army and naval forces. . . .

The salvation of the Negro in this country will depend chiefly upon his adherence to the principles of the Republican party and those liberal-minded men in the party of our oppressors who believe in law and order notwithstanding the principles taught by the party. . . . Of the two great political evils, take the lesser [the Republican Party]. . . . [The Negro] has proven himself loyal and true to the flag that doesn't protect him; true and loyal to the flag that waves over the dead victims of those who fought to uphold American independence against Spanish tyranny and for Cuban independence; a flag whose principles seem to be the obliteration of the black man; a flag that was raised upon San Juan Hill, through shot and shell, by the united charge of the black cavalry, while the American white man played the coward. . . . Notwithstanding his oppression and the present discrimination against him, he still holds out his hands to receive the accoutrements of war to continue himself under the oppression of a discriminating flag.

For these reasons and many others which I have not time to enumerate, is it strange that Afro-Americans are not enthused over the President's Philippine policy? Indeed we are against it, especially the methods used to advance it. . . .

Washington *Bee,* August 26, 1899

"Defends McKinley"

[The *Bee* replies to the Missouri *Colored Messenger*'s query, "What has McKinley done for the Negroes?"]

President McKinley has brought to a successful termination the Spanish-American War. He has brought prosperity to the country. . . . He is endeavoring to civilize a barbarous and rebellious race of people in the Philippines which have become recent possessions of the United States.

Perhaps the editor of the *Messenger* would be gratified if the President would catch the lynchers and allow the rapists to go free. Then, no doubt, the *Messenger* would conclude that the President had done something. On the other hand, the Democratic party is responsible for the political murders in the South and for that reason all on the *Messenger's* order will uphold the principles of that party.

*   *   *

[From the *Colored Messenger,* Kansas City, Missouri:]

The question is not whether the *Messenger* man is from the backwoods . . . but "What has McKinley done for the Negroes?" Our contemporary makes quite a bluster and says nothing. The *Messenger* is neither

Democratic nor Republican and cares as little about politics as the *Bee* about the interest of the race. Let the *Bee* stop dodging and answer the interrogatory or shut up.

Washington Bee, September 2, 1899

"NO ENTHUSIASM FOR THE PHILIPPINE POLICY"

[From the annual address to the National Afro-American Congress at Chicago by Bishop A. Walters, President:]

If to be an expansionist is a desire to see one's country enlarged by the acquisition of additional territory, larger field for commerce, opportunities to give a higher civilization to semicivilized peoples and to add prestige to the Nation, then I am an Expansionist. But while I believe in expansion, I do not think America is prepared to carry on the work of expansion at this time, especially if it be among the dark races of the earth. The white man of America is impregnated with colorphobia; he has been taught for centuries that the black man, no matter where he dwells, has no rights which the white man is bound to respect; hence, he is not prepared to grant to dark-skinned peoples the most favorable opportunities for development. No matter how intelligent or cultured a man may be, if his skin is dark, that is a sufficient reason at any time why his rights should be ignored.

Had the Filipinos been white and fought as bravely as they have, the war would have been ended and their independence granted long ago.

To subjugate and govern a people without their consent is contrary to the Declaration of Independence of the United States.

Indianapolis Freeman, September 2, 1899

"W. CALVIN CHASE FOR MCKINLEY"

The Frederick, Md., *Afro-American Speaker* publishes the "cut" of Hon. W. Calvin Chase, accompanied with the statement that he is the only Negro editor of national prominence who believes and thinks with the present McKinley administration.

This journal has that down about right. The administration will have to do some "mighty tall" hustling, too, to keep "Colonel" Chase in line until 1900.

We had hoped that Mr. McKinley would have seen his way clear to place him in command of a regiment bound for the Philippines.

Richmond Planet, September 2, 1899

"THE NEGRO SHOULD ENLIST"

Whatever may be the reason for discontinuing the recruiting of colored soldiers at Fort McPherson and vicinity, the Negro should be the last to raise the race question. If the regiments in the regular service are full, and no orders for the formation of any colored regiments have been given, that's all there is in it. The one thing to do is to be willing if called. . . . Let the color question alone and forget that he is a Negro so far as law and duty are concerned. He will always feel that he is not being treated properly if his uppermost thought is that he is a Negro. . . . Yes, whenever the opportunity presents itself, the Negro should enlist.

* * *

"WILL THE NEGRO FIGHT THE FILIPINO?"

[The following is from the Richmond, Va., *Dispatch* (white) in which the question of organizing volunteer Negro regiments is discussed:]

In discussing the policy to raise two negro regiments, an official in the War Department remarked to your correspondent: "I doubt whether half-disciplined negroes, under command of negro officers, if brought face to face with their colored Filipino cousins, could be made to fire upon them or make a fight. If the negro understands that the Filipinos are fighting for their liberty and independence, ten chances to one they would take sides with them." This view of the matter is shared by many others, who, however, are not strictly administration supporters.

Washington *Bee,* September 9, 1899

"THE FLAG MEANS DISCRIMINATION AGAINST DARKER RACES"

President McKinley, in a speech delivered at Orange Grove, N.J., recently said that the flag does not mean one thing in the United States and another in Puerto Rico and the Philippines.

Of course it doesn't, for it means discrimination against the darker race everywhere. The new version of the Declaration of Independence is that governments derive their just powers from the consent of some of the governed. . . .

Richmond *Planet,* September 9, 1899

"NO SUPPORT FOR THE TREATY UNTIL SLAVERY IS ABOLISHED IN THE PHILIPPINES"

Among the other resolutions adopted by the Indiana A.M.E. conference which met a few days ago in Indianapolis is the following:

> Be it further resolved, That we call upon the representatives of the people assembled in Congress to withhold their approval from said treaty until so much of it shall be stricken out as relates to the recognition of the institution of slavery and until in lieu thereof a clause shall be inserted abolishing forever slavery in the Philippines.

This resolution has in mind the treaty made with the Sultan of Sulu, which treaty recognizes slavery as existing. In trying to explain away this very ugly clause in the treaty, it is said that Sulu has been obtained merely as a coaling station from which the operations of war as conducted by the Americans will be more formidable etc., etc.

In other words, a subsidy of $12,000 is paid his highness, the Sultan of Sulu for his good will and other incorporeal hereditaments. Spain paid it; now we must pay it.

It is claimed that this country has no right to disturb the social customs as existing in this dependency. It is supposed that the institution of slavery is so deeply rooted that to have made the subject a subject for treaty considerations would have imperilled a successful termination of the negotiations.

It may be, as it has been mooted, that the occupation is but temporary and with the end in view of better conducting the war; but it will take considerable explanation to explain that this country was driven to such a sore distress as to make such large concessions for such seemingly small advantages.

It would argue that our country was glad of an opportunity to purchase peace as well as fight for it. The country has never before been informed that a coaling station on Sulu Island was a crying necessity. If Sulu is to be a part and parcel of this country, humanity, philanthropy, and the Negroes demand that no such relations be effected until slavery, polygamy, and other haremized conditions are quite impossible.

Indianapolis *Freeman,* September 9, 1899

"NEGROES SHOULD ANSWER THE CALL"

Now that an order for the organization of two colored regiments has been issued from the War Department, nothing remains now but a generous response. The question is not will Negroes fight Negroes? Citizens of the United States are asked to join hands with others of the government in subduing the hostilities in the Philippines. The time is now that all possessed of proper motives must lose sight of race belongings. The ball was set in motion when war was begun with Spain and must be kept going until the end desired is obtained.

The power and bravery of our colored soldiers are both known and appreciated by the government. Sufficient time has been spent in trying to subjugate the Philippines. No great achievement will ever be accomplished without the aid of the colored man. . . . There should be no worry on the part of the colored man for fear of not having something to do. In all things act well the part assigned.

While the field officers are to be white, a point is gained by having all the company officers colored. . . .

Washington *Bee,* September 16, 1899

"McKinley Is Today's George III"

Col. Wm. J. Bryan has likened Pres. Wm. McKinley unto King George. . . . If King Wm. McKinley continues to wage an unrelenting warfare upon the Filipinos he will be placed in the same category by the American people.

The platform adopted by the Anti-Imperialists who convened in this city (Chicago) the past week contains the right ring and it should rekindle the spirit and the flames of 1776 . . . and may the spirit of those immortal heroes rise up and blight the hands of those who are in favor of subjugating and governing any people without their consent.

King Wm. McKinley, while swinging around the circle, endeavored to make the farmers away out in Iowa believe that "ten million years ago God had decreed that the Philippine Islands should fall into the capacious pockets of the American people" or words to that effect. We admit that King McKinley has the right to hug such delusions to his breast. But we do not believe (if there is a God) that He had any more to do with the war in the Philippines than the devil has in conducting a good old-fashioned revival meeting.

Chicago *Broad Ax,* September 21, 1899

"Do Not Enlist"

[The following letter sent to the *Colored American* was reprinted in the *Weekly Blade*:]

To the Editor, *Colored American*:

I cannot see how any Afro-American who has one spark of manhood and race pride can enlist in Pres. McKinley's "colored regiment" to go to the Philippines, there to fight against their own color, who, like we in America, are fighting for liberty. Since all officers above captain are to be white, it requires that a colored man forget that he is a man if he would enlist. If President McKinley and the War Department deem it advisable to draw the color line in making up the ranks, why not draw the color line when awarding the shoulder straps and give us two real colored regiments, officers and men. . . .

R. W. Tyler
Columbus, O.

*   *   *

"Righteousness of Philippine Policy Doubted"

In his welcome address to the Nebraska soldiers, Assistant Secretary Meiklejohn remarked that "the dignity of warfare, the glory of a soldier depends on the cause for which he fights." Then he hinted broadly that those who doubted the righteousness of our war with the Philippines placed themselves in the infamous category headed by that prince of traitors—Benedict Arnold.

To assume that he is the patriot and that those who differ from him are traitors is the imperialist's way of dignifying the war. There are two sides to all questions—except this one.

But many people who have hitherto borne good reputations are skeptical. They do not believe there is any dignity in a war for 5 percent waged in behalf of men who boast their ability to snatch things against a people who long for liberty. Mr. Meiklejohn is begging the question.

Nor does he amend his logic by calling Aguinaldo a gold whistler and assuring his hearers that the Philippine chief offered his followers autocracy or death. Still less convincing is he when he says that Aguinaldo's "idea of honorable warfare justifies a massacre of innocent women and children."

Mr. Meiklejohn went to Nebraska as the President's spokesman. If McKinley thinks so poorly of his own policy that he discards argument for invective, calm statements for epithet and persuasion for bluster, he must be in a pitiable condition.

Parsons *Weekly Blade,* September 22, 1899

"PREDICTS REPUBLICAN VICTORY IN OHIO"

[John P. Green, the only Negro to occupy a seat in the upper house (Ohio) of any northern legislature, said:]

All those who favor the grand acquisition of territory which has been made under this administration and the efforts which are now being made under our flag in the Philippines to restore order and give to their unhappy inhabitants a free and stable government, will aid in our canvass in Ohio this year. . . .

*   *   *

"SHOULD THE NEGRO GO TO THE PHILIPPINES TO FIGHT"

[From the *Ascension Herald*, Donaldsonville, La.:]

"The Washington *Bee*, W. Calvin Chase, editor, thinks he should, and so do we, with certain provisions, chief among them that he should be treated, in all respects, just like all other American soldiers."

We have all along contended that it was not a question of the righteousness of the war, but that it was simply enough for all true Americans to know that their country was at war, and that she must win or compromise her honor, and lower her proud standard, and that too, before mere savages.

The question of imperialism, or expansion and non-expansion, pales into insignificance alongside this great fact.

These are after all questions which can be left to time and the patriotism of our people for final and righteous adjustment. The war must be fought out and victory must perch on the American banner or she must become the laughing stock of all the world. But, if the Negro must leave his home for the rigors of the battlefield and a tropical climate, he must have held out to him the advantages of honor and promotion that are offered to other races. He will be a fool to accept under any other conditions.

Washington *Bee,* September 23, 1899

"ATKINSON AND ANTI-IMPERIALISM BE DAMNED"

[From the *Herald*, Langston City, Oklahoma:]

The Atkinson pamphlets, being steeped in a traitor's guile, were excluded from the U.S. mails, and this same Atkinson, the brand of Cain, having deceived the American white man, has now turned to the American Negro and seeks to induce him to revile his country and blot his fair name. But the nation knows the Negro. He is loyal to the cause and is not only for the nation but for William McKinley and the Republican party as well. Mr. Atkinson be d——d.

Richmond *Planet,* September 29, 1899

"CAN TWO REGIMENTS OF NEGROES BE FOUND?"

[From the *Progress*, Omaha, Nebraska:]

Do you think it possible that two whole regiments of intelligent Negroes can be secured to help the Washington administration out of its Philippine pickle by going as soldiers to thrash the Filipino people, who love liberty so well that they will fight and die for it, people whom the white American soldiers have failed to defeat, much less conquer?. . .

Indianapolis *Freeman,* September 30, 1899

"BENJAMIN GRAVES WOULD RATHER TEACH THAN FIGHT"

[From the *Daily Record*, Washington, D.C.:]

Benjamin Graves, formerly an officer in the Sixth Virginia Volunteers, was recently appointed a captain in one of the new colored regiments now being recruited for services in the Philippines. Through his own application he was appointed a teacher in the public schools and rather than go to the Philippines to fight the Filipinos, he accepted the position of teacher. This is a commendable action. There is nothing for the colored man to gain by going to the Philippines. True, the salary of a captain is perhaps double the salary of a common teacher, but there are other things to be considered. The war in the Philippines is a most unrighteous one and the Negro has not the shadow of a right to ally himself with the forces of invasion [unless] his rights here were carefully guarded. As it is, his rights are gradually being withdrawn and yet he is called upon to aid the country in its merciless policy of subjugation of another nation.

Mr. Graves' action in refusing a commission is worthy of much praise and should be the course adopted by many of those who will be called upon to aid this country in this its hour of extremity.

Richmond *Planet,* September 30, 1899

"MAY BLACK REGIMENTS NEVER GO TO THE PHILIPPINES"

[From the *Progress,* Omaha, Nebraska:]

"We are not going to be rampant about the organization of the Forty-eighth and Forty-Ninth, the two new regiments to be composed of colored men. To express pleasure that the formation of these regiments has been ordered by the Secretary of War, Mr. Root, and to express a hope that their formation would be successful would be but little short of an acknowledgement of the justice of an imperialistic and cruel war policy of the administration as it is crystallized in William McKinley. It would be to acknowledge that Messrs. Green, Lyons, and Cheatham were eminently correct in informing the President that the intelligent and leading Negroes throughout the country, with a possible few insignificant exceptions, were loyally supporting McKinley in his war policy. No! We won't do that; nor will we whoop 'em up for the two new regiments. We hope that they will never be organized. In the event they are, we hope that they will never see service in the Philippines."

It is a very easy matter to give someone credit for what he does. Whether you do or not, the government at Washington is safe.

Washington *Bee,* September 30, 1899

"AGUINALDO KNOWS WHAT AMERICAN 'PROTECTION' IS"

[From the *Standard*, Lexington, Kentucky:]

The Dallas, Texas *Express* says that the more Aguinaldo reads the reports of how the colored people are being cut up for souvenirs in Georgia and hanged and shot to death in the other states, the more determined he is never to put himself under the protection of such a country, and who in the h—l can blame him?

Cleveland *Gazette,* September 30, 1899

"WILL OHIO NEGROES SUPPORT ANTI-IMPERIALIST AND ANTI-LYNCHING DEMOCRATIC CANDIDATES?"

Mr. James Russel, Columbus, Ohio.
Dear Sir and Friend: As I am a buckeye, have been born and brought

up in Newark, Licking County, Ohio, I am deeply interested in the welfare of the state, and more particularly in the success of my race politically, which depends on the result of the Negro vote in the November election. Friend Russel, I write to you to secure your honest opinion of Ohio—as you are one of the leading colored Democrats of the state and stand better than any man in Franklin County with the colored voters. . . . Will they give their votes to that spotless leader, financier and statesman, John R. McLean, who represents the true principles of the Democratic party as adopted in their platform at the recent convention held in Zanesville—which is anti-expansion, anti-imperialist, anti-trust, and anti mob law? The above declaration of principles protects the Negro in all his rights as a man and laborer, as he has nothing for sale except labor. Why not stand by a party that has the courage of its conviction, that has condemned lynchings and asks that a law be enacted to stop the outrages, and the same was incouched in their platform. That plank alone should justify every colored voter in that state who loves life, liberty, his race and family, in exercising his vote for the people's choice, Mr. McLean and the entire Democratic ticket, which will free themselves from political bondage, boss and Hannaism.

The Negroes of Ohio and other states have been voting for the party of promises—which is the Republican party, for over 30 years. John P. Green, his forty acres of land, and that mule he has been talking about lo these many years in Ohio, has never materialized yet, and John will come up with the same old chestnut in the campaign, but his arguments will be refuted by some of the ablest Negro Democratic debaters in the land. Two years ago I had the pleasure of following Mr. Green in the campaign, as you well know; I offered to meet him in joint debate but he refused. . . . The National Negro Anti-Expansion, Anti-Imperialist, Anti-Trust and Anti-Lynching League, of which I am the president, will take an active part for McLean of Ohio and Goebel of Kentucky, in the way of organizing clubs.

With your active campaign committee, headed by the Hon. James P. Seward of Mansfield, who knows no defeat, and his efficient lieutenants, with Col. I. R. Hill of Newark and ex-Director William of Columbus as aides, and a fair treatment of Negro votes, victory is certain. . . .

Yours respectfully,
W. T. Scott
President of the National Anti-Expansion,
Anti-Imperialist, and Anti-Trust League
409 Cone Avenue, Cairo, Illinois

Chicago *Broad Ax,* September 30, 1899

"Is the War Justified?"

Is the movement against the Philippines a just one after a hundred years of struggling for liberty?

Parsons *Weekly Blade,* October 6, 1899

"The Philippine War Is No Race War"

It pays to be a little thoughtful. Those papers and prominent citizens, who said that the Negro was a fool if he espoused the cause of our government as against the Philippines, have some considerable crow to eat, or in order to be consistent, prove to be the fools themselves. The strife is no race war. It is quite time for the Negroes to quit claiming kindred with every black face from Hannibal down. Hannibal was no Negro, nor was Aguinaldo. We are to share in the glories or defeats of our country's wars, that is patriotism pure and simple.

Indianapolis *Freeman,* October 7, 1899

"Dr. A. J. Carey Supports McKinley"

[On Sunday, Oct. 8 President McKinley was the guest of 400 Negroes at Quinn Chapel, Chicago. Rev. Dr. A. J. Carey, pastor of Quinn Chapel, said in part:]

I do not hesitate to say that to a man the Negroes feel that our war with Spain in the sight of God and man was a righteous war. Moreover, the vast majority of us feel that wherever the folds of Old Glory have been unfurled, whether it be in Cuba, Puerto Rico, Hawaii, or the faraway Philippines, there let the starry emblem continue to wave at least until a stable and satisfactory government has been established.

Iowa State Bystander, October 13, 1899

"West Virginia Paper Against Expansion"

[From the Washington *Post* (white):]

[Judge Daniel B. Lucas traveled through West Virginia and found disaffection for McKinley. He said in part:]

There is one element of his party which Mr. McKinley will not be able to count on in 1900—that is the solid Negro vote, which practically carried the South for him during the last campaign. To a man the Negroes are opposed to the policy of expansion. They look at the matter from a purely personal standpoint, and state that there are enough black people in this country now. They sympathize with the native Filipinos in their struggle against American domination, and on no account desire them for fellow citizens.

In Martinsburg, a Negro weekly paper [probably the *Pioneer Press*] has come out flat-footedly against President McKinley and his policy of annexation. I feel sure that the large, if not the dominant element of the black vote will be cast against the Republican party at the next election. This split in the Negro vote will be beneficial to the Negro race, as well as to the Democratic party.

Washington *Bee,* October 14, 1899

"McKINLEY SCORED IN BOSTON"

The colored people of Boston, Mass. held a meeting at the Charles St. A.M.E. church on the 3d inst. McKinley was scored and his administration condemned on account of its attitude towards the colored people of this country.

Hon. Archibald Grimke, ex-consul to San Domingo, read the resolutions which were the most caustic allegations as yet given to the public. [See Appendix IV—Ed.]

* * *

"THIS HIGHWAY ROBBERY"

[A colored soldier writing to the New York *Age* from Manila, Philippine Islands, under date of Aug. 11, 1899, says:]

"I have mingled freely among the natives and have had talks with American colored men here in business, and who have lived here for years, in order to learn of them the cause of their (Filipino) dissatisfaction and the reason for this insurrection and I must confess they have a just grievance. All this would never have occurred if the army of occupation had treated them as people. The Spaniards, even if their laws were hard, were polite and treated them with some consideration; but the Americans, as soon as they saw that the native troops were desirous of sharing in the glories as well as the hardships of the hard won battles with the Americans, began to apply home treatment for colored peoples. Curse them as damned niggers, steal and ravish them, rob them on the street of their small change, take from the fruit vendors whatever suited their fancy and kick the poor unfortunate if he complained, desecrate their church property, and after fighting began, looted everything in sight, burning, robbing the graves.

"This may seem a little tall—but I have seen with my own eyes carcasses lying bare to the broiling sun, the result of raids on the receptacles for the dead in search for diamonds. The troops, thinking we would be proud to emulate their conduct, have made bold of telling their exploits to us. One fellow, a member of the Thirteenth Minnesota, told me how his boys did; another, a Tennessean, told me of how some fellows he knew had cut off a native woman's arm in order to get a fine inlaid bracelet. On upbraiding some fellows one morning whom I met while on a walk (I think they belonged to a Nebraska or Minnesota regiment, they were stationed on the Malaban road) for the conduct of the American troops toward the native and especially as to raiding, etc., the reply was: "Do you think we could afford to stay over here and fight these damned niggers without making it pay all it's worth? The government only pays us $13 per month; that's starvation wages. White men can't stand it." Meaning they could not live on such small pay. In saying this they never dreamed that colored soldiers would never countenance such conduct. They talk with impunity of 'niggers' to our soldiers, never once thinking that they are talking to home "niggers" and should they be brought to remember that at home this is the same vile epithet they hurl at us, they beg pardon and make some effeminate excuse about what the Filipino is called.

"I want to say right here, if it were not for the sake of the 10,000,000 black people in the United States, God alone knows on which side of this subject I would be. And for the sake of the black men who carry arms and pioneer for them as their representatives, ask them not to forget the present administration at the next election. Party be damned! We don't want these islands, not in the way we ought to get them, and for Heaven's sake put the party in power that pledges itself against this highway robbery—expansion is too clean a name for it."

Our readers can draw their own conclusions. White soldiers have testified to a similar condition of affairs; but—we draw the curtain.

Richmond *Planet,* October 14, 1899

"Need For More Troops in the Philippines"

The United States will need at least three-fourths of that number [200,000] and we might as well get ready to send them. It is evident that Gen. Otis' rosy reports were based upon the hypothesis that we could buy up the Filipino leaders even as it is alleged Spain did.

This is the predicament in which we find ourselves after eight months' fighting. The declaration of President McKinley that forcible annexation would be criminal aggression will not only continue to confront us, but will tend to confound the nation in the eyes of the civilized world.

Richmond *Planet,* October 21, 1899

"Declaration of Independence Applies to All Peoples"

Last Sunday afternoon lawyer Beauregard F. Mosely addressed the Young Men's Sunday Club of Quinn Chapel on "Expansion". . . . Among other things the Colonel said: "As I am to talk to you this evening upon 'Expansion As The Colored Man Sees It,' I hope that none of you will be so unrelenting as to criticize my effort because it is the opposite of the position of greater men. We too often cling to men and measures, not because of their merit, but simply because some men, or set of men, advocate them. . . ."

In referring to the war in the Philippines the speaker said: "If the doctrine is true that all men are created free and equal and all governments derive their just powers from the consent of the governed, how can we take Puerto Rico without a plebiscite or Cuba with a sham or the Philippines with a naked sword? If the people of Cuba, Puerto Rico and the Philippines are not born free and independent, neither are we. If we are, so are they."

In closing the Col. declared: "The expansion we are sadly in need of is wise laws, free schools in Alton and everywhere which black and white may attend, the death penalty for lynchers, be they black or white; transportation alike for all the traveling public; a jail for operators of "Jim Crow cars" . . . a President who will recognize officially the outrages perpetrated on black men at home as well as outrages upon men in far away Armenia and France; a President who will enforce the law and protect the lives and liberties of men and women of color in Mississippi as well as appoint a few from Ohio to office; a President who will not tarnish the memory of Grant, Logan, and Lincoln by wearing Confederate badges; a President who is in favor in recognizing men for worth and merit without taking into consideration the color of their skin; a free ballot and a fair count in every state and territory, that is the expansion this country needs. It is an 'Expansion' besides which the dream of the 'Expansionist,' with his few beggarly islands, is a pitiful thing. This is the El Dorado for which the people justly sigh and which they must justly obtain without following double-faced, though single-hearted, dreamers to a goal of certain ruin down a path of splendid shame."

Chicago *Broad Ax,* October 21, 1899

"FROM LINCOLN TO MCKINLEY IS A LONG STEP DOWNWARD"

[From the *Progress,* Omaha, Nebraska:]

After waving for thirty-six years above a land without a slave, the stars and stripes once more waves over men in bondage. And the greatest concession that President McKinley could make in the cause of freedom was that the slaves beneath its folds might purchase their liberty whenever they could raise 'the market price.' From Lincoln to McKinley is a long step, and it is a step downward. In fact, it is a whole flight of steps.

*   *   *

The "best" people on earth, the white men of America, are committing criminal assaults upon the defenseless women of the Philippine Islands. Is this the civilization the American people would take to the inhabitants of their newly acquired possessions?

Chicago *Broad Ax,* October 28, 1899

"A WORLD MOVEMENT AMONG DARKER RACES HAS BEGUN"

Slowly but surely American interest is veering back from contemplation of economic and commercial questions towards which it turned by a natural reaction after the great Civil War for human rights, to justice and human rights again. With the forsaking of the effort to enforce and protect the citizenship of the Negro in 1876 came the great national struggles over the tariff, interstate commerce, money, and national prerogative. Now, the annexation of Hawaii, raising with the economic aspects the justice of raping a happy people of their government, is followed by similar questions of the morality of similar sequestration in the cases of Cuba and the Philippines. Strangely enough, too, all the people involved in the islands are dark races. If we further consider that almost all the other movements involving the existence and integrity of weaker governments are against the dark races in Africa and Asia, and add to that the domestic problem of the American Negro, we are struck with the thought that a startling world movement has begun which is no less than the stirring of the spirit of civilization and prowess among the dark-skinned races, to lead on, doubtless, to an adjustment which shall in the cycles change the present relation of oppressor and oppressed to that of coadjutors in the world's redemption. The intense hearts of these colored peoples, joined to the acute brain of the pale races, will close up the break that has always in history separated the segments of what God intends, we believe, to be the perfect human circles.

AME Church Review (Philadelphia, Pa.), October, 1899

"FORCING A WARPED CIVILIZATION ON THE PHILIPPINES"

[The *Bee* quotes from Nathan Sprague, son-in-law of Frederick Douglass, who resigned from the Maryland Committee of the Republican Party:]

"Again, this Administration goes to Cuba to keep Spain from murdering its citizens, leaving millions of American-born citizens to be lynched and burned at the stake, saying that they have no power to prohibit such crimes, and yet this Administration feels justified in forcing a warped civilization as this upon the Filipinos. This great Republican party is doing this bloody work after it has posed as a party fighting for liberty, independence, justice, and humanity. . . .

"I protest against having my political convictions estimated by the color of my face. As an American citizen, I claim the right to judge the issues that from time to time arise in the government of my country. . . ."

Washington *Bee,* November 4, 1899

TEXAS NEGROES SUPPORT McKINLEY

[The *Weekly Blade* reported a meeting of the Negro State Convention in Austin, Texas, October 25, at which the following resolutions were passed:]

Resolved, that we give our unqualified endorsement to our wise and

patriotic President, William McKinley, in that he has successfully prose-
cuted one of the most righteous wars and achieved some of the most
brilliant victories of modern times.

Resolved, that we recognize that the chief executive of this nation is
powerless to declare a policy for this country in the matter of the war
now being waged in the Philippine Islands but that such power is alone
with the Congress of the country, and though ever so deplorable be that
strife, the President has no alternative but to continue the prosecution of
the war until Congress shall bid him otherwise.

Parsons *Weekly Blade,* November 10, 1899

FILIPINOS ASK BLACK SOLDIERS
TO CONSIDER THEIR HISTORY

La Loma Church, Luzon, Philippines—A placard written in Spanish
was discovered nailed to a tree a few miles north of Angeles. . . . [It
read:]

> To the colored American soldier. It is without honor that you are
> spilling your costly blood. Your masters have thrown you in the most
> iniquitous fight with double purposes, in order to make you the
> instrument of their ambition; and also your hard work will make soon
> the extinction of your race. Your friends, the Filipinos, give you this
> good warning. You must consider your situation and your history, and
> remember that the blood of your brothers, Sam Hose and Gray [who
> were lynched in the United States earlier that year], proclaims
> vengeance.

*   *   *

"THE WAYS OF THE AMERICAN PEOPLE
SERVE AS A LESSON TO CUBANS AND FILIPINOS"

C. Melville, in the London *Daily Chronicle*, tells "How the Americans
Make War." The writer ostensibly undertakes to prove that the campaign
in Cuba against the Spaniards was not to aid the Cubans in securing their
independence as represented by the American press. Previous to the
military occupation of Cuba, it was the constant theme that the cause of
the oppressed should be vindicated upon the ample ground of liberty and
independence to all the inhabitants of the island. It was the enforced
opinion of President McKinley and Congress, and it was the accepted
view of the Christian world. No other belief was maintained but that
Cuba should enjoy the rights and privileges of an independent republic.
Americans held this idea foremost and it was received in good faith both
by the Cubans and the outside world as the unalterable and fixed
agreement on the part of all concerned.

It becomes then a great conundrum with the writer in the London
Chronicle as to the present American movement paving the way to the
demand for annexation in direct contravention of the solemn pledges

made in favor of Cuban independence. Very reasonable must it appear that the Cubans having for so many years of earnest toil, trial and struggle labored to this end, should have their highest aspirations contravened by a nation professedly their avowed friends. It should hardly seem that a brave and patriotic people as Americans are known to be can be charged with such undisguised tergiversation. But that there is a blind hand of double-dealing being played cannot be denied. Neither the Cubans nor Americans are very talkative at this time. A studied silence reveals the uncertainty of the strained situation. But coming events cast their shadows before and when this secret deadlock is broken, it will be found that by some artful scheming, the sublime idea of national independence has been only as a tale that is full of sound and fury, signifying nothing.

But regardless of all inducements conceived in the thought of expansion, of power and annexed territory, Americans cannot afford upon any ground of political expediency to violate its obligations implied or expressed. We must stand upon our promises, coveting nothing which may seem to us an easy prey through the power of a glutinous hand. We owe it to ourselves to stand as an example for other nations. The gross and impious insinuations offered by C. Melville must be repudiated through the verities of our past declarations and in a fair and honest maintenance of the "Monroe Doctrine" both in spirit and application. The best way by which we may assure the Cubans of our sincerity and sympathy is by encouraging and aiding them in their struggle for independence, and not by handicapping and embarrassing them nor by obligating them through terms given in a show of justice and magnanimity. Nothing smacks more of treachery and usurpation than the taking advantage of another in the moment of one's weakness. Let the Cubans enjoy the opportunity which has come to them and let them dictate the terms and conditions upon which they shall enroll themselves upon the list of nations.

Speaking of the Filipinos, Melville holds that the Americans, pretending friendship to the people of those islands, have actually bought them and have taken possession of the whole group of islands and exploited them for their own use. But the poor wretches, believing the Americans to be friends, had a rude awakening from this delusion when they found themselves bought like cattle, regardless of their wishes and opinions. Fired with a just indignation at this treatment, they entered upon another struggle for emancipation.

The demand of unconditional surrender is all that comes to their ears. Yet remembering the long series of heartless butchery and bloodshed so often recounted in the recent events of American life, it is with quailing sensations of horror and dismay that these savages now shrink from the appalling condition with which they are threatened. Already Americans are responsible for the massacre of thousands of natives whose only offense is that of being loyal to themselves and their honest convictions.

Mindful of the ways of the American people, such as the lynching of Afro-Americans and inoffensive foreigners, and especially the cruel and inhuman persecution, the murdering and torturing of ex-slaves whose only offense is that of a dark skin, very assuredly, the sable savages of the Philippines have very just reasons to repel the effort of this government to bring them under control of a powerful nation, the exercise of whose authority has been called in question by all Christendom. What shall be the outcome heaven only knows. It is evident that the ways of the American people serve as a lesson to Cubans and Filipinos.

Cleveland *Gazette,* November 11, 1899

"Forcible Annexation is Criminal Aggression"

We endorse Mr. Bryan's position on the Philippine question and his denunciation of imperialism.

We condemn Mr. McKinley's policy in the Orient and are opposed to his being a party to the slaughtering of women and men in the Philippine Islands.

We have not quoted, however, any extracts from Mr. Bryan's utterances because upon other questions we cannot bring ourselves to agree with this distinguished free silver leader.

We have no desire or inclination to train with the Democratic party.

The Republican party has not as yet taken a stand with reference to the questions now confronting the nation. Its records and traditions have always been diametrically opposed to that of President McKinley.

When that gentleman declared that forcible annexation would be criminal aggression, we agreed with him.

He has never declared that he was incorrect in making this statement, and until he does, we decline to be party to a policy which is unquestionably one of the foulest crimes ever attempted by a republic.

Richmond *Planet,* November 11, 1899

It is Not a War of Conquest

It is understood by every American citizen, and by the whole world, that this is not a war of conquest or an attempt at expansion, but it is simply an honorable struggle or effort to settle matters that were brought about through the chain of events, unforeseen, that such difficulties bring . . . there is only one thing to do and that is to maintain the dignity and hold up the standard of the country by bringing about good results regardless of time or cost.

Indianapolis *Recorder,* November 18, 1899

PHILIPPINE WAR UNJUST

Up to the present time more than 10,000 American soldiers have lost their lives on those islands, and the end is not yet in sight. This shows that the war which is being waged against the Filipinos does not meet with the highest approbation of the gods of war, and it is in the sight of all who prize and love liberty, unholy, unrighteous, unjust and wicked in every sense of the word. If this be treason, make the most of it.

Chicago *Broad Ax,* November 18, 1899

"END THE WAR IN THE PHILIPPINES"

The colored American is for "expansion," but he wants expansion on lines consistent with the human principles, for the establishment of which he has given his labor and shed his blood in four wars.

End the war in the Philippines. The American laborer can ill afford the expense and the nation cannot stand to lose so many valuable young men like Major John A. Logan.

The war in the Philippines can be stopped in thirty days if Congress can be prevailed upon to make a clean-cut statement of the policy of this government and arrange a settlement of all pending questions on an equitable basis.

Colored American (Washington, D.C.), December 2, 1899

"PHILIPPINE POLICY SUPPORTED"

They [the Filipinos] have been made to believe their rights and liberty and country are jeopardized by the Americans and to surrender would be to give up all they possess. The influence of such nefarious teachings has fastened such a hold upon the ignorant masses of the islands that it is almost impossible to reason or treat with them in a peaceable manner. But, to the contrary, they persist in following this sham leader whose sole occupation is stirring up troubles and revolutions. . . .

That the United States does not want their country is obvious but it is a settled fact that the islands will never be turned over to Aguinaldo and his followers, who are neither waging the war for the country nor for the interest of its people—but simply for self gain. . . .

Indianapolis *Recorder,* December 2, 1889

"EXPANSION WILL NOT BENEFIT THE RACE"

[In a dispatch from Boston, "Bruce Grit" (John E. Bruce) said:]

In the culmination of the conquest in the Philippines, soon to occur, the Eagle will scream and flap its wings and liberty will be assassinated in the name of Freedom. Expansion will expand and American ideas and customs will be transplanted beyond the seas and we shall be a world power with a vengeance. The Negroes who think expansion is going to benefit the race and that its opportunities for more and larger development will be greater are very much mistaken. There will be nothing in the new possessions for the Negroes except those things which are of no possible use or benefit to the whites, who will develop the resources of these new countries. Since we haven't the money to compete with white men in these countries, I do not know if there is any particular harm in a few of us painting pictures and building air castles in our minds and in the Philippines. As soon as the war there is over, millions of American money are going there. . . . How much will the Negro carry with him when he goes there and what will he do with it? Does anybody know?

Washington *Colored American,* December 9, 1899

"MCKINLEY'S MESSAGE CRITIZED"

He has completely changed fronts on his Philippine policy, and has refrained from recommending at this time a specific and final form of government for the people of those islands when peace is restored. Congress will be empowered to construct a form of government for the Filipinos. If the numerous reports are true, which have appeared in the various newspapers, then we can not agree with the President, when he maintains that "The progress of our troops has been marked by a humanity which has surprised even the misguided insurgents." Now if those reports are true, they inform us that our troops have, with the butts of their guns, slain little children, run their bayonets through women and boys, and committed many other crimes, upon those innocent and inoffensive people who have for over two hundred years been fighting for liberty and freedom, too horrible to mention.

Again, the President is in error when he contends that "These people whom providence has brought within our jurisdiction must feel that it is their liberty and not our power, their welfare and not our gain we are seeking to enhance. Our flag has never waved over any community but in blessing." Ah, Mr. President! There is the rub. Do you mean to tell us that the flag was a blessing to the millions of Indians who were exterminated and robbed of their rightful possessions, while it gloriously waved over their heads? That same flag for two hundred and fifty years waved over four million slaves, and how much of its blessings did they enjoy? And today under the divine guidance of providence, and you, Mr. President, it triumphantly waves over slavery and polygamy, which you and your party for many years declared were the twin relics of barbarism. But in the closing hours of the nineteenth century, after we have reached the highest point in civilization, you, Mr. President, or divine providence, have changed fronts concerning polygamy and slavery.

The President commends the new form of government which has gone into effect in the islands of Negros; its main feature prohibits its inhabitants from taking part in its affairs or voting unless they are property holders or pay a certain amount of rental, and can read and write the English language or one or two foreign languages. But the President many times has given expression to the opinion that it is outrageously wrong to require people in this country to be able to read or write, own property and pay taxes before they can be permitted to vote, so you see it all depends upon who is gored. His declaration that "Cuba must have an independent form of government" will meet with the very highest approbation of all true Americans and it is the brightest jewel in his long message.

Chicago *Broad Ax,* December 9, 1899

"FILIPINOS WILL NOT BE GIVEN LIBERTY"

[From the *Progress*, Omaha, Nebraska:]

That the United States does not propose to give the Filipinos the liberty for which they have fought so long and well to obtain is evidenced by the fact that Congress must provide "special laws" for their especial benefit. It is better that they fight and die rather than surrender to American rule.

Parsons *Weekly Blade,* December 15, 1899

"UNJUSTIFIABLE POLICY OF CONQUEST"

If the [Democratic] party could be trusted, there would be no question as to the proper course for every right-thinking, justice-loving citizen to pursue. We are engaging in an unjustifiable policy of conquest. We have forsaken the well-defined landmarks of our fathers. We are assassinating the eternal principles of the Bible, and the punishment which has been meted other nations who had forgotten God in prayer, will follow us, as surely as night follows day. The Democratic leaders have at last gotten right upon this question.

Richmond *Planet,* December 23, 1899

THE COWARDICE OF THE NATION AND PRESIDENT McKINLEY'S STATEMENT CONCERNING THE FILIPINOS

Treated by Hon. Frederick Douglass' Son—
Mr. Douglass Thinks We Should Settle the Race
Question Here Before Going 10,000 Miles Away.

[From an article by Lewis H. Douglass in the New York *Age*:]

Washington, D.C.—President McKinley, in the course of his speech at Minneapolis, said of the Filipinos under American sovereignty:

They will not be governed as vassals, or serfs, or slaves. They will be given a government of liberty, regulated by law, honestly administered, without oppressing exaction, taxation without tyranny, justice without bribe, education without distinction of social condition, freedom of religious worship, and protection in life, liberty, and the pursuit of happiness.

I do not believe that President McKinley has any confidence in the statement above. It cannot be successfully asserted that the great tariff statesman is blind to the fact of the race and color prejudice that dominates the greater percentage of the soldiers who are killing Filipinos in the name of freedom and civilization.

President McKinley knows that brave, loyal, black American soldiers, who fight and die for their country, are hated, despised and cruelly treated in that section of the country from which this administration accepts dictation and to the tastes of which the President undoubtedly caters. The President of the United States knows that he dare not station a regiment of black heroes in the state of Arkansas. He knows that at the race-hating command of a people who sought destruction of the nation his administration rescinded an order to send black soldiers to Little Rock. The administration lacks the courage to deal with American citizens without regard to race or color, as it clearly demonstrated in the weak and contemptibly mean act of yielding to the demands of those who hold that this is a white man's government and that dark races have no rights which white men are bound to respect.

It is a sorry, though true, fact that wherever this government controls, injustice to dark races prevails. The people of Cuba, Puerto Rico, Hawaii, and Manila know it as well as do the wronged Indian and outraged black man in the United States.

What hope for justice and fair dealing is there for a people who have shot down our soldiers in an attempt to maintain their freedom, and who are denounced as "niggers" by the officers of our army, when black men of the United States who fight gallantly and with distinguished heroism are subjected to ingratitude and unjust reproach? If the nation cruelly treats its dark friends who fight and die in its interest, what will it not do with its dark enemies when it has them in its power?

The question will be asked: How is it that such promises are made to Filipinos thousands of miles away while the action of the administration in protecting dark citizens at home does not even extend to a promise or any attempt to rebuke the outlawry which kills American citizens of African descent for the purpose of gratifying bloodthirstiness and race hate?

President McKinley says that the Filipinos will not be governed as vassals or serfs or slaves, but he does not say that they will not be treated as the people of the South are allowed to treat its black citizens of the United States. Can this government act more justly ten thousand miles away than it can at home? Will it be more true to the principles of the Declaration of Independence in the Philippine Islands after having paid $20,000,000 for control without consent of the governed than in this land where the evil effects of slavery are still visible? No sane, honest man in this country believes that equal and exact justice and that education without social distinctions will be had where the race hate indulged in by the men who denounce Filipinos as "niggers" and only fit to be subjected to the white race has full sway.

It is hypocrisy of the most sickening kind to try to make us believe that the killing of Filipinos is for the purpose of good government and to give protection to life and liberty and the pursuit of happiness. Let us have protection to life, liberty and the pursuit of happiness at home.

Knowing, as the colored voter does, the hollow hypocrisy of the profession that the way against the Filipino is a benevolent one, how can he be expected to support men for office who favor continuing a strife, the real purpose of which is to deprive a people of their liberty?

When the United States learns that justice should be blind as to race and color, then may it undertake to, with some show of propriety, expand. Now its expansion means extension of race hate and cruelty, barbarous lynchings and gross injustice to dark people.

Cleveland Gazette, December 23, 1899

"We Must Not War on a Liberty-Loving People"

[Dr. L. B. Weymenth of North Vassalboro, Maine wrote the following letter to the editor of the *Courant*:]

I must have the ablest, the paper most devoted to the republic's ideals, that we have in America. I regard the *Courant* as the truest exponent we have to teach the people why we have the grandest government when administered, as the founders declared it should be, "by the people and for the people." We have become a great nation. Isolated as we have been, it has proved an immense blessing. We have prospered exceedingly without having a large standing army to be sustained by the laboring people. Our flag was respected by all nations long before our Moses declared war on the Philippine Islands. To be serious, of all the arrant humbugs ever invented by evil men, chiefest is the idea that we must deprive a brave, liberty-loving people of their freedom in order to become a world power. Even a schoolboy of 10 years of age knows it is false. The present administration, if sustained, will overthrow our form of government. We cannot serve God and do the bidding of Satan. If we are to remain a republic, we must not war on a people who are struggling for self-government.

Courant (Boston, Mass.), January 6, 1900

"Senator Beveridge Commended"

The speech of Senator Beveridge delivered Tuesday . . . commends itself to every thoughtful citizen. . . . Briefly stated, the speech as presented embraced the great strategic and commercial value of the Philippines; the situation as created by and forced upon us by the war with Spain; the character of the inhabitants and their unfitness for self-government; the duty of the United States in the premises; the best form of government suitable for these people, and the urgent need for a clean administration.

Indianapolis *Recorder,* January 13, 1900

"PHILIPPINE POLICY SUPPORTED"

Senator Pettigrew may be full of sympathy with the Filipinos, but we suspect he is only looking for an opportunity to work them for a "wad." That class of sympathetic persons are frequently met in this day and generation.

Our duty in the Philippines is to lick those devils, who turned upon their friends, to an immortal stand-still, and Otis is going to do that thing to a queen's taste. All this Philippine sympathy in the United States is nothing more nor less than Bryan-Demo-Pop political clap-trap for campaign purposes.

If there are any gift swords left in stock, one might very appropriately be bestowed upon young Mr. Brile, who knocked an anti-expansion resolution out of the New York City Council.

Republican (Seattle, Washington), January 19, 1900

"PHILIPPINE POLICY APPROVED"

The eyes of the world are still on the United States' position in the Philippines. And the people here in America are equally as anxious for a complete settlement of differences and are looking forward to that end. As difficult as the situation has been we must give the Administration credit for the untiring efforts that have been and are still being put forth to subdue the barbarous and uncivilized portions of the Islands and pacify the better elements by assuring them with protection as against uprisings and sudden outbreaks that characterize the people of the Philippines. . . .

And in spite of the tirades and obstacles and other numerous schemes in the form of arguments used by designing demogogues to hinder and impede the progress of the good work being done by this government in the Islands, the agents, in whose hands this duty is intrusted, are ably pushing the people's claims in a manner that will soon bring the matter to an end.

We feel safe when we say that if the people will have a little more patience they will be more than rewarded. This problem is complicated and difficult but it must be solved regardless of time or cost—time is a small matter when the dignity and honor of this administration is involved. It behooves all people regardless of their political views or religious affiliations to stand man to man in defense of so noble a cause as is being contended for in behalf of humanity in the Orient.

We highly endorse Senator Beveridge's speech last week on this question and believe that every well-thinking man and wisher of good government civilization shares our feeling in this matter. The end is in sight; just a little more patience and all will be well.

Indianapolis *Recorder,* January 20, 1900

"INSIST THAT FILIPINOS HAVE JUSTICE"

Chaplain T. G. Steward of the United States Army, writing from Manila, in an article to the *Christian Recorder*, says that he is surprised at the cordiality with which the Filipinos receive "colored people from the United States." He found that same condition in Honolulu. . . .

We shall insist that the Filipinos have justice and fair play, and as soon as they get into the American Union we shall make common cause with them in fighting American prejudice, whatever shape the vile thing may take.

We are getting a large mixed population into the American Union. At the proper time the Afro-American citizens will join issues with all of them in the contention for a fair and square deal.

Ohio Standard and Observer (Xenia and Wilberforce, Ohio)
January 27, 1900

"ANTI-EXPANSIONISM IS TOMMYROT"

The Philippines will be held by the United States government, by virtue of the bill of sale made by Spain in Paris, as long as there is a drop of blood coursing through American veins. The simple-minded and emotional harangues of the anti-expansionists have no more show of stemming public sentiment in the matter than was accomplished by Don Quixote in his ludicrous assault on the windmill. It would look foolish to give up the islands when we have undisputed title to them guaranteed by international law and the demands of civilization under the beneficent folds of the American flag. If the United States forces were to be withdrawn from those islands the Philippines would be left to the grasping hand of Aguinaldo and his personal friends—the junta at Hong Kong with headquarters and treasury in the saddle, with horse and rider in the brush lying in wait for the victim, the producers of wealth—the working Filipino, Spaniard, or American—thus placing the islands under brigandage and plunder. All this sympathetic tommyrot of the anti-expansionists is very tiresome to the American people, who know that the demogogues don't mean a word they say.

Observer (Kansas City, Missouri), January 27, 1900

"Anti-Expansionists Should Concentrate On Disfranchisement and Mob Rule"

The great pow-wow of the anti-expansionists, anti-imperialists, alias anti-good governmentists, and anti-administrationists which opened up the cave-of-the-winds on last Sunday evening, demonstrates to what extend well-dressed platitudes and barren sentimentality can be utilized to bolster up party hopes and stimulate party antagonisms.

If they really wanted something to vent their pent-up notions of liberty, humanity, and fair dealing upon, they might have made disfranchisement, lynching, and mob rule appropriate topics.

Washington *Bee*, January 27, 1900

"William Jennings Bryan"

The newspapers under the control of the trusts, monopolists, and money powers might make light of the utterances of this wonderful man. . . . To defeat him the Republican party will be forced to meet him in the coming contest with a man shorn of imperialism and free from the domination of the rings and monopolies that are now controlling. . . .

* * *

"The Slaughter in the Philippines"

The slaughter in the Philippines is one of the most unrighteous acts ever perpetrated by any government even during the Middle Ages. The doings of Weyler in Cuba pale into insignificance by those of the nation, who, with hypocritical humanity, made haste to go stop the blood feud, to secure independence, happiness, and contentment to the natives. Spain stands aghast at America's cruelty upon her once colonists, rescued from her under such a hypocritical guise, without the power of protesting or aiding those who are being so mercilessly chastised by a government of liberty and justice. American manliness and the spirit of the fathers are trampled under the feet of the imperialists, and those who pretend to have the spirit of independence and human liberty in their breast are called traitors if they raise their voices against this diabolical outrage. The sages in the Senate, like Senator Hoar and others cradled in the spirit of constitutional liberty, are traduced and abused because they dare defend the Constitution of the Fathers and the rights of a people contending for their liberties. This is the condition of the affairs in the Philippines. The report coming every day from Gen. Otis is so wicked and bloody that it takes the form of a fox hunt or a rabbit expedition, as the cruelties are doled out to the American people—one hundred Filipinos killed and one American wounded; the rebels routed; the women and children made prisoners; Aguinaldo will be captured tomorrow; and a lot of provisions destroyed and a number of rifles taken with much ammunition; no casualties on our side. This is the daily farce that is being enacted as the Filipino slaughter goes on. It is time for Congress to call a halt, and if the imperialists are too strong and all hope of true Americanism is departed, it is time for the people to take a hand and wipe out the dynasty of imperialism at the polls in November next.

Defender (Philadelphia, Pa.), January 27, 1900

"ANTI-IMPERIALISM CRITICIZED"

The so-called anti-imperialist opposition to the administration policy in the Philippines has its humorous side, and it is from that side that it has been treated generally in the press of the country. . . . That the speeches of Senator Hoar and others, telegraphed to Hong Kong and thence to Manila, encouraged Aguinaldo and his followers, and that the continuance of the insurrection, and the blood of General Lawton and many others is directly chargeable to these treasonable encouragements of the armed enemies of our country, has been put beyond a doubt. It is time now to stop the foolishness.

The so-called anti-imperialists differ among themselves as to the policy to be pursued; but one thing all of them apparently are united on: that the United States, when it abandons the Philippines to Aguinaldo and the Hong Kong junta, shall guarantee that no other nation shall put a stop to the anarchy which would naturally result from the withdrawal of the United States forces, or take possession of the islands or any part thereof, for the time of ten years at least. This is the most definite proposition upon which all the anti-imperialists appear to be united. This is a policy which can only be characterized as a dog-in-the-manger policy. Does any one imagine, who has any sense, that the other nations who would be glad to get possession of the islands would acknowledge for a moment the right of the United States to withdraw from them, and at the same time announce to the world that no other nation should take them? So long as we hold the Islands, other nations acknowledge our right to do so; but the moment we withdraw, and allow the natives to make war on each other undisturbed, to violate the rights of traders, to pillage and massacre at their will, other nations are bound to see that the rights of their subjects are protected, and they will do so; and if we should undertake to prevent them we should have on our hands a world-wide war.

The guaranty which the anti-imperialists propose, therefore, is a guaranty of war with England and Germany and Russia and probably France, all in the interests of peace. A more absurd proposition was never formulated by a man insane.

There is not a single anti-imperialist, so far as their utterances disclose, who would have this country simply withdraw from the Philippines and leave them to their fate. Everyone wants the United States to guarantee them from interference by any other power. Such a guaranty involves all the responsibilities and none of the benefits which would come from an occupation by this country. That the Filipinos would have under our government a larger measure of individual freedom, a better administration of justice, and a better chance to "life, liberty and the pursuit of happiness" than under the dictatorship of an Aguinaldo, is not worth arguing. The question is whether this country, having undertaken a responsibility, shall flunk it. There is but one answer to such a question that can be given by the American people, and if Mr. Bryan and the majority of the Democrats in their next national convention shall declare that this country ought to adopt any such course as is now proposed by the Democratic leaders who seem to have most influence in the party, the popular verdict in the next election will be so overwhelming that the party will need a quarter of a century more to recruit its shattered forces enough to make a respectable contest.

Colorado *Statesman* (Denver, Colorado), January 27, 1900

"TO RECEDE IN THE PHILIPPINES WOULD BE WEAKNESS"

The Anti-Expansionists of our country are attempting to balk our government in endeavoring to maintain its standards in the Philippines. The cause of the quarrel is hardly to be considered at this juncture. We find ourselves in possession of the Philippines, and according to the policies of progressive nations, to recede would be simply a confession of weakness; that, this government does not mean to stand. The question of humanity is not at issue, but if so, our government is far more capable of insuring tranquility to the natives than the natives can ever insure. . . .

Indianapolis *Freeman,* January 27, 1900

"MAY NEGROES WHO VOLUNTEER GET BALL-STUNG"

Every colored soldier who leaves the United States and goes out to the Philippine Islands to fight the brave men there who are struggling and dying for their liberty is simply fighting to curse the country with color-phobia, jim-crow cars, disfranchisement, and lynchers and everything that prejudice can do to blight the manhood of the darker races, and as the Filipinos belong to the darker human variety, [it is] the Negro fighting against himself. Any Negro soldier that will cross the ocean to help subjugate the Filipinos is a fool or a villain, more fool, however, than villain, we trust. May every one of them get ball-stung is our sincere prayer.

Reporter (Helena, Arkansas), February 1, 1900

"NEGRO ANTI-IMPERIALISTS' NATIONAL ORGANIZATION MAY MEET IN KANSAS CITY"

Cairo Ill., Special.—Colonel W. T. Scott of this city, who is president of the National Negro Anti-Imperial and Anti-Trust League, states that he has been requested, through L. A. Newby, secretary of the society at Chicago, Ill., to call a meeting of the organization at Kansas City, Mo., about May 16, to formulate plans for the coming campaign.

The following are the members of the Executive Committee: J. Milton Turner, St. Louis, Mo.; Chas. H. Croswait, Nashville, Tenn.; James A. Ross, editor of the Buffalo *Globe,* New York; Dr. W. T. Peyton, Louisville, Ky.; F. W. Ernst, Detroit, Mich.; J.H.C. Howard, Philadelphia, Pa.; J.T.V. Hill, Indianapolis, Ind.; C. F. Armsted, Gallipolis, O.; Joseph Houser, editor of the *Negro World,* St. Paul, Minnesota; ex-Senator Stamps, New Orleans, La.; Edward I. Clark, San Francisco; John B. Vashon, St. Louis, Mo.; Dr. J. B. Riley, Seattle, Wash.; George T. Downing, Rhode Island; George E. Taylor, Oscaloosa, Ia.; Wm. E. Gross, Greater New York, N.Y.; D. T. Freemont, Virginia; T. C. Brown, Baltimore, Md.; A. B. Davidson, Newark, N.J.

* * *

"NEW POSSESSIONS MUST BE TERRITORIES, NOT COLONIES"

The question of expansion cannot be a burning question. We have expanded. We have possessed ourselves of Puerto Rico, Hawaii, the Sulus and the Philippines. What we have taken on as the fruits of war we cannot well throw off. Having broken the Spanish power and failed to give to the late subjects of Spain their independence, and having assumed the government of these countries where Spain left it off, the nations of the world look to us for a proper administration of affairs and for the meeting of such of the many and just obligations as came into our possession when we took on those countries. But the question of the government of these people is a burning question. We do no more than indicate this as one of the issues which will enter largely into the campaign of the current year. We will say, however, that those people in Congress and out of it who insist that we have colonies and must have colonial government are at fault. The Constitution of the United States provides for territories and states. It does not provide for colonies. As President McKinley has said: "Our priceless principles for the flag." If they do, and we think they do, [sic] then eventually the people in those new countries must take the same course in the formation of their territorial and state government that obtains in the United States proper.

Washington *Colored American,* March 24, 1900

"NEW POSSESSIONS MUST BE TERRITORIES"

Puerto Rico, Hawaii, and the Philippines are a part of the United States. They are territories in the process of civil organization—not colonies. Our country is a republic, not an empire. Put these points down as a "starter."

Washington *Colored American,* April 21, 1900

"Gods of War Are Not Smiling Upon American Troops"

No one can form any idea of the hardships which the American soldiers have to endure in the Philippine Islands. Two years ago many of them thought it would be great fun and sport for them to go to those far away Islands and shoot down without any justification the half-civilized "Niggers," as they call them to show their patriotism. But many of those same soldiers who have assisted in murdering innocent women and little children are now being brought home raving maniacs and Gen. Otis has recently ordered one thousand pair of handcuffs to be used in hand-cuffing the large number of demented soldiers and bringing them back to this country. The General says in his report, that "from May, 1898 one thousand men have been bereft of their reason and almost one hundred so far have taken their own lives." All this tends to prove that the Gods of War are not smiling upon the American troops.

Chicago *Broad Ax*, May 5, 1900

"Why Does the Negro Fight in the Philippines?"

[William Simms, a soldier in Bong a Bong, Philippine Isles, whose home is in Muncie, Ind., writing to the *Freeman* says:] "I was struck by a question a little boy asked me, which ran about this way—'Why does the American Negro come from America to fight us when we are much friend to him and have not done anything to him? He is all the same as me, and me all the same as you. Why don't you fight those people in America that burn the Negroes, that made a beast of you, that took the child from its mother's side and sold it?' " Simms admits that he was staggered. . . .

Indianapolis *Freeman,* May 11, 1900

"Disagreement With New England Anti-Imperalists' Attack on McKinley's Administration"

Information comes from Hartford, Connecticut that the Colonial Baptist Association of New England (colored), comprising thirty churches in Connecticut and Massachusetts, which met there May 19, adopted resolutions which criticized President McKinley and the administration because of the treatment of colored men in the South and denounced imperialism and lauded Grover Cleveland as a man who did his duty. Alluding to the Baker family outrages, these resolutions state that "the blood of this father and child is upon the skirts of the present administration."

The foregoing is an attack upon the administration that seems quite unwarranted. It appears that the association went out of its way and out of reason in trying to put itself on record as being opposed to the administration.

The denunciation of imperialism, so called, while in the province of such or any association, seems a little far-fetched for that kind of association. Imperialism and race issues have no connection. As an American citizen, any man or set of men may denounce what he sees fit, but the wisdom of a body of colored men meeting for religious purposes will be questioned when it deliberately enters into politics of such intense kind. The peculiar relation of the colored man to this country should forbid such rabid utterances against the party that has the reputation of making it possible for free speech.

This outburst will be attributed either to ignorance or insincerity. It cannot be imagined that that convention is alarmed to that extent over the expansion idea of this government.

. . . To laud Grover Cleveland is a fling at McKinley; yet, Cleveland has nothing to his credit as it affects the colored people. The condition of the South, it appears by that remarkable convention, was created by the McKinley administration. These men would have the President plunge the country in another civil war that in the end would afford no relief. . . .

Indianapolis *Freeman,* May 26, 1900

"BRYAN RIGHT AND WRONG"

Mr. Bryan is all right in wanting to give the so-called Negroes in the Philippines their independence but his party is all wrong concerning the rights of the Negroes in this country.

*   *   *

The frauds which have been exposed in Cuba have been a revelation to many people, and the attempt to shield the guilty parties shows that others have been the beneficiaries of these stupendous robberies. It will yet be ascertained that these cruel wars have been waged for the purpose of enriching the few at the expense of the many.

Richmond *Planet,* May 26, 1900

"AGUINALDO STRUGGLING FOR INDEPENDENCE"

W. Calvin Chase [at a meeting of the Negro Progressive Association, May 24, 1900] followed in a speech pointing out the Negro's faults. Aguinaldo was struggling for freedom and independence just the same as the Negro. "I am no apologist," he said, "and I am not afraid to express my sentiments. The man who says that Aguinaldo is not a patriot is a mere seeker after office, trying to cater to popularity."

Washington *Bee,* June 2, 1900

"Philippine Policy Approved"

The war begun for humanity has accomplished its purpose and covered American arms with glory. At its conclusion we find ourselves suddenly in possession of new and valuable territory and are confronted with the momentous questions which the just government of these new island possessions involve. The issue has been squarely met. Stable government has succeeded disorder in Cuba and Puerto Rico, and the work of pacification in the Philippines is going steadily onward. Despite the cry of imperialism and the prediction of dire disaster by the false prophet of the Platte, the ship of state has weathered the storm. . . .

Indianapolis *Recorder*, June 9, 1900

"Opposed to Policy in the Philippine"

[In its discussion of the National Republican Convention the *Planet* said:]

We are opposed to the policy of the administration in the Philippines, but in view of the Democratic attitude in disfranchising colored citizens by unconstitutional enactments in the several states, it seems that for him as yet "the Republican party is the ship—all else is the sea."

Richmond *Planet*, June 23, 1900

VII

CIVIL RIGHTS, IMPERIALISM, AND THE ELECTION OF 1900

The anti-imperialist sentiments of most black newspapers in 1899 were toned down in the spring and summer of 1900, when blacks who could vote had to choose between an out-and-out white supremacist party that was rapidly disfranchising them in the South and a Republican party whose imperialism they disliked and whose leader did nothing to protect them in their right to life, liberty and property.

Support of the Republican party on the part of such papers as the Washington *Bee*, which had scored McKinley's Philippine policy, was dictated by party loyalty and the conviction that the really dangerous enemy was the Democratic party and its standard-bearer, William Jennings Bryan, who was silent on his party's anti-democratic and frequently terroristic activities in the South. The *Bee* and other papers said that Bryan did not know what imperialism was and that anti-imperialism was only an issue he used to win votes. They pointed to the South as an illustration of domestic imperialism under the Democratic party and used Bryan's own words, that imperialism was rule without the consent of the governed, to denounce him as a hypocrite and unscrupulous politician. The Chicago *Inter-Ocean,* quoted in the *Bee*, asked: "Does Mr. Bryan's zeal for "consent of the governed" extend to native American citizens or is it limited to Malays?" Nevertheless, a few prominent blacks in the North switched to Bryan because they could not stomach McKinley's subjugation of the Filipinos and his *fainéant* southern policy.

The hostile feeling in 1900 among the black papers (most were Republican) against McKinley was enunciated by the Cleveland *Gazette*: ". . . our opposition to the policy of the administration in its desire to get possession of the Philippines is because of wrongs we have suffered at home." But twenty-three members of the Afro-American Press Association,* or five-sixths of the total membership, went on record as supporting the McKinley candidacy.

---

*This association was comprised of representatives from only one-fifth of all black newspapers in the country.

A number of black leaders, Thomas Wallace Swan, Bishop Alexander Walters, Bishop Levi Jenkins Coppin, Judge Edward C. Walker, and Rev. John P. Sampson, could see "neither wisdom or expedience" in supporting either party and sent out a call for the formation of a national Afro-American party to run national, state and municipal candidates in 1900. The proposed platform was vigorously anti-imperialist and pro-civil rights. [See Appendix III—Ed.]. That no action followed this call is indicated by the fact that by early September, Bishop Walters had signed a statement with some members of the Afro-American Council to "unreservedly endorse the foreign and domestic policy of the national Republican administration." Faced with the choice of a McKinley or a Bryan, many blacks chose "the lesser evil."

"Negro Republican Delegates From the South Unseated"

[From the *American Eagle,* St. Louis, Mo.:]

When McKinley was nominated years ago he depended almost entirely upon the Negro vote of the South, but his term of office having proved so beneficial to the trusts or money interests of the country, they rallied to him in such numbers that the Negro vote was not needed, hence the unseating of the delegations from the South, which were largely colored, and the recognition of the "lily whites" in the Mark Hanna Republican convention. Where the Republican party finds they can carry their point without the Negro, why Mr. Negro's not wanted.

Cleveland *Gazette*, July 7, 1900

Negroes for Bryan and Stevenson

The Negro National Democratic League, at its recent sixth biennial session in Kansas City, Mo., issued the following address to the public:

We, the chosen representatives of the Negroes of the United States, who are opposed to the reelection of President William McKinley and the Republican nominee for Vice President, Theodore Roosevelt, in national convention assembled, appealing to the intelligence, good reason and sober judgment of the Negroes of the country, do declare and set forth the following:

Republicans Arraigned

Since the Emancipation the Negro has been counted in all states as an ally to the Republican party, who owed it such faith and devotion that whatever the issues presented between the parties, or whatever treatment he received at the hands of those having the management of political, national and party affairs, he had no right and was counted an ingrate to refuse to vote the party ticket. His duty has been during all the time to fight the issues of the war again, while the Republican party has been engaged in exerting its every effort to forget, forgive and shake hands across the bloody chasm. Indeed, the white Republican never mentions the "late unpleasantness" except when he wishes to appeal to the Negro to remain loyal to the party. If it be the good of the white Republican to forgive and forget it is doubly so for the Negro.

Office should never be the inducement to party support; but the distribution of office has been made a part of practical politics. No Republican President since the election of Grant, in 1868, could have been elected without the vote of the Negro in the pivotal states of Ohio, Illinois, Indiana, Michigan, New Jersey or New York, yet the Republican party has never given any fitting recognition to the Negroes in these states.

Advice to Negroes

The citizen is of right entitled to the full enjoyment of all the rights, privileges and protection guaranteed by our constitution and its amendments. But the enforcement of these rights, the protection of life and property, Republican officials charged with that duty have repeatedly declared, was a matter exclusively in the keeping of the several states of the Union. A denial of either had no federal aspect is the answer given to the repeated appeals to the federal authority; and until this position is receded from, the Negro must turn to the sovereign states. It is, therefore, to use the words of Prof. Booker T. Washington, "the plain duty of the Negro to make friends of the southern white men." If peace and good will we would have, we will get it only upon the terms agreeable to and acceptable by the southern white men. If we would have these terms—agreeable and acceptable to ourselves, we must enter upon such friendly relations as we can treat with him. This we can only do by showing that we are not unfriendly to his aims and purposes.

Loyalty of Democrats

Democrats are not natural enemies of the Negro; the assertion that Republicans freed the Negro is not wholly true. There was not in the country 75,000 able-bodied Republicans when the call to arms to defend the Union was issued, and more than 60% of the soldiers that enlisted under this first call were loyal democrats.

A Division of the Negro Vote

The intelligence of the country—Republicans whose party loyalty cannot be doubted—agree that division of the Negro vote is a thing to be desired, and will work good for the nation and race. It is the Negro partisan alone who insists upon a blind adhesion to party without regard to the issues. The white Republican renounces his party faith and very quickly cancels his obligations to the party. When will the Negro be able to balance his account?

President McKinley Denounced

The record of President McKinley's administration has but little, if anything, to commend it to the Negro, or upon which it can make any claim for his support. The administration at Washington is expressly opposed to the appointment of Negroes as commissioned officers in the army, though President McKinley on account of dauntless courage and heroic bravery reluctantly commissioned nine Negroes second lieutenants. He nevertheless at his earliest convenient time gave them the option of being mustered out or returning to the companies as privates, and to emphasize his determination not to have the Negro placed on equal footing with the white soldier, refused to commission Negroes to office in the black regiments, enlisted for service in the Philippines higher than that of captain, and this is but in keeping with President McKinley's advice to our race at Tuskegee, that "the Negro youth should not aspire to the unattainable."

Patriotism and Loyalty of the Negro

The glorious and untarnished record of the Negro soldiers, in all the wars of the country, has been a source of pride to the race, and it remains for Colonel Theodore Roosevelt, now candidate for Vice President on the Republican ticket, to first reflect upon the bravery and heroism, first to slander the men and the race to which they belong, who saved the day at El Caney, San Juan Hill, and gave to him the opportunity to pose as he does, as the hero of the land forces in the Spanish-American War.

Must Study the Issues

We respectfully invite the men of our race to an earnest consideration of the issues to be determined in this campaign.

We hold that the policy known as imperialism is hostile to liberty and leans toward the destruction of government by the people themselves. We insist that the subjugation of any people is "criminal aggression" and is a pronounced departure from the first principles taught and declared by Washington, Lincoln, Jefferson, and all the great statesmen who have guided the country through the many dangers of the past. Whether the people who will be affected by such policy be or consider themselves Negroes, nor yet because the Majority of them are black, is of but little moment. They are by nature entitled to liberty and freedom. We being an oppressed people, to use the words of Daniel O'Connell, should be the "loudest in our protestations against the oppression of others." It may be that our government can and will govern the people of the Philippines and Puerto Rico better than they can govern themselves; but with equal force can it be said that the white men of the South can govern the localities in which the Negro is a majority better than they can govern themselves, and if we are prepared to support an administration that is engaged in suppressing liberty and freedom in our so-called possessions, why not be consistent and cease to complain of the same thing being done in any part of our own land? A nation cannot oppress a people without the borders of the country without sooner or later introducing some such oppression within its borders.

Condemnation of the Gold Standard

We declare that Congress can fix the money of the land, and whatever ratio it fixes that will be the money. The Negro is not an investor of capital. Those who insist that gold alone shall be the money of the land give no employment to the Negro, though employing thousands of laborers. He is not affected by the money market, the more the volume of money in the country, the more he will have, and gold will always be controlled by the few.

The control of the commodities and necessities of the country by the aggregation, concentration and combination of capital, commonly called "trusts," threatens the life of the businesses and industries of the country, making a vast army of unemployed, to make room for which the Negro will find himself pushed aside in those avenues in which he now has but small representation, and into which he may seek entrance, and in the avenues where we are already shut out and discriminated against, our opportunities of entering are lessened and our ventures hampered by the direct influence of the trusts.

Endorse Democratic Principles and Ticket

To the end that our country, its constitution and its government as established by the fathers be maintained; that the Declaration of Independence be not construed away; that the Negro take his place among the people that compose our citizenship, thinking out the issues and acting upon them with that high intelligence that characterizes the highest type of American citizenship; that the rights of the common people be given as much sober thought as the rights of capital; that a bond of friendship be welded between the Negro and the white men among whom he lives, thus insuring protection of life and property and the enjoyment of all the rights guaranteed in the constitution; that hypocrisy be defeated; we urge that our race support the Democratic party in the coming election of that great commoner of the plain people, the tribune of the rights of man as against money—William Jennings Bryan and Adlai E. Stevenson.

> F. L. McGhee, Chairman, Committee on Address; Geo. F. Taylor, President of League; W. T. Scott, Vice President; Jas. A. Ross, Secretary; A. E. Manning, Chairman, Executive Committee; Julius F. Taylor; Lawrence A. Newby; Prof. H. R. Graham; J. L. Edmonds; C. J. Walker; W. J. Johnson; Dr. J. C. Williams; Theodore Frye; and J. H. W. Howard

Chicago *Broad Ax*, July 21, 1900

"BOXER REBELLION HURTING THE REPUBLICANS"

The situation in China is attracting much attention in this country. It is indeed unfortunate that it has become necessary for us to withdraw troops from the Philippines for service in the Celestial Kingdom. It tends towards the further embarassment of the administration and works to the benefit of the Democratic leaders, who have declared that Imperialism is the paramount issue in the campaign.

Richmond *Planet*, July 21, 1900

"The Democratic Party Represents Domestic Imperialism"

This Democratic candidate for the Presidency represents the principles of a party that knows no law or reason, and neither does it regard human rights, nor civil and political liberty. The Democratic party, as it is represented by Mr. Bryan, is the unequivocal advocate of imperialism. . . .

Washington *Bee*, July 28, 1900

"Why Albert M. Thomas Switched to Bryan"

[Albert M. Thomas, "a well-known New York attorney and Republican of color," recently said:]

My reason in a nutshell is my conviction that it will be in the best interest of the country and incidentally for my race to elect Bryan and Stevenson this fall. To be more specific, I cannot agree with the administration's policy towards the Philippines, Cuba, and Puerto Rico. I do not believe in the first place that we should have purchased for $20,000,000 or any sum Spain's hopeless war in the Philippines, nor the avowed purpose of forcibly retaining the possession of or suzerainty over the islands against the will of the people, after their subjugation, purchased also by some of the best blood of our American citizens. I condemn the dilatory tactics towards Cuba. I do not believe the Puerto Rican tariff just for the Puerto Ricans or even consistent with ourselves, and I condemn discrimination no less against the individual than against any part of our domain. . .

Cleveland *Gazette*, August 4, 1900

"North Carolina Imperialism"

[From the Chicago *Inter-Ocean*:]

Does Mr. Bryan's zeal for "consent of the governed" extend to native American citizens or is it limited to Malays? This interesting question is raised by the playful antics of Mr. Bryan's Democratic "Red Shirt" supporters in North Carolina. There is pending in that state a constitutional amendment whose avowed purpose is to deprive Negroes of their suffrage. This measure is advocated with great fervor by Democratic Bryanites. Why does not Mr. Bryan hasten to the old North State and point out to his Red Shirt followers their imperialistic error? Can it be that for the sake of votes Mr. Bryan is willing to waive "consent of the governed" in North Carolina?

Washington *Bee*, August 11, 1900

"IMPERIALISM LEADS TO DESPOTISM"

[From a letter to the editor of the *Freeman* written by George E. Taylor, President, National Negro Democratic League, dated Oskaloosa, Ia., July 30th, 1900:]

That a large percentage of the two million and a half Negro voters of this country are to-day arrayed with the Democratic party no well-informed person will deny. And . . . I desire to say through the *Freeman* that we believe that imperialism leads to despotism and we consider that the present administration has strong imperialistic tendencies; we also believe in the right of all men to govern themselves, hence we oppose the policy of the administration towards the Filipinos; we are firm believers in the Monroe Doctrine, and since the present administration has practically annulled this doctrine we oppose the action; we are opposed to the propagation of private trusts and combines, and consider that the administration is in full sympathy with such trusts. . .

Indianapolis *Freeman*, August 11, 1900

"NEGROES SHOULD NOT FIGHT IN CHINA"

[In a letter to the editor of the N.Y. *Age*, written July 27, the venerable Bishop Henry M. Turner, of Atlanta, Ga., said:]

"Suppose the Chinese have murdered and killed a few diplomats and missionaries, they have not done half or one-third of the devilment that has been done in this country to our race.

"They want black men to enlist in the United States Army, in this section, but none shall if I can prevent it, and none will but the low, ignorant and scullion class. This is not our war, and the black man that puts a gun upon his shoulder to go and fight China should find the bottom of the ocean before he gets there."

The bishop, as usual, strikes out swift and strong. There are many who think as he does in this matter. From a race standpoint there are plenty of "Boxers' (Red Shirts, Ku Klux and the like) in the South who are greatly in need of the presence of soldiers. For the protection of the life and property of *citizens*, as well as government property, a goodly portion of our army should be kept in that section as well as out west where Indians are feared.

Cleveland *Gazette*, August 13, 1900

"Against the Democratic Party Platform"

The Democratic platform declares that any government not based on the consent of the governed is a tyranny. By justifying the Philippine insurgents it declares also that any portion of the population has the inherent right to withdraw its allegiance. And it holds further that coercion cannot justly be used against a section of the people in rebellion.

All the claptrap contained in this platform about the primary right of man and the Declaration of Independence does not avail to conceal these plain enunciations of policy and principle. They stand out clearly and impressively. They fix an issue about which the battle at the polls may intelligently be fought. They were the doctrines of the Southern Confederacy, and are the doctrines of secession wherever found. They also are the doctrines of crimes and riot. . . .

In adopting such a platform the Democratic party was clearly within the province of free thought and free speech. No one will gainsay the right to revive the issue which the American people thought was settled. . . .

Kansas City *American Citizen,* August 17, 1900

"Afro-American Council Should Endorse Neither Party"

We heartily concur with the *Colored American* that it would be a mistake for the council to endorse either political party as a whole. While we are uncompromisingly democratic we would not undertake to impugn the motives of that organization by securing a political endorsement for our party. We are led to believe that the sober-thinking race men will not insist upon such a step.

Hon. W. Calvin Chase, of D.C.; Col. James Hill of Miss., and Congressman White [all Republicans] are successful politicians. Aye, more than this, they are statesmen of the first rank. . . .

Indianapolis *Freeman,* August 18, 1900

"Grand Old Party Opposed in its Philippine Policy"

The revolt against McKinley and Hannaism among the Afro-Americans is spreading to all parts of the country and there is not a day but what we receive letters and information setting forth the fact that influential colored men in their respective communities are cutting loose from the grand old party which is now engaged in establishing slavery and polygamy in the new territorial possessions and shooting liberty and civilization into the Philippines.

The following letter is one of the many we have lately received.

Charleston, W. Va., Aug. 12, 1900.
Julius F. Taylor, Esq., Editor of the
Broad Ax, Chicago, Ill.

Dear Sir:—Please send to our headquarters some of your papers. As you can see by our headings, we have organized to support Democracy's principles and would be pleased to circulate your papers. . . .

Yours respectfully,
John Patton, Chairman, State Committee of Negro Democrats of West Virginia; Elijah Hurt, Vice Chairman; Allen Dehoney, Secretary; Prof. Barnert and Spencer, Hayden, Huntington, Charles Baines, McDowell, Wm. Hayney, Point Pleasant; Charles Smith, Anthony Harris, Andrew Jefferson, Wm. Brannon, Floyd Hairston and Peyton Carr, members of the State Committee. . . .

Chicago *Broad Ax*, August 18, 1900

"IMPERIALISM IS A SUBTERFUGE OF THE DEMOCRATIC PARTY"

Certainly the Democratic candidate for the Presidency doesn't know what imperialism means. He must be either ignorant as to its definition or he is of the opinion that he and his Democratic satellites can fool the ignorant masses. If there is not an imperial government in the South, then the Empire of China is not an imperial government. There is . . . a certain class of people [in the] South who have been disfranchised and are compelled to be governed by a set of renegades and cutthroats against their consent. This class must submit to those who have no regard for human rights or civil liberty. Where, then, is the consistency of the Democratic party and those who claim to be not favorable to expansion?

*   *   *

The people should not be misled as to the term of imperialism because it is only a subterfuge of the Democratic party.

*   *   *

"A NEGRO BRYAN PAPER"

We have received the *Colored Citizen*, an eighteen-page paper edited and published in the city of New York, Charles E. Brown and Ralph E. Langston, business managers. This paper is published in the interest of Bryan and the Democratic party. New York is the only State in the Union where the Democrats treat the Negro as a man and a citizen.

The Bee knows Mr. Langston and several of the New York United Colored Democracy. . . . The *Colored Citizen* has the sympathy of *The Bee* in this hour of democratic struggle for existence.

Washington *Bee*, August 18, 1900

"NEGRO DEMOCRATS IN MARYLAND"

Baltimore, Md., Aug. 22, 1900.

The colored people of Maryland are very much dissatisfied. Meetings are being held throughout the city. Loome is the biggest Negro democrat in the State. The Negro democrats and independents denounced *The Bee* as the paid organ of the Republicans.

Washington *Bee*, August 25, 1900

"AGAINST BRYAN"

The speech of Mr. Bryan accepting the Democratic nomination, with the exception of an avowal for a "scuttle" policy in the Philippines, is a waste of political truisms and a violation of fact. Mr. Bryan's text is his favorite mystery, that this campaign is a contest between the man and the dollar . . . he apologizes for approving the Paris treaty by saying he thought it "safer to trust to the American people than to diplomacy with an unfriendly nation." In other words, he favored taking sacred obligations to other nations in Paris, merely to repudiate those obligations later. . . .

Mr. Bryan admits that Spain's title to the Philippines was extinguished and that we made no promise of independence to the Filipinos. Yet he questions our title, falsely asserts that "we accepted the services of the Filipinos with full knowledge that they were fighting for independence," and says that "history furnishes no example of turpitude baser than ours." This is a slanderous distortion of fact. The Filipinos never fought for independence until a minority of them fought us. When Dewey went to Manila they were not fighting at all. We have kept every promise we ever made to the Filipinos.

Mr. Bryan speaks of "forcible annexation," and says we are not "innocent purchasers of the Philippines, because certain Tagals disputed our title." Certain Indians once disputed our title to this continent. . . . According to Mr. Bryan's theory, George Washington, who sent Wayne to conquer Ohio, and Thomas Jefferson, who bought Louisiana, were respectively a thief and a receiver of stolen goods. If it is a theft to keep the Philippines—and that is what Mr. Bryan says—then it was a theft to keep Texas and California. The Mexicans disputed our title to both.

"A republic can have no subjects," solemnly asserts Mr. Bryan. Then this has never been a republic, for it has always had what Mr. Bryan chooses to call "subjects"—people whom it governed without their consent. We have ruled red men without their consent for more than a century. Jefferson, Mr. Bryan's model, ruled white subjects in Louisiana. Mr. Bryan's friends in North Carolina have just added 75,000 black men to the number of our subjects.

Mr. Bryan dodges the practical question of the present fitness of the Filipinos for self-government by solemnly reiterating Clay's dictum that "it is the doctrine of thrones that man is too ignorant to govern himself."

Indianapolis *Recorder,* August 25, 1900

"McKINLEY ENDORSED"

As a result of the resolution adopted at the Afro-American Press Association Monday night a number of the members of the association met Tuesday evening and prepared the following statement:

The undersigned members of the National Afro-American Press Association very much regret that the impression has gone abroad from the action of the association last night that the association is unfriendly to the administration of President McKinley. This is not true. It has been the uniform policy of the association not to commit itself to any partisan endorsement as an organization.

The undersigned members of the association, who constitute more than five-sixths of the membership present, unreservedly endorse the foreign and domestic policy of the national Republican administration, and believe that the best interests of the country at large, and the Afro-American people in particular, will be served by a consistent support of McKinley and Roosevelt in the coming election.

Cyrus Field Adams. *The Appeal*, Chicago, Ill.
T. Thomas Fortune. *The Age*, New York City
W. H. Stewart. *American Baptist*, Louisville, Ky.
George L. Knox. *The Freeman,* Indianapolis, Ind.
John C. Dancy. *A.M.E. Zion Review*, Charlotte, North Carolina
D. R. Wilkins. *The Conservator*, Chicago, Ill.
J. W. Wheeler. *The Palladium,* St. Louis, Mo.
I. B. Scott. *S.W. Christian Advocate,* New Orleans, La.
W. A. Pledger. *Age*, Atlanta, Ga.
J. H. Deveaux. *Tribune*, Savannah, Ga.
J. Chavis. *Express*, Dallas, Texas.
C. H. Tandy. *The Afro-American,* St. Louis, Mo.
T. T. Allain. *The Forum,* Houston, Texas.
George P. Stewart. *The Recorder*, Indianapolis, Ind.
L. T. Fox. *Preacher-Safeguard*, Kosciusko, Miss.
J. R. Marshall. *The Bee*, Paducah, Ky.
R. R. Wright. *College Journal*, Savannah, Ga.
H. T. Kealing. *A.M.E. Church Review*, Philadelphia, Pa.
James Lewis. *Republican Courier*, New Orleans, La.
J. Q. Adams. *The Appeal*, St. Paul, Minn.
J. P. Green. *The Bee*, Washington, D.C.
W. V. Penn. *The Appeal*, Louisville, Ky.
George H. White. *True Reformer*, Littleton, N.C.

Indianapolis *Recorder,* September 1, 1900

"Support for the Administration"

The cry of imperialism is a twin attraction set up to garner the discontents and the disgruntled ones. It is but a shield under which those who are opposed to the administration owing to disappointments may safely and respectably masquerade. Happily, they are but few. We glory in the ascendency of the American flag. Chance and the fortunes of war brought us our foreign possessions, fortitude and valor will secure them for us. No fear of oppression from the government at Washington needs to obtain.

Indianapolis *Freeman,* September 8, 1900

"Negroes Support the Republican Party"

The undersigned members of the Afro-American Council "unreservedly endorse the foreign and domestic policy of the national Republican administration but this is not an action of the council per se":

Bishop A. Walters, Ernest Lyons, Cyrus Field Adams, John P. Green, J.R.A. Crossland, Nelson C. Crews, J. Silas Harris, C. H. Tandy, J. W. Wheeler, O. M. Wood, A. R. Chime, J. H. Pelham, W. E. Henderson, John C. Dancy, J. W. Thompson, J. S. Caldwell, T. W. Whittaker, George W. Lytle, T. T. Allain, Jordan Chavis, J. P. Rivers, Hugh A. Rouse, J. E. Rodgers, John J. Blackshear, Edward E. Gilliam, Judson W. Lyons, S. A. Furniss, John A. Puryear, O. V. Royall, G. W. Hardimon, E. L. Bell, Gurley Brewer, Foster Barnett, P. A. Lord, W. A. Pledger, D. M. Roberts, W. S. Scarboro, J. Frank Blagburn, O. W. Mitchem, G. L. Knox, C. W. Newton, J. B. Colbert, A. Wakefield, W. A. Alexander, James Lewis, F. D. Welch, A. L. Murray, David Jenkins, Bishop G. W. Clinton, W. A. Kersey and J. Raynor.

Indianapolis *Recorder,* September 8, 1900

"Send Negro Troops to the South, Not China"

Prominent Afro-Americans of Chicago are opposed to colored troops being sent by the government to fight in China. An expression of disapproval of the war department's determination to use for that purpose the Ninth cavalry, now en route to the Philippines, was forwarded to the President in a petition praying that the order be revoked and that the men be sent to the southern part of the United States.

Cleveland *Gazette,* September 8, 1900

"McKinley Not Endorsed"

[From the *Weekly Echo,* Hot Springs, Arkansas:]

Fifty delegates were in attendance to the Afro-American Press Association. The resolution for the endorsement of President McKinley's administration was defeated. Editor Lewis, of the *Freeman,* introduced the resolution. The fight against it was on the ground of McKinley's failure to stand by the Negroes of the South. T. Thomas Fortune of the New York *Age* took a prominent part in the discussion. He said that the Negroes of the United States had supported the Republican administration, shed their blood on the soil of Cuba, Puerto Rico, and the Philippines and will follow the Old Flag wherever she goes.

Indianapolis *Freeman,* September 15, 1900

"Negro Democrats Oppose Imperialism"

Colored Democratic voters of Maryland and Virginia, who temporarily reside in Washington, met last Tuesday night to perfect an organization [whose name is] The United Colored Democratic League of Maryland and Virginia.

The following officers were elected: President, Prince Robinson; Vice President, John Duker; Secretary, George Bowie; Treasurer, William Bell; Chaplain, James Anderson; Sergeant at Arms, Richard Cook; Chairman of the Executive Committee, R. W. Gillam; Chairman of the Campaign Committee, Horace Williams.

The following resolution was presented and adopted:

Resolved that we do endorse the platform adopted by the Democratic party at Kansas City, which antagonizes the trusts and imperialism. . . .

Washington *Bee,* September 22, 1900

"Bryan Misleads the People"

[From a communication of John E. Bruce:]

How easy it is for a shrewd man like Mr. Bryan to mislead the common people by specious argument and to appeal to their passions with such sublimated rot as the following from his recent Chicago speech: "If the people in Puerto Rico are to be denied the protection of the Constitution, we can well imagine that the Filipinos will not fare any better."

Why does not Mr. Bryan say something about the people in the southern states of America who are denied the protection of the constitution and tell his hearers why they are denied the protection which he craves for the Puerto Ricans and the Filipinos and who it is that denies them the protection of the constitution?

Before the administration has had a fair opportunity to show to the people of these new possessions what it is trying to do to promote their welfare and advance their civil and political interests, the calamity howlers . . . are prejudging it and impugning its motives without any positive knowledge or proofs of the heinous offenses they are charging up against the administration.

Indianapolis *Freeman,* September 22, 1900

IMPERIALISM—THE DEMOCRATIC TOCSIN

(Prepared by Dr. Ernest Lyon)

According to Democratic definition, and we take the highest Democratic authority, viz., Mr. Bryan himself, the standard-bearer of that Party: "Imperialism is government without the consent of the governed," or government by force, pure and simple. This form of government, Mr. Bryan declares, exists in the Philippine Islands, and he charges the Republican party with responsibility for its existence.

It is unnecessary to enter into the history of the acquisition of these Islands. . . . It is sufficient to say, however, that the Philippine Islands, in the main, have been acquired in the same manner in which the territory of Louisiana, Alabama and other portions which now constitute the geographical area of the United States [were acquired] namely by purchase and without the consent of the inhabitants. In the same manner these Islands now in question came into our possession.

It will be remembered that the Louisiana purchase . . . was purchased from France. . . . The result of that purchase has been so beneficial that no American citizen, Democrat or Republican, would now say aught against the wisdom of that transaction. It was the policy of Jefferson's administration to annex that territory to the United States, and it did annex it. But it is not the policy of the present administration to annex the Philippine Islands. The policy is to put down insurrection, to establish a stable government, and to turn over the same to the Filipino as soon as he is capable of self-government.

But for the sake of argument, let us see which of the two parties is guilty of Imperialism. Let us see whether there is any sincerity in the boasted sympathy of the Democratic party for the Filipino, thousands of miles away, whose right and liberty they declare the Republicans have robbed.

The constitution of the United States says: "All governments derive their just powers from the consent of the governed." Now Imperialism is to govern citizens without their consent, through force and intimidation. Such being the case, we charge that the Democratic party has violated the constitution of the United States in that they are now governing seven or eight millions of Negro citizens without their consent. For example in North Carolina, in South Carolina, Louisiana and Mississippi they have directly disfranchised three millions of Negro citizens, and they are now governing them without their consent. Therefore, the Democratic Party is not only guilty of the theory, but of the practice of the imperialism which they feign to repudiate. Now Mr. Bryan knows that this code of fraud, intimidation and disfranchisement, which is the very embodiment of imperialism, exists in the South among the Negroes, his own fellow citizens, yet he is silent. He never says one word against this imperialistic mode in the South, and what is more alarming, he is the close friend and companion of Ben Tillman and the other enemies of our constitution.

Compared with this we state the policy of the Republican party, which accords to every citizen the right to cast his ballot and to have it counted and cast. It is the policy of the Republican party to protect every man in his constitutional rights in the peaceful enjoyment of happiness, in the acquisition of property and the preservation of life. . . .

* * *

"DEMOCRATS IGNORE LACK OF 'CONSENT OF THE GOVERNED'
IN THE SOUTH"

[From a communication of W. T. Menard, Washington, D.C., Sept. 5, 1900:]

William Jennings Bryan, the octopus candidate for the Presidency; Senator J. K. Jones; Ben Tillman; John T. Morgan; J.S.C. Blackburn, and other high priests of Democracy are shouting themselves hoarse over the treatment of the Filipinos and Puerto Ricans, contending that the McKinley Administration is forcing upon these people a "government without the consent of the governed." The inhabitants of the Philippines and Puerto Rico are, as yet, citizens de facto of the United States, and are being accorded the same government and treatment shown the inhabitants of Alaska, New Mexico, and other territorial jurisdiction of this country. It is a notorious fact that the Democratic party has always ruled the South "without the consent of the governed," not alone its Negro "subjects," but white ones also, a case in point being Kentucky, where Taylor, the Republican candidate for governor, received 2,500 votes more than did his Democratic opponent. Still the Democratic legislature and courts of that State decided that Taylor was not entitled to the office. . . .

Washington *Colored American,* September 29, 1900

"OUTRAGED FEELINGS OF A LOYAL AMERICAN SOLDIER—
SPOKEN FROM THE TOMB"

Steubenville, Ohio—Following is an extract from a letter received here, written by Patrick Mason, sergeant of Company I, Twenty-fourth United States Infantry, who died recently in our new possessions:

Corregidor, P. I., Nov. 18, 1899

I have not had any fighting to do since I've been here and don't care to do any. I feel sorry for those people and all that have come under the control of the United States. I don't believe they will be justly dealt by. The first thing in the morning is the "Nigger" and the last thing at night is "Nigger." You have no idea the way these people are treated by the Americans here. I know their (American) feeling toward them (Filipinos) as they speak their opinions in my presence, thinking I am white. . . . The poor whites don't believe that anyone has any right to live but the white American, or to enjoy any rights or privileges the white man enjoys. I must stop here. You are right in your opinions. I must not say much, as I am a soldier. The natives are a patient, burden-bearing people.

Cleveland *Gazette,* September 29, 1900

"IMPERIALISM NOT A VITAL QUESTION FOR NEGROES"

The highflown notion of Imperialism will have no terrors for the Negroes. It is not the question which agitates them at all. And should it be an issue, an alarming one, it could not at this stage of the Negroes' progress be a vital one.

* * *

"EXPANSIONISM IS NOT IMPORTANT"

The present campaign presents issues of a very mixed kind. Both parties are opposing the "trusts." The Democratic party is opposed to expansion simply because the Republicans espouse it. They espouse it not from a spirit of territorial or mercenary greed but because chance and fortune has so decreed. They stoutly and justly maintain that the nation had no choice in the matter. But as to the thing of expansion itself, the nation could get along as well in either event: expansion or anti-expansion.

Indianapolis *Freeman,* October 6, 1900

AS TO EXPANSION

"Prof. Kelley Miller and Hon. A. H. Grimke
Express Their Views on This Important Issue"

Washington, D.C.—Prof. Kelley Miller, in his interview in the Washington *Post* some months ago, expressed the prevalent opinion among colored people when he said:

To be plain about the matter, I don't think there is a single colored man, out of office and out of the insane asylum, who favors the so-called expansion policy. Whether or not they will organize under the banner of Mr. Atkinson is another question. I don't think we are yet ready for a departure so radical.

President McKinley may not know it and his henchmen may attempt to disguise it, but it is nevertheless a fact that in the states north, east, and west where they constitute the balance of power, there is a great deal of unrest and hostile feeling against the administration among the colored people. They are not so much concerned about the policy of expansion as they are about the cruel and inhuman treatment which they receive at home and the desertion of a President. . . . In fact our opposition to the policy of the administration in its desire to get possession of the Philippines is because of wrongs we have suffered at home. Ex-Consul A. H. Grimke puts it aptly when he says:

> From my own observation I know that the expansion policy of the administration is very unpopular with the Negro. The absolute supineness of the chief executive on the subject of Negro lynchings makes them shudder for other peoples who may come under the yoke.

Cleveland *Gazette,* October 13, 1900

"JOHN E. BRUCE AGAINST IMPERIALISM"

The letter subjoined was published in the Washington, D.C. *Colored American* a few months ago and was written by the Afro-American, J. E. Bruce, now employed at the national Republican committee headquarters in New York City to write political letters to our newspapers. . . .

> We know of no instance where it has ever thrown the ægis of its protection around outraged citizens on our own shores. As Bishop Holly pointedly says: 'A race vaunting its materialistic achievements in the arts of destruction as well as utility also boasts because of its brute strength that it is destined to dominate the whole earth in its self-conceited ambition! But in their solid stupidity they forget that the inheritance of the earth is not promised to the haughty and proud. . . .'
> American brag and bluster just now permeates the entire country and has crossed the seas, where it is doing duty lauding American prowess on sea and land and spelling brotherhood with five letters—P-O-W-E-R. After the conquest of the Philippines is complete, the partition of China accomplished and the subjugation of Turkey, which is to be frightened to death by an American war vessel, is a fixed fact, the great American nation will turn its attention to conquering one or two new worlds. Just now it is drunken with power, flushed with victory, strong in its own strength. . . .
> We are on the threshold of a new century, and awful responsibilities devolve upon this nation. If in discharging them it eliminates the element of righteousness as successfully as it has eliminated the Negro while coming forward as a world power, it will need no prophet or seer to read the final chapter in its history. . . .
> The Anglo-Saxon race has gotten the idea that the earth belongs to

it—the way it is staking off claims in Africa, Asia, North and South America and wherever it gets a foothold.

Bruce Grit [John E. Bruce]
Albany, N.Y., July 2, 1900

Cleveland *Gazette,* October 20, 1900

To Colored Voters
An Address by Three Eminent Friends of Their Race

Headquarters of the Colored Democratic Central Committee.

Dear Sirs: Enclosed you will find a copy of an address issued by three eminent friends of our race, men whose loyalty to it has never been questioned. This copy is sent you in order that you may read it and ponder over its contents.

In addition to the above letter referred to, we will ask you as a race lover and upholder of right and justice whether you are in favor of the following:

Slavery in the Sulu Islands?

Polygamy in the Sulu Islands?

Do you favor taxing Puerto Ricans without giving them representation?

Are you in favor of freedom and independence of thought and action in the United States?

Then why do you sanction, favor and support McKinley in his effort to shoot the Filipinos because they want liberty and freedom under an independent government of their own?

Lawrence A. Newby, Chairman
Colored Democratic Central Committee
S.A.T. Watkins, Secretary

*   *   *

Boston, Mass., Oct. 4.—To the Colored People of the United States: We, the undersigned, address you at one of the most important points in your history. If ever there was a war of races in this world the war now going on in the Philippine Islands is precisely that. Yet if there is anything which the colored race in this country has to dread, and the white race also, it is just such a war.

Every day in the Philippines is already training our young American soldiers to the habit of thinking that the white man, as such, is the rightful ruler of all other men. This is seen, for instance, in the fact that these very soldiers, in writing home letters from the seat of war, describe the inhabitants of the Philippines more and more constantly as "niggers," thus giving a new lease on life to a word which was previously dying out among us. Every defender of the war in Congress sustains the contest on the assumed ground that the Filipinos are unfit for freedom, although

Admiral Dewey at first described them as more fit for it than the Cubans; and Senator Hoar describes them to be probably better fitted than any race on the two American continents south of ourselves.

In other words, freedom is to become for the new Republican party a matter of complexion. If this doctrine is to prevail, what hope is there for the colored race in the United States? The answer is easy; there is in that case no hope at all. In the name of the old anti-slavery sentiment we call upon you to resist this great danger, even if you have for that purpose to turn your backs on the party you once had reason to love.

This danger can evidently not be resisted by any further voting for the Republican party. In other days that party freed the slaves and passed Amendments to the United States Constitution for the protection of those who had been slaves. These Amendments are now steadily set aside and the Republican party shows no sign of raising a finger in their defense. There have been far more outrages on the American Negro during one term of McKinley than two terms of Cleveland. On the other hand, the southern Democrats are at least doing the colored race this service; that they as a rule oppose the national policy of imperialism. This may seem an inconsistency, but it is really very simple. The very fact of their unwillingness to give equal rights to the American Negro makes them unwilling to undertake the government of ten millions more belonging to the colored race. This much, at least, experience has taught them. Thus far, at any rate, they are on your side.

The undersigned, trained from youth in the strictest school of anti-slavery convictions, are following up the same early training when they now write to you. We wish to warn you that the imperialistic Republican party of today is not the liberty-loving party of that name which it was formerly. . . . The time is past when you can safely give to it your implicit support. We warn you that the American Negro must henceforth think for himself and must cut adrift from every organization which wars on darker races, as such, and begins to talk again of the "natural supremacy of the Anglo-Saxon." We fought through a four years' war to get rid of that doctrine, and enlisted nearly 200,000 black soldiers for the purpose. It is too soon to see such a theory brought up again. It rests with you to make it impossible.

> Thomas Wentworth Higginson
> William Lloyd Garrison Jr.
> George S. Boutwell

*   *   *

REPUBLICAN DOCTRINE

One who steals a ham is a thief.
One who steals a fortune is a financier.
One who assists in stealing the Philippines is a patriot.

*   *   *

"An Anti-Imperialist Negro Reader"

Against the tyrannical colonial despotism of England, our forefathers protested, rebelled, fought and conquered. Today, McKinley has forced this government to occupy the position assumed by England in the 1770's while the so-called semi-civilized Filipinos are strugglers for liberty, freedom, independence. Shall we, the Negroes, be so forgetful of the bondage under which we were ground for two hundred and fifty years as not to sympathize with the benighted, down-trodden Filipino? Can we forget that the Filipino is related to us as are the Cuban and Puerto Rican? Is it not clear that the present administration has shown clearly that dark races have no favorable consideration?

If one-half the Negroes of the country should vote for Bryan next month and thus teach the Republicans that they are no longer political slaves, it would be a broad strike in the direction of establishing political standing for the race.

Why should Negroes vote for McKinley this year, because of the action he took in not bringing the murderers of Postmaster Baker to trial?

Should the Negroes vote for McKinley because he went to Atlanta and wore a Confederate badge and exclaimed, "This is the proudest moment of my life"? I hope not.

> Respectfully,
> A Negro Reader

Chicago *Broad Ax,* October 27, 1900

"Bryan A Demagogue"

William Jennings Bryan shows himself a demagogue of the first class when he whines about the warring Filipino being denied the right to a voice in his government, when the governing part of his party, southern Democracy, is disfranchising Afro-American citizens by hundreds of thousands. . . .

Cleveland *Gazette,* October 27, 1900

"Pro-Filipino Bryan Ignores the Negro at Home"

Mr. Bryan has trimmed his sails to every gale that blows except to the Negro at home. Even the poor Filipinos come in for a very respectable share of attention. He has the hardihood to declare in favor of their independence, total, absolute independence, and yet here stands the American Negro, right in the bosom of the country, the people that the National Convention at Philadelphia felt its duty or policy to notice, whom the convention at Kansas City failed to notice either as a duty or policy. This same unconcern is shared by Mr. Bryan. He has been asked dozens of times about North Carolina, and while he has replied as many times, he has never yet once answered.

Indianapolis *Freeman,* November 3, 1900

NEGRO PRESS SUPPORTS THE REPUBLICANS

There are more than 200 Afro-American papers published in the United States, and of these but six are supporting the Democratic ticket. The others are true to the Grand Old Party.

Indianapolis *Recorder,* November 3, 1900

"THE ANTI-IMPERIALISM OF THE SAVANNAH *Gazette*"

[From the *Gazette*, Savannah, Georgia:]

"The President offers many inducements to the Filipinos to lay down their arms and accept such terms as this government chooses to give them. While we are Americans and honor the American flag, we cannot fully endorse the Filipino policy of this government, especially since the people of that faraway country are mostly Negroes—our distant kindred —and with us 'blood is thicker than water' and a common destiny more than a non-protecting flag at home."

Well, suppose you don't endorse it? Neither do you endorse the policy of being disfranchised in Georgia but what are you going to do about it? The Filipinos will adopt the American policy and the Savannah, Ga. *Gazette*, to the contrary, notwithstanding.

Washington *Bee,* December 22, 1900

APPENDIXES

APPENDIX I

[Political affiliation notations are from Ayer's *American Newspaper Directory for 1898-1900*]

A.M.E. Church Review. Philadelphia, Pa.: H. T. Kealing, editor, T. W. Henderson, publisher.

Afro-American Sentinel. Omaha, Nebr.: Cyrus D. Bell, editor, Walter W. Bell, publisher—Silver Democrat.

American. Coffeyville, Kansas: L. D. Fuller, editor and publisher.

American Citizen. Kansas City, Kansas: George A. Dudley, editor and publisher.

Bee. Washington, D.C.: W. Calvin Chase, editor and publisher—Independent.

Broad Ax. Salt Lake City, Utah: Julius F. Taylor, editor and publisher—Democratic (Moved to Chicago in the summer of 1899.)

Colorado Statesman. Denver, Col.: S. H. Hobson, editor.

Colored American. Washington, D.C.: Edward E. Cooper, manager.

Courant. Boston, Mass.: J. Gordon Street, editor.

Defender. Philadelphia, Pa.: H.C.C. Astwood, editor, George A. Astwood, publisher—Republican.

Freeman. Indianapolis, Ind.: George L. Knox, editor.

Gazette. Cleveland, Ohio: H. C. Smith, editor and publisher—Republican.

Illinois Record. Bloomington, Ill.: Charles E. Hall, editor.

Iowa State Bystander. Des Moines, Iowa: J. L. Thompson, editor—Republican.

Kansas State Ledger. Topeka, Kansas: F. L. Jeltz, editor and publisher—Independent.

Observer. Kansas City, Mo.: L. C. Williams, publisher.

Ohio Standard and Observer. Xenia and Wilberforce, Ohio: D. H. V. Purnell, editor.

Planet. Richmond, Va.: John P. Mitchell, Jr., editor and publisher—Republican.

Recorder. Indianapolis, Ind.: William H. Porter and George P. Stewart, editors and publishers.

Reporter. Helena, Ark.: Rev. W. A. Holmes, editor.

Republican. Seattle, Wash.: H. R. Cayton, editor, Susie Revels Cayton, associate—Republican.

Tribune. Wichita, Kansas: D. L. Robinson, editor, R. Covington, publisher—Republican.

Weekly Blade. Parsons, Kansas: J. Monroe Dorsey, editor.

Wisconsin Weekly Advocate. Milwaukee, Wisc.: A. G. Burgette, proprietor, P. L. Stangl, city editor—Republican.

World. Seattle, Wash.: D. W. Griffin, editor—Republican.

APPENDIX II

Age. Atlanta, Ga.: W. A. Pledger and A. M. Hill, editors and publishers—Republican.

Age. New York City: T. Thomas Fortune and Peterson, editors and publishers—Republican.

American Baptist. Louisville, Ky.: William H. Steward, publisher.

American Eagle. St. Louis, Mo.: E. W. Newsome, editor.

Appeal. St. Paul, Minn.: Adams Bros., editors and publishers.

Ascension Herald. Donaldsonville, La.

Christian Banner. Philadelphia, Pa.: Rev. G.L.P. Taliaferro, editor.

Christian Recorder. Philadelphia, Pa.: Rev. H. T. Johnson, editor, T. W. Henderson, publisher.

Colored Messenger. Kansas City, Mo.: R. Edward Lee Bailey, editor —Republican.

Conservator. Chicago, Ill.: F. L. Barnett, publisher—Republican.

Daily Record. Washington, D.C.; Alexander L. Manly, editor.

Enterprise. Omaha, Nebr.: G. F. Franklin, editor and publisher.

Express. Dallas, Texas: W. E. King, editor and publisher—Republican.

Florida Evangelist. Jacksonville, Fla.: Rev. J. M. Waldron, editor.

Gazette. Savannah, Ga.

Herald. Brunswick, Ga.; H. A. Hagler, editor—Republican.

Herald. Langston City, Okla.: W. L. Eagleson, editor—Republican.

Odd Fellows Journal. Philadelphia, Pa.: J. C. Asbury, editor and publisher.

Observer. Xenia, Ohio: J. M. Summers, editor—Republican.

Pioneer Press. Martinsburg, W. Va.: J. R. Clifford, editor and publisher—Republican.

Progress. Omaha, Nebr.: F. L. Barnett, editor—Republican.

Radical. St. Joseph, Mo.: Isaac Frederick, editor—Independent Republican.

Rising Sun. Smithville, Texas: L. W. Mackey, editor and publisher.

Southern Republican. New Orleans, La.: Joseph LeBlanc, editor and publisher—Republican.

Standard. Lexington, Ky.: Rev. R.C.O. Benjamin, editor— Republican.

Star of Zion. Charlotte, N.C.: Rev. J. W. Smith, editor.

True Reformer. Littletown, N.C.: George H. White, editor.

Tribune. Philadelphia, Pa.: John W. Harris, editor, Chris J. Perry, publisher—Republican.

Tribune. Savannah, Ga.—Republican.

Union. Augusta, Ga.: A. W. Wimberly, editor—Republican.

Voice of Missions. Atlanta, Ga.:

Weekly Call. Topeka, Kansas: J. B. Bass, editor and publisher—Republican.

Weekly Echo. Hot Springs, Ark.: E. S. Lockhart, editor—Republican.

Weekly Triumph. New York City.

Western Enterprise. Colorado Springs, Col.—Independent Republican.

World. Indianapolis, Ind.: Christy and Christy, editors and publishers.

World Herald. Omaha, Nebr.: R. L. Metcalfe, editor—Independent.

APPENDIX III

[Sen. Henry C. Lodge had the following letter read into the *Congressional Record*:]

Harvard University, Cambridge, Mass.

To the Senate of the United States:

A largely attended mass meeting of colored citizens of Boston and vicinity, at which some white citizens were present, was held on February 28 in Faneuil Hall, to protest against the murder of the colored postmaster of Lake City, S.C., by a mob on the night of February 21. And the sentiments expressed at that meeting are echoed by the finest culture and best manhood of both races.

The Independent truly says: "There are other general causes of the ill will to America for which we are to blame. The enormous number of murders and lynchings in our Southern and Western States makes an impression on the European mind, as it should. Here we are verily guilty."

Indeed, the national honor is as much at stake in failing to protect the rights and lives of American citizens at home as it is in failing to protect the rights and lives of American citizens abroad. And whenever America criticizes Spain for her treatment of Cuba, France for her treatment of Zola, and Turkey for her treatment of Armenians; whenever America protests against the wrongs committed against Cuba, the fact that the United States allows so many murders and lynchings to go unpunished will always be a taunt in the mouths of other nations. The United States bears the disgrace of permitting more unpunished murders and lynchings than any other civilized nation in the world.

There are two reasons why the fiendish murder of Postmaster Baker and the infant in its mother's arms, the dastardly attack upon unarmed and helpless women, is possible in America.

In the first place, there is an apparent apathy at the fact that men for no other reason than that negro blood flows in their veins are at the mercy of a lawless mob. Public sentiment has in the past apologized for the lynchers instead of condemning them.

In the second place, neither the Federal Government nor the local authorities have in the past made any effort to discover or prosecute the perpetrators of this awful crime.

In case of war with Spain this Government would not hesitate to call upon negro soldiers to protect the rights of white American citizens abroad; and yet will not this Government protect the lives of colored American citizens at home? When we are threatened with war, ought not this government so to treat the negro that he shall continue in the future to be as patriotic and as loyal to his country as he has been in the past?

As one of the invited speakers at the Faneuil Hall meeting, I know that I am voicing the sentiment of all those white and colored persons assembled in Faneuil Hall when I say that the Senate of the United States should listen to the cry of the *Charleston News and Courier* when it declares: "We hope that the United States authorities will move in the Lake City case without delay, and that no guilty man will be suffered to escape." It is the unmistakable duty of the Federal Government to discover and prosecute those who shot a negro postmaster and burned the United States mail. It will be to the undying shame of this country if Congress and the Federal Government take no action with regard to the matter.

Those who called the Faneuil Hall meeting and all of those assembled there wait to hear an expression from the Senate of the United States upon the same.

Respectfully,
William Henry Ferris, Harvard Divinity School, Cambridge, Mass.; J. N. Wolff; Edward Everett Brown; Robert T. Teamoh; W. D. Johnson; E. G. Walker; Isaac B. Allen.

Congressional Record, U.S. Senate, 55th Congress, 2nd Session, pp/2404-5—March 3, 1898

APPENDIX IV

Open Letter to President McKinley
by
Colored People of Massachusetts

The Colored People of Boston and vicinity, through the Colored National League, at a mass meeting held in the Charles Street Church, Tuesday, evening, October 3d, 1899, addressed an Open Letter to *President McKinley.*

The reading of the letter by *Mr. Archibald H. Grimke,* Chairman of the Committee, was listened to with marked attention and interest, and at the conclusion of its reading the letter was adopted by the meeting with significant unanimity.

The letter was forwarded to President McKinley, signed by the officers of the meeting and others.

Boston, Mass., October 3, 1899
Hon. *William McKinley,*
President of the United States

Sir: We, colored people of Massachusetts in mass meeting assembled to consider our oppressions and the state of the country relative to the same, have resolved to address ourselves to you in an open letter, notwithstanding your extraordinary, your incomprehensible silence on the subject of our wrongs in your annual and other messages to Congress, as in your public utterances to the country at large. We address ourselves to you, sir, not as suppliants, but as of right, American citizens, whose servant you are, and to whom you are bound to listen, and for whom you are equally bound to speak, and upon occasion to act, as for any other body of your fellow countrymen in like circumstances. We ask nothing for ourselves at your hands, as chief magistrate of the republic, to which all American citizens are not entitled. We ask for the enjoyment of life, liberty, and the pursuit of happiness equally with other men. We ask for the free and full exercise of all the rights of American freemen, guaranteed to us by the Constitution and laws of the Union, which you were solemnly sworn to obey and execute. We ask you for what belongs to us by the high sanction of Constitution and law, and the Democratic genius of our institutions and civilizations. These rights are everywhere throughout the South denied to us, violently wrested from us by mobs, by lawless legislatures, and nullifying conventions, combinations and conspiracies, openly, defiantly, under your eyes, in your constructive and actual presence. And we demand, which is a part of our rights, protection, security in our life, our liberty, and in the pursuit of our individual and social happiness under a government, which we are bound to defend in

201

war, and which is equally bound to furnish us in peace protection, at home and abroad.

We have suffered, sir—God knows how much we have suffered!—since your accession to office, at the hands of a country professing to be Christian, from the hate and violence of a people claiming to be civilized but who are not civilized, and you have seen our sufferings, witnessed from your high place our awful wrongs and miseries, and yet you have at no time and on no occasion opened your lips in our behalf. Why? we ask. Is it because we are black and weak and despised? Are you silent because without any fault of our own we were enslaved and held for two centuries in cruel bondage by your forefathers? Is it because we bear the marks of those sad generations of Anglo-Saxon brutality and wickedness, that you do not speak? Is it our fault that our involuntary servitude produced in us widespread ignorance, poverty, and degradation? Are we to be damned and destroyed by the whites because we have only grown the seeds which they planted? Are we to be damned by bitter laws and destroyed by the mad violence of mobs because we are what white men made us? And is there no help in the federal arm for us, or even one word of audible pity, protest and remonstrance in your own breast, Mr. President, or in that of a single member of your cabinet? Black indeed we are, sir, but we are also men and American citizens.

From the year 1619 the Anglo-Saxon race in America began to sow in the mind of the negro race seeds of ignorance, poverty, and social degradation, and continued to do so until the year 1863, when chattel slavery was abolished to save the union of these states. Then northern white men began, in order to form a more perfect union, to sow this self-same mind of the negro with quite different seeds—seeds of knowledge and freedom; seeds garnered in the Declaration of Independence for the feeding of the nations of the earth, such as the natural equality of all men before the law, their inalienable right to life, liberty, and the pursuit of happiness, and the derivation of the powers of all just governments from the consent of the governed. These seeds of your own planting took root in the mind and heart of the negro, and the crop of quickening intelligence, desire for wealth, to rise in the social scale, to be as other men, to be equal with them in opportunities and the free play of his powers in the rivalry of life, was the direct and legitimate result.

The struggle of the negro to rise out of his ignorance, his poverty and his social degradation, in consequence of the growth of these new forces and ideas within him, to the full stature of his American citizenship, has been met everywhere in the South by the active ill-will and determined race-hatred and opposition of the white people of that section. Turn where he will, he encounters this cruel and implacable spirit. He dare not speak openly the thoughts that arise in his breast. He has wrongs such as have never in modern times been inflicted on a people, and yet he must be dumb in the midst of a nation which prates loudly of democracy and humanity, boasts itself the champion of oppressed people abroad, while it looks on indifferent, apathetic, at appalling enormities and inequities at home, where the victims are black and the criminals white. The suppression, the terror wrought at the South is so complete, so ever-present, so awful, that no negro's life or property is safe for a day who ventures to raise his voice to heaven in indignant protest and appeal against the deep damnation and despotism of such a social state. Even teachers and leaders of this poor, oppressed, and patient people may not speak, lest their institutions of learning and industry, and their lives pay for their temerity at the swift hands of savage mobs. But if the peace of Warsaw, the silence of death reign over our people and their leaders at the South, we of Massachusetts are free, and must and shall raise our voice to you and through you to the country, in solemn protest and warning against the fearful sin and peril of such explosive social conditions. We, sir, at this crisis and extremity in the life of our race in the South, and in this crisis and extremity of the republic as well, in the presence of the civilized world, cry to you to pause, if but for an hour, in pursuit of your national policy of "criminal aggression" abroad to consider the "criminal aggression" at home against humanity and American citizenship, which is in the full tide of successful conquest at the South, and the tremendous consequences to our civilization, and the durability of the Union itself, of this universal subversion of the supreme law of the land, of democratic institutions, and of the previous principle of the religion of Jesus in the social and civil life of the Southern people.

With one accord, with an anxiety that wrenched our hearts with cruel hopes and fears, the colored people of the United States turned to you when Wilmington, N.C. was held for two dreadful days and nights in the clutch of a bloody revolution; when negroes, guilty of no crime except the color of their skin and a desire to exercise the rights of their American citizenship, were butchered like dogs in the streets of that ill-fated town; and when government of the people by the people and for people perished in your very presence by the hands of violent men during those bitter November days, for want of federal aid, which you would not and did not furnish; on the plea that you could not give what was not asked for by a coward and recreant governor. And we well understood at the time, sir, notwithstanding your plea of constitutional inability to cope with the rebellion in Wilmington, that where there is a will with constitutional lawyers and rulers there is always a way, and where there is no will there is no way. We well knew that you lacked the will, and therefore, the way to meet that emergency.

It was the same thing with that terrible ebullition of the mob spirit at Phoenix, S.C., when black men were hunted and murdered . . . and driven out of that place by a set of white savages, who cared not for the Constitution and the laws of the United States any more than they do for the constitution and the laws of an empire dead and buried a thousand years. We looked in vain for some word or act from you. Neither word nor act of sympathy for the victims was forthcoming, or of detestation of an outrage so mad and barbarous as to evoke even from such an extreme Southern organ as is the *News and Courier*, of Charleston, S.C., hot and stern condemnation. Hoping against hope, we waited for your annual message to Congress in December last, knowing that the Constitution imposed upon you a duty to give, from time to time, to that body information of the state of the Union. That, at least, we said, the President will surely do; he will communicate officially the facts relative to the tragic, the appalling events, which had just occurred in the Carolinas to the Congress of the United States. But not one word did your message contain on this subject, although it discussed all sorts and conditions of subjects, from the so-called war for humanity against Spain to the celebration of the one hundredth anniversary of the founding of the national capital in 1900. Nothing escaped your eye, at home or abroad, nothing except the subversion of the Constitution and laws of the Union in the Southern States, and the flagrant and monstrous crimes perpetrated upon a weak and submissive race in defiance of your authority, or in virtual connivance therewith. Yes, sir, we repeat, or in virtual connivance therewith.

And, when you made your Southern tour a little later, and we saw how cunningly you catered to Southern race prejudice and proscription; how you, the one single public man and magistrate of the country, who, by virtue of your exalted office, ought under no circumstances to recognize caste distinctions and discriminations among your fellow-citizens, received white men at the Capitol in Montgomery, Ala., and black men afterward in a negro church; how you preached patience, industry, moderation to your long-suffering black fellow-citizens, and patriotism, jingoism, and imperialism to your white ones; when we saw all these things, scales of illusion in respect to your object fell from our eyes. We felt that the President of the United States, in order to win the support of the South to his policy of "criminal aggression" on the Far East, was ready and willing to shut his eyes, ears, and lips to the "criminal aggression" of that section against the Constitution and the laws of the land, wherein they guarantee civil rights and citizenship to the Negro, whose ultimate reduction to a condition of fixed and abject serfdom is the plain purpose of the Southern people and their laws.

When, several months subsequently, you returned to Georgia, the mob spirit, as if to evince its supreme contempt for your presence and the federal executive authority which you represent, boldly broke into a prison shed, where were confined helpless negro prisoners on a charge of incendiarism, and brutally murdered five of them. These men were American citizens, entitled to the rights of American citizens, protection and trial by due process of law. They were, in the eyes of the law, innocent until convicted by a jury of their peers. Had they been in legal custody in Russia or Spain or Turkey they had not been slaughtered by a mob under like circumstances; for the Russian military power, or the Spanish or the Turkish, would have guarded those men in their helpless and defenceless condition from the fury of the populace who were seeking their blood. Sir, they were men; they were your brothers; they were God's children, for whom Jesus lived and died. They ought to have been sacred charges in hands of any civilized or semi-civilized State and people. But almost in your hearing, before your eyes (and you the chief magistrate of a country loudly boastful of its freedom, Christianity, and civilization), they were atrociously murdered. Did you speak? Did you open your lips to express horror of the awful crime and stern condemnation of the incredible villainy and complicity of the constituted authorities of Georgia in the commission of this monstrous outrage, which out-barbarized barbarism and stained through and through with indelible infamy before the world your country's justice, honor, and humanity?

Still later, considering the age, the circumstances and the nation in which the deed was done, Georgia committed a crime unmatched for moral depravity and sheer atrocity during the century. A negro, charged with murder and criminal assault, the first charge he is reported by the newspapers to have admitted, and the second to have denied, was taken one quiet Sunday morning from his captors, and burned to death with indescribable and hellish cruelty in the presence of cheering thousands of the so-called best people of Georgia, men, women, and children, who had gone forth on the Christian Sabbath to the burning of a human being as to a country festival and holiday of innocent enjoyment and amusement. The downright ferocity and frightful savagery of that American mob at Newman outdoes the holiday humor and thirst for blood of the tiger-like populace of Pagan Rome, gathered to witness Christian martyrs thrown to the lions in their roaring arenas. The death of Hose was quickly followed by that of the negro preacher, Strickland, guiltless of crime, under circumstances and with a brutality of wickedness almost matching in horror and enormity the torture and murder of the first; and this last was succeeded by a third victim, who was literally lashed to death by the wild, beast-like spirit of a Georgia Mob, for daring merely to utter his abhorrence of the Palmetto iniquity and slaughter of helpless prisoners.

Did you speak? Did you utter one word of reprobation, of righteous indignation, either as magistrate or as man? Did you break the shameful silence of shameful months with so much as a whisper of a whisper against the deep damnation of such defiance of all law, human and divine; such revulsion of men into beasts, and relapses of communities into barbarism in the very center of the republic, and amid the sanctuary of the temple of American liberty itself? You did not, sir, but your Attorney-General did, and he only to throw out to the public, to your meek and long-suffering colored fellow-citizens, the cold and cautious legal opinion that the case of Hose has no federal aspect! Mr. President, has it any moral or human aspect, seeing that Hose was a member of the negro race, whom your Supreme Court once declared has no rights in America which white men are bound to respect? Is this infamous dictum of that tribunal still the supreme law of the land? We ask you, sir, since recent events in Arkansas, Mississippi, Alabama, Virginia, and Louisiana, as well as in Georgia and the Carolinas, indeed throughout the South, and your own persistent silence, and the persistent silence of every member of your Cabinet on the subject of the wrongs of that race in those States, would appear together to imply as much.

Had, eighteen months ago, the Cuban revolution to throw off the yoke of Spain, or the attempt of Spain to subdue the Cuban rebellion, any federal aspect? We believe that you and the Congress of the United

States thought that they had, and therefore used, finally, the armed force of the nation to expel Spain from that island. Why? Was it because "the people of the Island of Cuba are, and of right ought to be free and independent?" You and the Congress said as much, and may we fervently pray, sir, in passing, that the freedom and independence of that brave people shall not much longer be denied them by our government? But to resume, there was another consideration which in your judgment gave to the Cuban question a federal aspect, which provoked at last armed interposition of our government in the affairs of that island, and this was "the chronic condition of disturbance in Cuba so injurious and menacing to our interests and tranquillity, as well as shocking to our sentiments of humanity." Wherefore you presently fulfilled "a duty to humanity by ending a situation, the indefinite prolongation of which had become insufferable."

Mr. President, had that "chronic condition of disturbance in Cuba so injurious and menacing to our interests and tranquillity as well as shocking to our sentiments of humanity," which you wished to terminate and did terminate, a federal aspect, while that not less "chronic condition of disturbance" in the South which is a thousand times more "injurious and menacing to our interests and tranquillity," as well as far more "shocking to our sentiments of humanity," or ought to be, none whatever? Is it better to be Cuban revolutionists fighting for Cuban independence than American citizens striving to do their simple duty at home? Or is it better only in case those American citizens doing their simple duty at home happen to be negroes residing in the Southern States?

Are crying national transgressions and injustices more "injurious and menacing" to the Republic, as well as "shocking to the sentiments of humanity," when committed by a foreign state, in foreign territory, against a foreign people, than when they are committed by a portion of our own people against a portion of our own people at home? There were those of our citizens who did not think that the Cuban question possessed any federal aspect, while there were others who thought otherwise; and these, having the will and power, eventually found a way to suppress a menacing danger to the country and a wrong against humanity at the same time. Where there is a will among constitutional lawyers and rulers, Mr. President, there is ever a way; but where there is no will, there is no way. Shall it be said that the federal government, with arms of Briareus, reaching to the utmost limits of the habitable globe for the protection of its citizens, for the liberation of alien islanders and the subjugation of others, is powerless to guarantee to certain of its citizens at home their inalienable right to life, liberty, and the pursuit of happiness because those citizens happen to be negroes residing in the Southern section of our country? Do the colored people of the United States deserve equal consideration with the Cuban people at the hands of your administration, and shall they, though late, receive it? If, sir, you have the disposition, as we know that you have the power, we are confident that you will be able to find a constitutional way to reach us in our extremity, and our enemies also, who are likewise enemies to great public interests and national tranquillity.

I. D. Barnett, President; Edward D. Brown, Vice-President; Edward H. West, Secretary; Archibald H. Grimke; Edwin G. Walker; James H. Wolff; Emery T. Morris; William O. Armstrong; Thomas P. Taylor; and others.

Schomburg Collection, New York
Public Library, October 3, 1899

APPENDIX V

NATIONAL AFRO-AMERICAN PARTY

(Proposed)
411 South Eleventh St.
Philadelphia, Pa.

June, 1900
Editor, Howard's American Magazine

Dear Sir: A well-organized movement is under way to place in nomination a National Afro-American ticket to nominate candidates for President and Vice-President, members of Congress, the different State Legislatures, and/or all elective positions to be voted for by the people at the forthcoming general election.

The promoters of this effort realize that this movement is revolutionary in character, but they feel justified in their proposed action, because of the ruthless betrayal of popular government by both the two great political parties. We recognize in the spirit of Imperialism, inaugurated and fostered by the administration of President McKinley, the same violation of *Human Rights* which is being practiced by the Democratic party in the recently reconstructed States, to wit: the wholesale disfranchisement of the Negro. We can see neither wisdom nor expediency in supporting any one of the many other political parties now extant, for reasons which must be obvious.

We, therefore, submit the enclosed platform of principles and advise the calling of a conference to meet in the City of Philadelphia at an early date to consider the advisability of nominating a straight-out ticket for President. . . .

We would be pleased to have an expression of your views upon the proposed movement. . . .

> Very truly yours,
> Thomas Wallace Swan, Acting Secretary,
> On behalf of Committee on Organization

OUTLINE OF PLATFORM

The Afro-American Party

First: We maintain that the Constitution of the United States follows the flag into the most remote parts of the United States territory, affording to the inhabitants thereof, without regard to creed, color, or previous condition, the protection and benefits of its guarantees of life, freedom of speech, freedom of the ballot, freedom of the press, *habeas corpus*, trial by jury, and uniform taxation.

Second: We favor the "Monroe Doctrine."

Third: We are opposed to all monopolies and trusts, and favor the ownership and control of the public highways by the general government, such as railroads, telegraph and telephone, so as to prevent unjust discrimination of the people or the burdening of them with unnecessary taxation.

Fourth: We demand the immediate independence of Cuba and the Philippine Islands, and a tariff for revenue only, with such reciprocal treaties that would best subserve our foreign and commercial relations.

Fifth: Taxation without representation being unjust, we favor an unlimited, rather than a restricted suffrage, and are unqualifiedly in favor of the extension of suffrage to women.

Opinions

Rt. Rev. Alexander Walters, Bishop of the African Methodist Zion Episcopal Church, and President of the National Afro-American Council:

The systematic movement now going on in this country against the Negro is at no distant period destined to overthrow and throttle all the good that has been accomplished through and by the Emancipation Proclamation and the Fourteenth and Fifteenth Amendments to the Constitution.

As a remedy for the betterment of the Negro race in this country, I want to suggest that the Negro race leaders everywhere in this land get together, and, if need be, organize a Negro National Party, and thereby show ourselves a force in the body politic and a power in this country. We are numerically strong and financially strengthening, and I venture to say that if the Negroes do get together in a political or in any other kind of a compact, our power will be felt. In this I do not advocate a division of the Negro vote, but rather to create a policy and platform of our own.

Rt. Rev. Levi Jenkins Coppin, Bishop of the African Methodist Episcopal Church:

We purpose to force recognition, we have votes enough to determine elections in doubtful States. We can do it in New York, and we will do it. The party is not to be formed for selling out purposes. It will put up its ticket and vote for it. And we will keep in the field until we see beyond the shadow of doubt that our rights will be conserved. We have splendid material among the colored men of this country for Presidential timber, and our race will rally to their support.

Judge Edward C. Walker, of Boston:

This action of the colored people seeking a new party is no doubt inspired by the recent talk about abolishing the Thirteenth Amendment. The United States will never abolish the Fifteenth Amendment. I was sorry to see that Bourke Cochran made that speech down South. I always admired Cochran for his fair-mindedness, but I believe that the only effect of his speech was to hurt himself.

There is a pretty general feeling among the colored people that they will vote and work against the Republican party this coming election if President McKinley is the standard-bearer. McKinley has no sympathy for the Negro.

Rev. John P. Sampson, D.D.. Presiding Elder, African Methodist Episcopal Church:

We are tired of being used as puppets by the Republican party. Our rights are trampled upon; our protests ignored. We shall declare for the full measure of citizenship for the Negro, as guaranteed by the Constitution. We are deprived of privileges enjoyed by the ragamuffin of the white race; are compelled to ride in cars hardly fit for cattle; refused entertainment at hotels and restaurants; barred out of decent seats in theatres—in fact, discriminated against in every way, as though we were not citizens or even human beings. And the Republican Party sits by supinely and sees us outraged, lynched, murdered and driven from our homes as though we were odious pets.

John Edward Bruce Papers, Schomburg
Collection, New York Public Library

BLACK HISTORY

Other Books of Interest

Individual titles in Series I, II, and III of the Arno Press collection THE AMERICAN NEGRO: HIS HISTORY AND LITERATURE are listed on the following pages. These reprints are, in many instances, the actual records of those who were part of the Negro experience; they encompass the economic, political, and cultural history of the Negro from colonial time to the present. The 139 cloth-bound books in the collection are listed alphabetically by author/editor; immediately following is a list of the titles which are also available in paperback.

The books in THE AMERICAN NEGRO collection were selected by an Editorial Advisory Board made up of the following members:

William Loren Katz, General Editor, and author of **Eyewitness: The Negro in American History** and **Teacher's Guide to American Negro History**

Arthur P. Davis, Professor of English, Howard University

Jean Blackwell Hutson, Curator, The Schomburg Collection, New York Public Library

Sara D. Jackson, National Archives, Washington, D.C.

Ernest Kaiser, The Schomburg Collection, New York Public Library

Ulysses Lee (deceased), Professor of English, Morgan State College

James M. McPherson, Professor of History, Princeton University

Dorothy B. Porter, Curator, Negro Collection, Howard University

Benjamin Quarles, Professor of History, Morgan State College

Darwin T. Turner, Dean of the Graduate School, North Carolina A & T College

Doxey A. Wilkerson, Professor of Education, Yeshiva University

To order, or for an annotated brochure, please write to:
ARNO PRESS, 330 Madison Avenue, New York, N.Y. 10017.

The American Negro Academy Occasional Papers, Numbers 1-22...............
.... ISBN 0-405-01913-0 $21.50

Andrews, Sydney **The South Since the War:** As Shown by Fourteen Weeks of Travel and
Observation in Georgia and the Carolinas.............ISBN 0-405-01847-9 $12.00

The Anglo-African Magazine, Volume 1, 1859...........ISBN 0-405-01803-7 $12.50

Anti-Negro Riots in the North, 1863...................ISBN 0-405-01848-7 $ 3.50

Atlanta University **Atlanta University Publications, Numbers 1, 2, 4, 8, 9, 11, 13, 14, 15,
16, 17, 18** ....ISBN 0-405-01804-5 $30.00

Atlanta University **Atlanta University Publications, Numbers 3, 5, 6, 7, 10, 12, 19, 20**
.... ISBN 0-405-01914-9 $33.00

Bell, Howard H. (editor) **Minutes of the Proceedings of the National Negro Conventions,
1830-1864** ....ISBN 0-405-01916-5 $17.00

Bell, Howard H. **A Survey of the Negro Convention Movement, 1830-1861**............
.... ISBN 0-405-01915-7 $12.00

Bonner, T. D. **The Life and Adventures of James P. Beckworth, Mountaineer, Scout, and
Pioneer, and Chief of the Crow Nation of Indians**......ISBN 0-405-01850-9 $16.00

Botume, Elizabeth Hyde **First Days Amongst the Contrabands**......................
.... ISBN 0-405-01805-3 $10.50

Brown, Sterling **The Negro in American Fiction and Negro Poetry and Drama**.........
.... ISBN 0-405-01851-7 $10.50

Brown, Sterling; Davis, Arthur P. and Lee, Ulysses (editors) **The Negro Caravan**.......
.... ISBN 0-405-01852-5 $35.00

Brown, William Wells **Clotel, or, the President's Daughter**..ISBN 0-405-01853-3 $ 8.00

Carleton, George W. (editor) **The Suppressed Book About Slavery!**.................
.... ISBN 0-405-01806-1 $13.50

Cashin, Herschel V., et al. **Under Fire With the Tenth U.S. Cavalry**.................
.... ISBN 0-405-01854-1 $12.00

Chestnutt, Charles W. **The Marrow of Tradition**..........ISBN 0-405-01855-X $10.00

The Chicago Commission on Race Relations **The Negro in Chicago:** A Study of Race
Relations and a Race Riot.........................ISBN 0-405-01807-X $15.00

Child, Lydia Maria **An Appeal in Favor of That Class of Americans Called Africans**......
.... ISBN 0-405-01808-8 $ 7.00

Child, Lydia Maria **The Freedmen's Book**.................ISBN 0-405-01809-6 $ 8.50

Clark, Peter **The Black Brigade of Cincinnati:** Being a Report of Its Labors and a Muster-
roll of Its Members; Together With Various Orders, Speeches, etc. Relating to It....
.... ISBN 0-405-01917-3 $ 4.50

Coffin, Levi **Reminiscences of Levi Coffin, the Reputed President of the Underground
Railroad:** Being a Brief History of the Labors of a Lifetime in Behalf of the Slave, With
the Stories of Numerous Fugitives, Who Gained Their Freedom Through His Instrumen-
tality, and Many Other Incidents...................ISBN 0-405-01810-X $16.50

Commissioner of Education in the District of Columbia **History of Schools for the Colored
Population:** Part I: In the District of Columbia; Part II: In the United States........
.... ISBN 0-405-01918-1 $ 7.50

Craft, William and Ellen **Running a Thousand Miles for Freedom:** Or, the Escape of
William and Ellen Craft From Slavery................ISBN 0-405-01923-8 $ 5.00

Cullen, Countee **Color** ....ISBN 0-405-01919-X $ 4.50

Culp, D. W. (editor) **Twentieth Century Negro Literature:** Or, a Cyclopedia of Thought on
the Vital Topics Relating to the American Negro by One Hundred of America's Great-
est Negroes ....ISBN 0-405-01856-8 $20.00

Cummings, John **Negro Population in the United States, 1790-1915**.................
.... ISBN 0-405-01811-8 $23.50

Daniels, John **In Freedom's Birthplace:** A Study of Boston Negroes................
.... ISBN 0-405-01857-6 $12.50

Delany, Martin Robinson **The Condition, Elevation, Emigration, and Destiny of the Colored People of the United States:** Politically Considered . ISBN 0-405-01812-6 $ 6.50

Donnelly, Ignatius **Dr. Huguet**.......................ISBN 0-405-01920-3 $11.00

Douglass, Frederick **My Bondage and My Freedom**.......ISBN 0-405-01813-4 $14.50

Du Bois, W. E. B. **The Black North in 1901:** A Social Study . . ISBN 0-405-01921-1 $ 4.00

Du Bois, W. E. B. **The Quest of the Silver Fleece**.......ISBN 0-405-01922-X $13.00

Dunbar, Paul Laurence **Lyrics of Lowly Life**.............ISBN 0-405-01858-4 $ 7.00

Dunbar, Paul Laurence **The Sport of the Gods**............ISBN 0-405-01859-2 $ 8.00

Dunbar, Paul Laurence **The Strength of Gideon and Other Stories**...................
.... ISBN 0-405-01860-6 $11.50

Emilio, Luis F. **History of the Fifty-Fourth Regiment of Massachusetts Volunteer Infantry, 1863-1865** .... ISBN 0-405-01861-4 $14.50

Epstein, Abraham **The Negro Migrant in Pittsburgh:** A Study in Social Economics......
.... ISBN 0-405-01924-6 $ 4.50

Fisher, Rudolph **The Walls of Jericho**...................ISBN 0-405-01862-2 $ 9.50

Flipper, Henry Ossian **The Colored Cadet at West Point**....ISBN 0-405-01863-0 $ 8.00

Foley, Albert S. **Bishop Healy:** Beloved Outcaste.........ISBN 0-405-01925-4 $10.00

Foley, Albert S. **God's Men of Color:** The Colored Catholic Priests of the United States, 1854-1954 .... ISBN 0-405-01864-9 $10.00

Fortune, Timothy Thomas **Black and White:** Land, Labor, and Politics in the South.....
.... ISBN 0-405-01814-2 $ 9.00

Frazier, E. Franklin **The Free Negro Family:** A Study of Family Origins Before the Civil War
.... ISBN 0-405-01815-0 $ 2.50

Garrison, William Lloyd **Thoughts on African Colonization:** Or, an Impartial Exhibition of the Doctrines, Principles, and Purposes of the American Colonization Society Together With the Resolutions, Addresses, and Remonstrances of the Free People of Color .... ISBN 0-405-01816-9 $ 9.00

Gibbs, Mifflin Wister **Shadow and Light:** An Autobiography With Reminiscences of the Last and Present Century.......................ISBN 0-405-01817-7 $12.00

Griggs, Sutton E. **Imperium In Imperio**.................ISBN 0-405-01865-7 $ 8.00

Hall, Charles **Negroes in the United States 1920-32**......ISBN 0-405-01866-5 $25.00

Haynes, George Edmund **The Negro at Work in New York City:** A Study in Economic Progress .... ISBN 0-405-01818-5 $ 4.50

Haynes, George Edmund and Brown, Sterling **The Negro Newcomers in Detroit** and **The Negro in Washington** ....ISBN 0-405-01926-2 $ 4.50

Heard, William H. **From Slavery to the Bishopric in the A.M.E. Church:** An Autobiography
.... ISBN 0-405-01867-3 $ 3.50

Henson, Matthew A. **A Negro Explorer at the North Pole**...ISBN 0-405-01868-1 $ 6.00

Herndon, Angelo **Let Me Live**........................ISBN 0-405-01869-X $12.50

Higginson, Thomas Wentworth **Black Rebellion**...........ISBN 0-405-01870-3 $ 7.00

Higginson, Thomas Wentworth **Cheerful Yesterdays**.......ISBN 0-405-01819-3 $11.50

Hinton, Richard J. **John Brown and His Men:** With Some Account of the Roads They Traveled to Reach Harper's Ferry...................ISBN 0-405-01820-7 $23.00

Holmes, Dwight Oliver Wendell **The Evolution of the Negro College**.................
.... ISBN 0-405-01871-1 $ 7.50

Howe, Samuel Gridley **The Refugees from Slavery in Canada West:** Report to the Freedmen's Inquiry Commission, 1864 .... ISBN 0-405-01872-X $ 3.50

Hurston, Zora Neale **Dust Tracks On A Road**: An Autobiography....................
.... ISBN 0-405-01927-0 $12.00

Jacques-Garvey, Amy (editor) **Philosophy and Opinions of Marcus Garvey, Volume I**....
.... ISBN 0-405-01821-5 $ 3.50

Jacques-Garvey, Amy (editor) **Philosophy and Opinions of Marcus Garvey, Volume II**....
.... ISBN 0-405-01873-8 $10.00

Jay, William, and Clarke, James Freeman **The Free People of Color**: On the Condition of
the Free People of Color in the United States; Present Condition of the Free Colored
People of the United States....................... ISBN 0-405-01928-9 $ 4.50

Johnson, James Weldon **Black Manhattan**............... ISBN 0-405-01822-3 $13.00

Jones, Thomas Jesse (editor) **Negro Education**: A Study of the Private and Higher Schools
for Colored People in the United States.............. ISBN 0-405-01874-6 $35.00

Katz, Bernard (editor) **The Social Implications of Early Negro Music in the United
States** .... ISBN 0-405-01875-4 $ 7.50

Katz, William Loren (editor) **Five Slave Narratives**: A Compendium..................
.... ISBN 0-405-01823-1 $15.00

Keckley, Elizabeth H. **Behind the Scenes**: Or, Thirty Years a Slave, and Four Years in the
White House .... ISBN 0-405-01824-X $ 9.00

Kerlin, Robert T. **The Voice of the Negro 1919**........... ISBN 0-405-01825-8 $ 7.50

Kester, Howard **Revolt Among the Sharecroppers**........ ISBN 0-405-01876-2 $ 3.50

King, Edward **The Great South**: A Record of Journeys in Louisiana, Texas, the Indian
Territory, Missouri, Arkansas, Mississippi, Alabama, Georgia, Florida, South Carolina,
North Carolina, Kentucky, Tennessee, Virginia, West Virginia, and Maryland........
.... ISBN 0-405-01929-7 $28.50

Langston, John Mercer **From the Virginia Plantation to the National Capitol**: Or, the First
and Only Negro Representative in Congress From the Old Dominion................
.... ISBN 0-405-01877-0 $18.00

Larsen, Nella **Passing** .... ISBN 0-405-01930-0 $ 8.00

Livermore, George **An Historical Research Respecting the Opinions of the Founders of
the Republic on Negroes as Slaves, as Citizens, and as Soldiers**..................
.... ISBN 0-405-01878-9 $ 6.50

Locke, Alain **The Negro and His Music** and **Negro Art, Past and Present**.............
.... ISBN 0-405-01879-7 $ 8.00

Locke, Alain (editor) **The New Negro**: An Interpretation... ISBN 0-405-01826-6 $ 9.00

Lockwood, Lewis C. J., and Forten, Charlotte **Two Black Teachers During the Civil War**:
Mary S. Peake, the Colored Teacher at Fortress Monroe; Life on the Sea Islands....
.... ISBN 0-405-01931-9 $ 5.00

Love, Nat **The Life and Adventures of Nat Love, Better Known in the Cattle Country as
"Deadwood Dick"** .... ISBN 0-405-01827-4 $ 6.00

Lynch, John R. **The Facts of Reconstruction**............. ISBN 0-405-01828-2 $10.00

McKay, Claude **A Long Way From Home**................ ISBN 0-405-01880-0 $12.00

May, Samuel J. **Some Recollections of Our Anti-Slavery Conflict**...................
.... ISBN 0-405-01829-0 $10.50

Mayer, Brantz **Captain Canot, or Twenty Years of An African Slaver**: Being an Account of
His Career and Adventures On the Coast, In the Interior, On Shipboard, and In the
West Indies .... ISBN 0-405-01830-4 $14.50

Miller, Kelly **An Appeal To Conscience**: America's Code of Caste, a Disgrace to Democracy
.... ISBN 0-405-01881-9 $ 3.50

Miller, Kelly **Out of the House of Bondage**............. ISBN 0-405-01882-7 $ 7.50

Miller, Kelly **Race Adjustment**: Essays on the Negro in America, and The Everlasting Stain
.... ISBN 0-405-01831-2 $20.50

National Association for the Advancement of Colored People **Thirty Years of Lynching
in the United States, 1889-1918** .... ISBN 0-405-01932-7 $ 4.50

National Negro Conference **Proceedings of the National Negro Conference, 1909**......
.... ISBN 0-405-01890-8 $ 7.00

Nell, William C. **The Colored Patriots of the American Revolution, With Sketches of Several Distinguished Colored Persons:** To Which Is Added a Brief Survey of the Condition and Prospects of Colored Americans........ISBN 0-405-01832-0 $12.00

Nesbit, William, and Williams, Samuel **Two Black Views of Liberia:** Four Months In Liberia, or African Colonization Exposed; Four Years In Liberia, a Sketch of the Life of Rev. Samuel Williams ....ISBN 0-405-01936-X $ 5.50

Nichols, J. L., and Crogman, William H. **Progress of a Race:** Or, the Remarkable Advancement of the American Negro From the Bondage of Slavery, Ignorance, and Poverty To the Freedom of Citizenship, Intelligence, Affluence, Honor, and Trust............
.... ISBN 0-405-01883-5 $16.50

O'Connor, Ellen M., and Miner, Myrtilla **Myrtilla Miner: A Memoir** and **The School for Colored Girls in Washington, D.C.**....................ISBN 0-405-01933-5 $ 5.50

Ottley, Roi **New World A-Coming:** Inside Black America....ISBN 0-405-01833-9 $11.50

Ovington, Mary White **The Walls Came Tumbling Down**....ISBN 0-405-01884-3 $ 9.50

Payne, Daniel A. **History of the African Methodist Episcopal Church**.................
.... ISBN 0-405-01885-1 $15.00

Payne, Daniel A. **Recollections of Seventy Years**........ISBN 0-405-01834-7 $10.00

Pearson, Elizabeth Ware (editor) **Letters From Port Royal, Written at the Time of the Civil War** .... ISBN 0-405-01886-X $10.50

Penn, I. Garland **The Afro-American Press and Its Editors**..ISBN 0-405-01887-8 $18.00

Porter, Dorothy (editor) **Negro Protest Pamphlets:** A Compendium.................
.... ISBN 0-405-01888-6 $ 7.00

Porter, James A. **Modern Negro Art**....................ISBN 0-405-01889-4 $10.00

Rollin, Frank A. **Life and Public Services of Martin R. Delany:** Sub-Assistant Commissioner, Bureau Relief of Refugees, Freedmen, and of Abandoned Lands, and Late Major 104th U.S. Colored Troops ....ISBN 0-405-01934-3 $13.00

Schurz, Carl **Report on the Condition of the South**........ISBN 0-405-01938-6 $ 5.00

Scott, Emmett J. **Negro Migration During the War**........ISBN 0-405-01891-6 $ 6.00

Scott, Emmett J. **Scott's Official History of the American Negro in the World War**......
.... ISBN 0-405-01892-4 $18.00

Siebert, Wilbur H. **The Underground Railroad from Slavery to Freedom**.............
.... ISBN 0-405-01835-5 $14.50

Silvera, John D. **The Negro in World War II**.............ISBN 0-405-01893-2 $14.00

Simmons, William J. **Men of Mark:** Eminent, Progressive, and Rising..............
.... ISBN 0-405-01836-3 $39.50

Sinclair, William A. **The Aftermath of Slavery:** A Study of the Condition and Environment of the American Negro ....ISBN 0-405-01894-0 $11.00

Smedley, R. C. **History of the Underground Railroad:** In Chester and the Neighboring Counties of Pennsylvania .... ISBN 0-405-01895-9 $14.00

South Carolina Constitutional Convention **Proceedings of the Constitutional Convention of South Carolina:** Held at Charleston, S. C., Beginning January 14th and Ending March 17th, 1868 ....ISBN 0-405-01837-1 $28.00

Spiller, G. (editor) **Papers on Inter-Racial Problems:** Communicated to the First Universal Race Congress Held at the University of London, July 26-29, 1911.............
.... ISBN 0-405-01935-1 $17.50

Steward, T. G. **The Colored Regulars in the United States Army:** With a Sketch of the History of the Colored American and an Account of His Services in the Wars of the Country, From the Period of the Revolutionary War to 1899...................
.... ISBN 0-405-01896-7 $10.50

W. P. A. Writer's Project **The Negro in Virginia**..........ISBN 0-405-01910-6 $12.00

W. P. A. Writer's Project **These Are Our Lives**............ISBN 0-405-01911-4 $13.50

Wright, Richard R., Jr. **The Negro in Pennsylvania:** A Study in Economic History......
.... ISBN 0-405-01908-4 $ 7.00

Wright, Richard **Twelve Million Black Voices:** A Folk History of the Negro in the United States .... ISBN 0-405-01909-2 $10.00

Paperbacks

Baker, Henry E. **The Colored Inventor:** A Record of Fifty Years....................
.... ISBN 0-405-01943-2 $ 1.00

Brown, William Wells **Clotel, or, the President's Daughter**..ISBN 0-405-01951-3 $ 2.45

Delany, Martin Robinson **The Condition, Elevation, Emigration, and Destiny of the Colored People of the United States:** Politically Considered..ISBN 0-405-01952-1 $ 2.45

Douglass, Frederick **My Bondage And My Freedom**........ISBN 0-405-01967-X $ 3.95

Dunbar, Paul Laurence **The Strength of Gideon and Other Stories**...................
.... ISBN 0-405-01953-X $ 3.45

Fisher, Rudolph **The Walls of Jericho**...................ISBN 0-405-01954-8 $ 3.25

Fortune, Timothy Thomas **Black and White:** Land, Labor, and Politics in the South....
.... ISBN 0-405-01955-6 $ 3.25

Garrison, William Lloyd **Thoughts on African Colonization:** Or an Impartial Exhibition of the Doctrines, Principles, and Purposes of the American Colonization Society Together With the Resolutions, Addresses, and Remonstrances of the Free People of Color....
.... ISBN 0-405-01956-4 $ 3.25

Griggs, Sutton E. **Imperium in Imperio**.................ISBN 0-405-01957-2 $ 2.45

Herndon, Angelo **Let Me Live**....................... ISBN 0-405-01958-0 $ 3.75

Higginson, Thomas Wentworth **Black Rebellion**........ ISBN 0-405-01959-9 $ 2.45

Jacques-Garvey, Amy (editor) **Philosophy and Opinions of Marcus Garvey** 2 volumes in 1
.... ISBN 0-405-01960-2 $ 4.50

Katz, Bernard (editor) **The Social Implications of Early Negro Music in the United States**
.... ISBN 0-405-01961-0 $ 2.45

Katz, William Loren (editor) **Five Slave Narratives:** A Compendium.................
.... ISBN 0-405-01962-9 $ 3.75

Locke, Alain **The Negro and His Music** and **Negro Art, Past and Present**...........
.... ISBN 0-405-01964-5 $ 2.95

Lynch, John R. **The Facts of Reconstruction** ....ISBN 0-405-01965-3 $ 3.25

McKay, Claude **A Long Way From Home** .... ISBN 0-405-01986-6 $ 3.45

Ottley, Roi **New World A-Coming:** Inside Black America....ISBN 0-405-01966-1 $ 3.45

Payne, Daniel A. **Recollections of Seventy Years**.........ISBN 0-405-01968-8 $ 3.45

Pearson, Elizabeth Ware (editor) **Letters from Port Royal, Written at the Time of the Civil War** .... ISBN 0-405-01969-6 $ 3.45

Porter, Dorothy (editor) **Negro Protest Pamphlets:** A Compendium..................
.... ISBN 0-405-01963-7 $ 1.95

Porter, James A. **Modern Negro Art** .... ISBN 0-405-01970-X $ 2.95

Scott, Emmett J. **Negro Migration During the War** ...... ISBN 0-405-01971-8 $ 1.95

Sinclair, William A. **The Aftermath of Slavery:** A Study of the Condition and Environment of the American Negro .... ISBN 0-405-01972-6 $ 3.45

Stowe, Harriet Beecher **The Key to Uncle Tom's Cabin:** Presenting the Original Facts and Documents Upon Which the Story is Founded, Togther With Corroborative Statements Verifying the Truth of the Work .... ISBN 0-405-01973-4 $ 3.95

•Walker, David, and Garnet, Henry Highland **Walker's Appeal in Four Articles** and **An Address to the Slaves of the United States of America** . . ISBN 0-405-01901-7 $ 1.75

Washington, Booker T; DuBois, W. E. B; Dunbar, Paul Laurence, et al. **The Negro Problem:** A Series of Articles by Representative American Negroes of Today.......... .... ISBN 0-405-01975-0 $ 2.45

Webb, Frank J. **The Garies and Their Friends** .... ISBN 0-405-01976-9 $ 3.45

Weld, Theodore Dwight **American Slavery As It Is:** Testimony of a Thousand Witnesses .... ISBN 0-405-01977-7 $ 2.45

Wells-Barnett, Ida **On Lynchings**...................... ISBN 0-405-01978-5 $ 1.95

White, Walter **Rope and Faggot:** A Biography of Judge Lynch .... ISBN 0-405-01979-3 $ 3.25

Four New Compilations

Gilbert, Peter (ed.) **The Selected Writings of John Edward Bruce: Militant Black Journalist** .... ISBN 0-405-01982-3 $ 9.00

Marks, George P. III (ed.) **The Black Press Views American Imperialism, 1898-1900** .... ISBN 0-405-01985-8 $11.00

Porter, Kenneth W. **The Negro on the American Frontier** .. ISBN 0-405-01983-1 $15.00

Redkey, Edwin S. (ed.) **Respect Black: The Writings and Speeches of Henry McNeal Turner** .... ISBN 0-405-01984-X $ 9.00

To Be Published Fall 1971

Fisher, Rudolph **The Conjure-Man Dies: A Mystery Tale of Dark Harlem** .... ISBN 0-405-02800-8 $ 5.95

McKinney, Richard I. **Religion in Higher Education Among Negroes** .... ISBN 0-405-02804-0 $ 7.00